Queen Adelaide's Church
Valletta

by

Alan Keighley

With All Best Wishes for 2002
Epiphany 2nd Jan

Copyright © Alan Keighley

First published in 2000 by Alan Keighley

All rights reserved

ISBN 0 9537335 0 5

Typeset by Academic and Technical, Bristol
Printed and bound by Redwood Books, Trowbridge, Wiltshire

Introduction

Although Malta is rich in history, the detailed story of Queen Adelaide's Church, nowadays called St. Paul's Anglican Pro-Cathedral, has not previously been told. A few articles have appeared in Maltese newspapers and journals over the years based on limited information, but regretfully many of them contain factual errors copied from earlier publications.

With the advent of laptop computers, scanners, and opening up of the access to records for the general public it is now possible to see and copy the original documents themselves, so this book is an attempt to present an accurate record of the history of St. Paul's.

It covers the range of years from the original concept of building an Anglican Church for the English residents shortly after Malta came under the protection of the British Crown, until the present day.

Holy Trinity Church Sliema, and the other Anglican places of worship are only touched upon when entering the story of St. Paul's since they are worthy of a book in their own right.

By gracious permission of Her Majesty I include two portraits of Queen Adelaide, which are in the Royal Collection, and also thank the National Portrait Gallery for permission to reproduce the portrait of Queen Adelaide which appears on the cover.

For the text my thanks are given to Mr. Donald H.Simpson, sometime Diocesan Archivist, who made my task easier by his earlier research work. Apart from the information, which he had gleaned from the Diocesan records, he built up a list of sources in the Public Record Office at Kew, which was invaluable. Having accessed these files I would like to thank the Staff at PRO Kew for their attention.

I am also grateful to Canon Cousins and Canon Woods for their assistance and for dealing with my queries. My thanks must also go to the current Cathedral Archivist, Air Commodore Malcolm Jolly, and Mrs. Peggy Kirkpatrick who both read the initial draft and gave additional information and comments.

Alan Keighley 1999

Contents

Chapter 1.	Early Days	1
Chapter 2.	The Government Chapel	4
Chapter 3.	First Church Cancelled	7
Chapter 4.	Queen Adelaide	11
Chapter 5.	Construction of St. Paul's	18
Chapter 6.	Consecration	26
Chapter 7.	Bishop Tomlinson Era	32
Chapter 8.	Bishop Trower Era	45
Chapter 9.	Government Chaplain's Post Abolished	52
Chapter 10.	Anglican Church Commission	58
Chapter 11.	Bishop Sandford's Visits	64
Chapter 12.	St. Paul's v Barracca Church – First Round	68
Chapter 13.	Collegiate Status Established	76
Chapter 14.	St. Paul's v Barracca Church – Second Round	80
Chapter 15.	Canon Marshall's Improvements	86
Chapter 16.	Canon Nicholl's Influence	93
Chapter 17.	St. Paul's Interior Appearance Pre-War	101
Chapter 18.	Outbreak of World War II	105
Chapter 19.	Siege of Malta 1940 – 1942	107
Chapter 20.	Centenary of Consecration	123
Chapter 21.	Reconstruction Plans	129
Chapter 22.	Re-Hallowing and Memorial Shrine	132
Chapter 23.	1950's Changes in Malta and Britain	138
Chapter 24.	British Defence Cuts cause Crisis	143
Chapter 25.	Royal Marines Memorial	146

Chapter 26.	Independence for Malta	150
Chapter 27.	Memorial Services	154
Chapter 28.	British Forces farewell to Malta	160
Chapter 29.	St. Paul's and Holy Trinity United	163
Chapter 30.	Early 1990's	166
Chapter 31.	150th Anniversary of Consecration	169
Chapter 32.	St. Paul's Interior Appearance 1999	172
Chapter 33.	Latest Events	184
Appendix 1.	Diocese of Gibraltar	186
Appendix 2.	1895 Declaration	189
Appendix 3.	Memorial Shrine Naval Units	192
Appendix 4.	Clergy	195

Chapter 1

Early Days

An early connection of England with the Mediterranean area dates from Elizabethan days, when in 1582 Grand Master Verdala, the head of the Knights of St. John of Jerusalem, better known as the Knights of Malta, granted passports to two English merchants, Edward Alderman and Richard Staper, to trade with the island.

It seems that many men working with the early trading companies in the Mediterranean area were devout Christians, but little is known of the religious life of non-Catholics. The Levant Company, which was established in 1581, provided Chaplains for many of its trading communities, but its influence did not extend to Malta. Also, there was no provision by the Church of England to provide for the needs of such communities.

It was not until 1633 that the jurisdiction of the Bishop of London over all English congregations abroad was recognised and confirmed by an Order in Council. It was a start and although Malta came under his control, it was obviously unsatisfactory since the Bishop could not be in direct touch with such a collection of wide spread congregations.

Prior to 1800 the English community on Malta was very small, but once the combined Maltese and British forces had expelled the French in the September of that year, the number of English civilians and troops increased. The early arrivals were merchants[1] and their families from other Mediterranean ports, since Sir Alexander Ball, the Civil Commissioner, actively encouraged the growth of trade. The war against Napoleon was still being continued on mainland Europe and his troops were in possession of nearby Italy and Sicily, so there was a build up of British soldiers in the Malta garrison, as well as men of the Royal Navy, on His Majesty George the Third's men-of-war.

Since the Maltese had invited the British Crown to protect them, in these early years an effective Government and Civil Service was set up, as well as an expansion of the dockyard facilities to meet the needs of the Royal Navy. By the Treaty of Paris in 1814,[2] the Maltese islands became part of the British Empire, and with the end of the Napoleonic Wars in 1815, there was increased immigration by English citizens of all trades and professions, plus their wives and children.

Malta also became known as a health resort, and was favoured by English men and women wishing to avoid the cold winter months at home. Several prominent personalities visited the island, including Lord Byron, Benjamin Disraeli, Sir Walter Scott, and Queen Adelaide the widow of King William IV. Others became permanent residents, such as the distinguished diplomat, scholar and writer John Hookham Frere and his family.

The first Chaplain to the Garrison, was the Reverend William Pargeter, a Naval Chaplain who had served on board the *Alexander*, at the Battle of the Nile in 1798. He officiated at the funeral of Sir Ralph Abercrombie on 29th April 1801. The British Commander-in-Chief had died of his wounds in Egypt in the successful expedition against the French, but was brought back to Malta for burial in the bastions of Valletta.

Apart from the Reverend Pargeter, other Chaplains to the Forces in 1801 were the Reverend Hare and the Reverend David Peloquin Cosserat until his death in 1809. From April 1805 to July 1813 the Reverend John Castleton Miller also acted as Chaplain to the Forces, and the long serving Reverend John Thomas Howe Le Mesurier[3], from 1813 till 1846 followed him. Without their own Chaplain, the first civilian residents were looked after by the Chaplains to the Forces.

The earliest registers of births, deaths and marriages, were made by the Reverends Cosserat and Miller, and in those days each clergyman kept his own records. They were later deposited in the Cathedral archives, but disappeared some time after 1952, and copies made that year are currently held in St. Paul's, but are incomplete.[4]

The first Chaplain to Government was appointed by Sir Alexander Ball in 1807; he was the Reverend Francis Laing, the son of an Edinburgh architect, who had been the tutor to Ball's son Keith, as well as being private secretary to Ball himself. This office was held from 2nd December 1814 to 31st March 1824 by the Reverend John Castleton Miller, after his service as Chaplain to the Forces. He was recommended by Sir Thomas Maitland in 1813, since he had been very helpful during the plague that had ravaged Malta that year. He also acted as interpreter at the Vice-Admiralty Court.

However, by 1823 he had created a difficult situation vis-à-vis the Reverend Le Mesurier, and refused to enter into his Births and Deaths registers either of these duties carried out by Le Mesurier, and also refused to visit Protestants in the 'Three Cities', insisting that they be brought over to Valletta. Clearly, in the case of the dying this was impossible. He also seems to have offended some of the English civilians.

2

Maitland was forced to write to England:[5]

> "Under all these circumstances therefore I have found it my duty to request that Mr. Miller be removed from the situation of Civil Chaplain to the Government.... His general behaviour for some years past both in private life and in the exercise of his religious function has been of such a nature as to bring disgrace upon the Protestant church here and to create general discontent and disgust among the British inhabitants."

Miller was dismissed and the Reverend John Cleugh took over, and held the post for fifty-three years.

Notes

[1] See Mercanti Inglesi a Malta 1800 1825, Michela D'Angelo, Franco Angeli Libri, Milan 1990.

[2] The Treaty of Paris dated 30th May 1814. Under Article 7: " The Island of Malta and its dependencies shall belong in full right and sovereignty to His Britannic Majesty." thus Malta became a British Colony.

[3] A grandson of John Le Mesurier, hereditary Governor of Alderney, and son of a former Lord Mayor of London.

[4] In September 1996, the surviving original registers of Births, Deaths and Marriages, were sent to the Guildhall Library, London, to be preserved. Copies are kept at St. Paul's.

[5] PRO Kew CO.158/39 20th November 1823.

Chapter 2

The Government Chapel

The exact date when the Government Chapel was opened has not been verified, but three items of Communion Plate bear the inscription 'Malta Government Chapel A.D.1809'[1]. It was located in the Governor's Palace, and had to serve the needs of the civil population as well as the garrison families. It was a room on the ground floor, off what is known today as the Neptune courtyard, and had formerly been the kitchen of the Grand Masters. Accommodation for about 350 people was available, but Government officials appropriated most of the pews and the remaining thirty-two badly situated under the gallery were rented.

It was in the charge of the Chaplain to the Government, who held two services on a Sunday. He was assisted by a retired sergeant from the Royal Artillery, employed as his clerk at £16.10.0d per annum. For those who did attend the Chapel, matters were far from satisfactory, since the acoustics were very bad, and there was neither organ nor choir and the music depended on the chance services of a military band.

There were numerous British officials, mostly attached to the Naval Dockyard, living in Senglea, Vittoriosa, and Cospicua, the 'Three Cities' on the opposite side of the Grand Harbour to Valletta. For them a sail loft in Cospicua was set aside for worship, and was known as the Dockyard Chapel. It was first used on 12th September 1819 and was enlarged in 1824, with a gallery being built later. No minister was appointed so the Reverend Le Mesurier added it to his duties.

As the Chaplain to the Forces Le Mesurier worked exceedingly hard. He looked after the religious needs of about 3,000 British troops in the garrison, and for many years he did a Sunday round of duty covering eight miles by land and water, often in bad weather. At 8.30 a.m. he took divine service for troops in Valletta, in a room of the prison, or on rare occasions in the open air on the barrack square. He then travelled to Cospicua, and held a service in the Dockyard Chapel at 10.45 a.m., this was followed by services for the troops of Fort Tigne and Fort Manoel at 2 p.m. He was back at the Dockyard Chapel by 3.30 p.m. and up to Bighi Naval Hospital, to which he was Chaplain at 5 p.m. In addition he undertook to visit any Protestant patients in hospital, supervised the regimental schools for around 120 children, and visited ships calling at Malta which had no Chaplain of their own, no easy task when the sea was rough.

Neither of these Chapels were really suitable places of worship, and from time to time approaches were made by the Governor to the Secretary of State for the Colonies, for a proper church to be provided for the British Protestant community.

The British Government in fact had in its possession two churches, which it had taken over as part of the property of the Knights of Malta. The Jesuits Church in Strada Mercanti, Valletta, which the Knights themselves had confiscated in 1768 when they expelled the Jesuits, and the Conventual Church of St. John.

It was suggested from England that St. John's Church should be used by the English residents for Anglican worship but the Governor, Sir Thomas Maitland, strongly opposed this idea, and expressed his views in his despatch of 27th January 1814, to the Secretary of State[2]. He wrote:

> "... but a very material question is whether or not the Church of St. John should be made into an English Church. At the present time and I own my opinion clearly is that it would be inexpedient to insist upon this measure ... it appears that it would be a measure militating most severely against the prejudices of the people here, were we to insist of adopting as our own a place of worship which has been celebrated for ages as one of the first of the Roman Catholic persuasion and in which are the burial places of all the great men who have ever belonged to that order of religious knighthood more particularly as there is within a hundred yards of it the Jesuits Church also the property of the Crown .... This I think I can certainly get without difficulty the other I am convinced would give great difficulty – and occasion infinite disgust.... I shall adopt no measure upon this subject till I receive further instructions from your Lordship."

The Secretary of State replied on 2nd May 1814[3], agreeing with this point of view:

> "You will not, upon any account, occupy the Church of St. John as a place of Protestant worship, but have it as heretofore, for His Majesty's Catholic subjects.... It appears to me to be far more advisable to enlarge the existing chapel in the Palace and continue to make use of that building as the Place of Worship for persons of the Protestant faith."

Maitland, presumably much relieved, answered[4] on 13th June 1814:

> "...I am extremely happy to find your Lordship entertains so strong an opinion in regards to not occupying any of the Catholic churches as a place

of worship for the English. It will save me a considerable degree of trouble and certainly give great satisfaction to the people."

Nevertheless, a few years later, Lord Liverpool, the British Prime Minister, gave official sanction for the use of the Jesuits Church by the Church of England, provided that no public money was spent on the necessary alterations. Though funds could be raised from other sources, it was found that, in addition to the structural changes, there would be the cost of purchasing the foundations of private altars, amounting to some £5,000 and also the removal of Roman Catholic graves in the Church if desired by their relatives. The scheme was therefore abandoned, and the Government Chapel continued to be used.

Notes

[1] A Silver paten, a large Silver Flagon, and a Silver chalice.
[2] PRO Kew CO.158/39
[3] PRO Kew CO.159/4
[4] PRO Kew CO.158/39

Chapter 3

First Church Cancelled

The position of Malta, in the centre of the Mediterranean, made it an attractive location for Missionary work, which increased after 1815. The London Missionary Society had commenced on a small scale in 1808, and kept going for many years. Their target was Greece, so tracts and translations in the Greek language were prepared, for use particularly on the Ionian Islands, when they came under British control in 1815. The Church Missionary Society opened a school in Malta in 1815. A branch of the Bible Society was founded in 1817 by Henry Drummond, with Mr. Isaac Lowndes, Dr. Cleardo Naudi[1] and the Reverend William Jowett as Secretaries.

In 1824 the Methodists established a Church in Valletta at No. 55 Strada Britannica, on the corner with Old Bakery Street, under the control of their Minister, John Keeling. Not only was this the first Methodist Church on Malta, but also the first church for the Protestant religion. Another Methodist Minister, William Harris Rule, held services in the Cospicua district.

The activities of these groups during the 1820's frequently came into conflict with the Roman Catholic Church, which led to protests from the Maltese hierarchy, they also caused friction with the Governor and some members of the Civil Government. Sir Richard Plasket, the Chief Secretary to the Government wrote to England on 20th April 1823[2]:

> "...a few days before Sir Thomas Maitland left Malta, the Bishop demanded an audience and at this meeting made a formal complaint against a set of gentlemen here who have established themselves into a Malta Bible Society ... the principal complaint of the Bishop is that this Society have got a translation made by some ignorant person here of chosen selections from the scriptures in the Maltese and Italian languages that they have had this work printed in England and copies sent out here expressly for distribution amongst the natives of the island."

The non-conformists also drew some of the civilian worshippers away from the Government Chapel. With the arrival and departure of different army regiments quite a large number of non-conformist soldiers did their tour of duty on Malta, so boosting their congregations.

The shortage of Anglican clergy would have been alleviated to some extent if there had been more adequate church accommodation, so the whole responsibility fell upon the shoulders of the Reverend Cleugh and Reverend Le Mesurier.

Since the decision in 1814 to continue with the Government Chapel for religious services nothing happened for the next ten years to improve the situation. This may have been due to the influence of Governor Maitland. However, after his death, and before his successor was appointed, on February 16th 1824, two estimates for building a Protestant Church were sent to the Colonial Office[3] by Sir Richard Plasket. The first plan seating 340 people without a gallery, and 460 with, would cost £4,645 or £5,045, whilst the second one to seat 490 or 620 people, was estimated to be £6,880 or £7,280 and by October authority to proceed had been given.

The church had been designed by Colonel George Whitmore, Royal Engineers, and work commenced to prepare the site. The corner of the Great Prison nearest the Lower Barracca, at the junction of Strada Cristofero and Strada Irlandais, was demolished. A new Chief Secretary, Sir Frederick Hankey took over in 1825, and reported that work had begun, but when he submitted a fresh estimate to the Secretary of State on April 23rd 1825[4], saying that the building alone would cost £7,625 the answer from England requested further explanation of the increased costs. More details and a ground plan were sent but these were not accepted, and at the beginning of December all work was suspended.

When in June 1824 the Marquess of Hastings arrived as the new Governor he was all in favour of the project, since it would help to bring a boost to the local economy[5]. With the church building now at a halt, the Colonial Office put forward to Hastings[6] the old idea of using an existing church. He rejected the Jesuits Church, on the same grounds as Maitland, i.e. the high cost of purchasing private altars and removing private graves, but when in April 1826 he visited the other suggestion, the church of St. Giacomo in Strada Mercanti he decided it was too small.

So everything came to a standstill again. However, Hastings died on 28th November 1826, and the following year, 1827, the Whitmore project was abandoned and other buildings were erected on the site.

More years passed without any progress, then in 1834 during the Governorship of Sir Frederick Ponsonby, it was officially announced that some surplus from the island's revenue would be devoted to the erection of an English church, but he would leave the decision to the Secretary for State[7]. Two years later another attempt was made, on 7th January 1836 when a report compiled by John Mackenzie, Director of Government Works, proposed a building on the corner of Strada Reale and Strada Mezzodi[8], or an alternative site at 91 Strada Vescovo. It would be Gothic in style, seating 1,500 people, 500 in pews and 1000 on benches, and the cost was estimated to be around £8,000 or with a bombproof roof £10,000[9]. From London the reply asked for more details to be sent, but it seems that once again the matter was allowed to lapse.

Ill health forced Sir Frederick Ponsonby to resign in 1836, and he was succeeded as Governor by Sir Henry Bouverie. To some degree the action by the Church Missionary Society brought the subject to the fore again when in January 1837 their representative, the Reverend Christopher Frederick Schlienz, asked the Colonial Office and Governor Bouverie for a site on Malta, as a gift, on which they could build a church. This caused considerable correspondence between London and Malta, since it raised many questions; should the C.M.S. build a church? or the Government? what about possible proselytising causing protest from the Roman Catholic clergy? what site should be chosen? how would such a church be financed? the use of the Church of St. Giacomo was proposed again and rejected again. For over eighteen months letters went back and forth.

In 1838 Bouverie put forward a proposal to adapt part of an existing building, the Auberge D'Italie, though he understood that such a scheme would not satisfy those who wanted an impressive English church, but it would show a substantial saving of public funds[10]. However, this only sparked off another round of correspondence between Malta and London.

A writer in a local paper voiced the feelings of many when in 1838, he wrote:

> *"Ballrooms, clubs and racket courts have been fitted up but our officials have baulked every desire to raise a Temple to the Living God. The Saviour of the world was born in a stable and they appear to think that a cellar is a fitting place to worship Him in."*

By 1838 there were about 2,000 English civilians on the island, mostly resident in Valletta. A large number of the English population attended non-conformist services, or stayed away from church altogether. This was the situation when Queen Adelaide, the widow of King William IV, visited Malta for the benefit of her ever-delicate health at the end of the year.

Notes

[1] Born 3rd June 1781, Strada San Paolo, Valletta, Dr. Cleardo Naudi formally renounced the Church of Rome and received the Sacrament at the English Chapel. Letter 7th December 1824, C.M.S. Archives, University of Birmingham.

[2] PRO Kew CO.158/40
[3] PRO Kew CO.158/35
[4] PRO Kew CO.158/41
[5] PRO Kew CO.158/36
[6] PRO Kew CO.159/8
[7] PRO Kew CO.158/79
[8] This site was later used for the Opera House, now in ruins.
[9] PRO Kew CO.158/88
[10] PRO Kew CO.158/100

Chapter 4

Queen Adelaide

Adelaide was born at Meiningen[1], Germany, on the 13th August 1792, the daughter of Duke George I of Saxony-Meiningen and his wife Princess Luisa Eleonore of Hohenlohe-Langenburg. She was given the full title of 'Princess Amalie Adelheid Luise Therese Karolina', but became known as Princess Adelaide.

She was the eldest child, followed by a sister Ida born 1794, and a brother Bernhard in 1800. Their father died when Adelaide was eleven years old in 1803, leaving his widow with the three young children.

Being a member of this minor German court she led a sheltered life but with strong family bonds between the three children themselves, and their mother. Her younger sister Ida married Prince Bernhard of Saxe-Weimar in 1816, and two years later the marriage of Adelaide to the Duke of Clarence, a son of King George III of England, was arranged.

Not only was her future husband much older than herself, but she faced a considerable change for a young woman from a small German Court to an important role in one of the major Courts of Europe. The wedding took place in Kew Palace on 11th July 1818, five weeks short of her 26th birthday but he was six weeks short of his 53rd birthday.

They were resident in Hanover when their first child, Charlotte Augusta Louisa, was born prematurely on 27th March 1819, but the baby died a few hours later. The sons of King George III were competing to produce an heir to the throne, and so when Adelaide became pregnant again the following year, the Duke of Clarence was anxious that the child should be born in England. They set out on the journey from Germany, but harsh travelling conditions caused her to have a miscarriage at the French port of Dunkirk.

The couple moved to England and on the 10th December 1820, Adelaide gave birth to another girl, Elizabeth Georgiana Adelaide, at St. James's Palace, but the child only lived until the 4th March 1821. Her last pregnancy produced twin boys, which were still born, on 23rd April 1822. These must have been three traumatic years of personal tragedy for her.

Many years before his marriage the Duke had formed an attachment with an actress, Dorothea Bland, known as 'Mrs.Jordan'[2]. By him over a period of twenty years, she bore ten children, whom he acknowledged, and were known by the name of Fitzclarence. The relationship with Mrs. Jordan ended in 1811. Though greatly saddened by the loss of her own children in infancy, Adelaide became devoted to her stepchildren, step-grandchildren, and her niece, Victoria, the future queen.

When his brother George IV died on 26th June 1830, the Duke of Clarence became King William IV, and reigned for seven years until he died from pneumonia on 20th June 1837. Adelaide[3] became the Queen Dowager, and resumed a quiet life. She suffered from ill health, in particular from chest ailments, and it was for this reason that in 1838 she decided to spend the winter months in Malta.

On the voyage out from England she had called at Gibraltar in October and had been present on the 18th at the consecration of the Holy Trinity Church, later to become Gibraltar Cathedral. She arrived at Malta on board HMS *Hastings* on the 30th November[4], and her feelings regarding the lack of a Protestant church on the island were immediately apparent.

Within two weeks of her arrival she wrote[5] to her niece, Queen Victoria:

Palace, Valetta, 13th December 1838.

MY DEAREST NIECE, – The English mail going today gives me another opportunity to address you, and to name a subject to you which I think deserves your consideration, and about which I feel most anxious. It is the want of a Protestant church in this place which I mean. There are so many English residents here, it is the seat of an English Government, and there is not one church belonging to the Church of England... The consequence of this want of church accommodation has been that the Dissenters have established themselves in considerable number, and one cannot blame persons for attending their meeting when they have no church of their own.

I address myself to you, as the Head of the Church of England, and entreat you to consider well this important subject, and to talk it over with your Ministers and the Archbishop, in order to devise the best means of remedying a want so discreditable to our country. Should there be no funds at your disposal to effect this object, most happy shall I feel to contribute to any subscription which may be set on foot, and I believe that a considerable sum may be raised among the Protestants of this island, where all parties are most anxious to see a proper place of divine worship erected; without assistance from England, however, it cannot be effected. I therefore most humbly and confidently submit this subject to you, dearest Victoria, who will bestow upon your Protestant subjects of this island an everlasting benefit by granting them what they want most...

I hope this will find you quite well and happy, and that I shall soon again have the pleasure of hearing from you. Give my affectionate love to your dear Mother, and all my dear sisters, and believe me ever, my dearest Niece, your most devoted and faithfully attached Aunt, ADELAIDE"

It must have been uppermost in her mind, and without doubt she discussed the subject with the Governor, Sir Henry Bouverie, who probably made it clear to her that from his experience since taking office, funding from the British Government for such a project was unlikely to be forthcoming. However, he was the President of the Malta District Committee of the Society for Promoting Christian Knowledge (S.P.C.K.), and apart from agreeing with her views from the spiritual aspect, he could also see the benefit that the building project would bring to employment on the island.

Without waiting for a reply from Queen Victoria, Adelaide made her own decision, as shown by extracts from the letter[6] written by the Governor to the Secretary of State on the 6th January 1839:

"Since I had the honour of addressing your Lordship on the subject of the building of a Protestant Church in Malta, Her Majesty the Queen Dowager has expressed her determination to supply the funds required for the undertaking. Anxious as I have ever been to see a Church erected upon a scale commensurate with the dignity of Great Britain and the spiritual wants of the Protestants of Malta both residents and travellers the number of which latter class is daily increasing it has never appeared to me likely that that measure would be effected otherwise than by a grant of Money by Parliament, and I have always imagined that great difficulty could be thrown in the way of such a Grant, and that this great object so essential to the welfare of so many would therefore continue to be, as it has been for so many years, postponed again and again to the great injury of the interests of the Church of England, your Lordship will not therefore be surprised at the difficulty which I experienced in finding adequate terms in which to express the admiration and gratitude which I in common with all well wishers to the Church of England must be impressed, on this most gracious and most beneficent determination of Her Majesty being made known....

...On the part of the Government I have engaged to give up the site on which the house now occupied by Sir John Stoddart stands in the Strada Ponente. To this site there is no objection on the part of the Commanding Engineer.... On no other would a Church be built at so small a sacrifice of income and under the very unlooked for circumstances of the case I trust Your Lordship will approve of my having given orders to proceed with the pulling down of the building immediately, having engaged also on the Government

to clear the site for the erection of the Church and Her Majesty being most anxious that the work should be begun without delay.

Her Majesty's intention is to furnish the funds necessary for the building which is to contain 1000 persons, to be used by the Garrison who will have a separate Service and with sittings for the families of the Officers, and the Soldiers wives and children, as well as for such Officers and Seamen of the Fleet as may choose to attend the regular service, and the expense of which is calculated at from £6000 to £8000 . . . .

The Plan of the Church has not yet been definitely decided upon by Her Majesty, but plans have been called for and will soon be presented."

Lord Glenelg's reply of February 2nd, approved Bouverie's prompt action in arranging the demolition of the building, which was formerly the Auberge d'Allemagne, but now housed part of a Naval Bakery for the Mediterranean Fleet, and the residence of Sir.John Stoddart, but had fallen into disrepair.

The Protestants on Malta sent an Address dated 5th February 1839 to Queen Adelaide:

"We, the Protestant population of these Islands, impressed with the highest admiration at Your Majesty's munificent and pious intention to build a church for our use, desire, with the profoundest respect to offer in common some testimony, unworthy indeed but sincere, which shall mark the heartfelt gratitude with which we receive so inestimable a gift.

From the hour of Your Majesty's connexion with the British Empire, we have not failed to perceive with the rest of our countrymen, the excellent influence of Your Majesty's quiet example in the cause of virtue and religion upon the whole community, nor, less so, Your Majesty's attachment to the pure and apostolic branch of Christ's Church established in the realm of England. Many have been the splendid occasions wherein Your Majesty has been gratefully hailed as the liberal patroness of our Christian institutions; but, manifest as were these indications of Your Majesty's pious zeal, we were unprepared to expect from Your Majesty this accomplishment of our long cherished and most ardent wishes, and we are confident, that the sacred edifice, now about to adorn this city, will not be reckoned the least of those noble acts which will render the honoured name of Your Majesty conspicuous in the page of history and in the pious annals of the Church.

By means of Your Majesty's Christian benevolence, a bright prospect has now opened upon us, and soon all our protestant brethren, from the least to the greatest, will be enabled to join together in the public exercises of our holy faith.

Your Majesty's visit to this island has been productive of great good to all. May it be blessed to Your Majesty in a perfect restoration of health.

Queen Adelaide when Duchess of Clarence.
Painted shortly after her marriage. c. 1818, by Mrs. James Green.

Fervently, we pray the Almighty that Your Majesty may live long to hear of, if not to witness in person, the prosperity of this your labor of love and zeal for the glory of God. And may the Lord God cause righteousness and praise to spring forth from it a glorious proof of the faithfulness of his word, that 'Kings shall be the nursing fathers and their Queens the nursing mothers of the Church' "[7].

Six weeks later, on the 20th March 1839, Queen Adelaide laid the foundation stone. It was an impressive ceremony, described in the Malta paper 'The Harlequin':

"On Wednesday last 20th of March p.m. Her Majesty Queen Dowager of England left the Palace accompanied by His Excellency the Governor and her Suite, to lay the foundation stone of the new Protestant Church. The day was fair and bright but very windy. Her Majesty as had been her wont since her residence here rode in a carriage of the country and was preceded by a band of the Garrison playing 'God save the Queen' and also, there preceded Her Majesty twelve clergymen of the Church of England, chiefly Chaplains of the Navy. A very large concourse of British residents and of the Maltese, had already assembled on the arrival of Her Majesty in Strada Ponente the site of the new church....

All the officers of the Garrison and the Fleet were present in full dress, whose rich and massy uniforms cast an air of grandeur over the solemn scene. Her Majesty herself attired in a splendid dress of black silk velvet looked at once most graciously condescending and regal - and with His Excellency in grand uniform on her left and the lovely Lady Sheffield on her right, she took her seat on a chair of state, under a warm and commodious booth, richly carpeted, constructed for Her Majesty and the ladies. The Reverend Chaplain of the Forces, Mr. Le Mesurier, then opened the service by reading the 132nd psalm, which was responded to by the children of the military schools, and the company present.

Her Majesty afterwards descended with a firm step to lay the stone amidst the most intense anxiety of the spectators.... Her Majesty assisted by His Excellency, Lady Sheffield, Earl Howe, the Chief Secretary the Hon. Sir Hector Greig, and Mr. Lankesheer the architect took the square of the mason and adjusted the stone as it was lowered down by pulleys over the cement lying beneath."

In a cavity within the stone she placed a glass vessel containing a collection of English coins, namely, a sovereign, a half-sovereign, a crown, a half-crown, a shilling, and a six-pence, a four penny silver piece, a penny, a half-penny, a farthing and a British grain, also a coronation medal of their Majesties William and Adelaide in bronze, together with a parchment with the following English inscription:

> "Glory to God in the highest, and on earth peace, good will towards men. This foundation stone of the Church of St. Paul in the City of Valletta, for the celebration of Divine Worship, according to the ritual of the Church of England, and to be erected out of the free and Christian bounty of Her Majesty Adelaide, the Queen Dowager, was laid by Her Majesty in person on the 20th day of March A.D.1839."

A brass plate with the Latin inscription was immediately placed over the opening and fastened down. After completing this part of the ceremony, Queen Adelaide returned up the steps to her former position. A twenty-one gun Royal Salute was fired, and the Guard of Honour presented arms, whilst the band played the National Anthem. This was followed by the children from the regimental schools singing the 100th Psalm, and the ceremony was concluded by the Reverend John Cleugh, the Government Chaplain, reading a prayer, then the Lord's Prayer and pronouncing the Blessing.

Just twelve days later on the 1st April, Queen Adelaide left Malta with the satisfaction of knowing that construction of her church had commenced.

Notes

[1] Meiningen is a small town about 90 kilometres south west of Erfurt. At the time of the partition of Germany it was just inside the East German border.

[2] She was born in London in 1761. Prior to her meeting with William, she had a daughter by Richard Daly, a Dublin stage manager, and two daughters by Sir Richard Ford. She died in France on 8th July 1816.

[3] The previous year on 13th July 1836, King William IV founded a town in South Australia, and gave it the name 'Adelaide'.

[4] Her Suite consisted of: The Countess of Sheffield, the Hon.Miss Hudson, the Earl Howe, the Earl of Denbigh, Captain Curzon, the Reverend John Ryles Wood, and Sir David Davies, Physician.

[5] The Letters of Queen Victoria 1837 1861 Vol.1

[6] PRO Kew CO.158/105

[7] Her letter of reply is in St. Paul's Archives.

Chapter 5

Construction of St. Paul's

The architect selected for this project was Richard Lankesheer, who had been Head Superintendent of Civilian Artificers in the Land Revenue and Public Works Department of Malta since 1830. None of his plans or sections showing his intentions for the interior of the church have survived, just two exterior drawings. The Malta Penny Magazine published an illustration and description of the proposed church in November 1839.

> *"The accompanying drawing is the intended side elevation of the building, which is now in rapid progress. The first stone was laid by Her Majesty on the 20th March 1839, and the work has so far advanced that the groundwork may be said to be completed. No labour has been spared by the superintending architect to render the edifice durable; and tho'often with immense difficulty, every part of the foundation has been based upon the solid rock, which in many instances was found covered with thirty feet of rubbish.*
>
> *According to a drawing already published, the front of the edifice facing N.E. will be adorned with a portico supported by four Ionic pillars, and surmounted by a bas-relief design illustrative of St. Paul's casting the viper off his hand into the fire immediately after his shipwreck. (Acts xxviii 3).*
>
> *Each wing of the front will be ornamented with a statue of the two great apostles of the Christian Church, St. Peter and St. Paul. The tower or steeple will be 130 feet high, terminating with the emblem of Christianity, the cross.*
>
> *The dimensions of this building exceed those of any of the modern churches in London: the length of the area will be 110 feet, breadth 67 feet and height 45 feet. Mary-le-Bone, one of the largest parish churches in the metropolis measures only 105 by 70 feet, and serves a congregation in which 3000 baptisms take place yearly; and that of St. Pancras 117 by 60 ft, including the altar. The church of St. Paul at Malta will contain seats for upwards of 1500 persons."*

The building work commenced and all went well for a while but after about twelve months problems began to arise due to the inexperience of the architect, Mr. Lankesheer. He died on 8th March 1841, aged 38 years[1], and whilst it was officially reported 'after a short illness', the rumour at the time was that he had committed suicide when his plans for St. Paul's were found to be unsafe.

A prominent member of the English community, and a Committee member of the S.P.C.K., Robert Clement Sconce[2], the Agent Victualler to the Royal Navy, wrote to a friend in June 1841:

> *"Our poor church is in a bad way. Queen Adelaide was not lucky in her choice of an architect. She was probably guided in her choice by the high-constituted authorities here; but, however, by her, or by somebody, a cabinetmaker, a Mr. ... was chosen to design and execute the work. Well, some cracks, splits and crushings began to appear in the columns of the portico before half the pediment was built upon it.*
>
> *The Admiralty engineers were summoned to survey and pronounce; and what they pronounced was that the portico must all be immediately pulled down and down it all is, accordingly. The columns within the church, for the support of the gallery and the roof, must come down too. All the work is suspected; but it would be so great a pity to throw away £6000 already spent, that I believe they mean to try and coax the walls to bear a roof. Perhaps, after all, it may not tumble down; or if it does, it may not be when all the people are in it. The Governor will just arrive in England to impart the pleasing news to the Queen.*
>
> *As soon as the accident was discovered, Captain Brandreth came to me, and said he hoped I had had nothing to do with the church! He and Mr. Scamp (who is a first-rate clever fellow) say they never saw in all their lives such an exhibition of ignorance.... I only begged Lady Louis to tell the Queen, which I believe she did, that* one *thing was absolutely necessary, and that was to get an architect from England, even at any price. What a disgrace it would have saved us!"*

"*Isn't this a dainty dish to set before the Queen*" he commented in a subsequent letter; but there appears to be no record of Queen Adelaide's reaction to the disastrous news.

The project was placed in the hands of a Naval Architect, William Scamp, and though work resumed in November 1841 under his direction, his task was not easy. Another letter written by Sconce in December 1841 gives the details:

> *"... They say our bishop is not to be appointed till the church is built. Scamp hoped to complete it by the close of next year, but every step he takes, discloses a new imperfection in the old work, and the poor man is puzzled everywhere. He has just found a part of the substructions based, not, as they ought to have been, upon the rock, but upon the remnants of an old and imperfect wall; so he is afraid to trust the foundations anywhere; and the underground*

Front entrance to St. Paul's Church, Valletta,
as designed by Richard Lankesheer

work is so deep, that he would have to dig down, more or less in different parts from ten to fifty feet, to examine them.

Eight or ten inches of the base of a principal column was found projecting beyond the intended foundation of it, and resting upon nothing; and what has been used for cement has so little cementing or tenacious property, that it pulverizes under the touch, so that snuff would have been quite as useful a material."

Scamp was forced to demolish most of the previous work, and eventually overcame the difficulties and completed the building, though he modified the original design very considerably. In particular he dispensed with the steeple behind the portico and added instead a tall and graceful spire of his own design, independent of the main building and overlooking the Marsamuscetto Harbour.

Scamp submitted a report to the Building Committee on the state of the work as at the 25th November 1842, accompanied by drawings, a detailed abstract of expenses, and list of work still to be carried out on the interior and exterior of the building.[3]

He stated:

"The Portico. A difficulty has hitherto existed in obtaining stone of sufficiently good quality for the columns. Men are now employed in quarrying stone at St. George's Bay for the works of the Navy[4] of the required quality and arrangements are made for delivering the quantity required at the Church at a low price; this work therefore will be proceeded with immediately.

The Spire: From the bottom of the foundation to the level of the Walls as at present built is about 65 feet, tho' this is less than a third of the whole height of the spire, there is a greater quantity of masonry in this part executed than will be contained in the part yet to be built and when the arches upon which the workmen are now employed are constructed, the next 30 feet are plain walls that will be executed with dispatch and at less cost and the quantity of masonry will be reduced in proportion as the work proceeds upwards.

In originally forming the estimate for completing the church – £1,000 was allowed for rectifying the defects- reconstructing the columns and a portion of the walls but in providing for permanent stability instead temporary security, this sum has been unavoidably greatly exceeded – to keep the actual cost therefore within the money remaining to be expended the interior work must be executed in the most simple manner and if the sum remaining after the interior work, portico, etc., is completed should be insufficient for constructing the spire as represented on the drawing, this feature may terminate with the tower only."

Whilst the number of men employed on the site varied from week to week he gives details for week ending 25th November, showing their daily rate of pay: 7 Masons 1/9d. to 1/6d., 63 Stone Cutters 1/3d., 39 Stone Carriers/Labourers 11d., 47 Boys 7d. to 5d., 3 Sculptors 3/-d., 14 Carpenters 1/8d. to 1/1d., a total of 173 workmen.

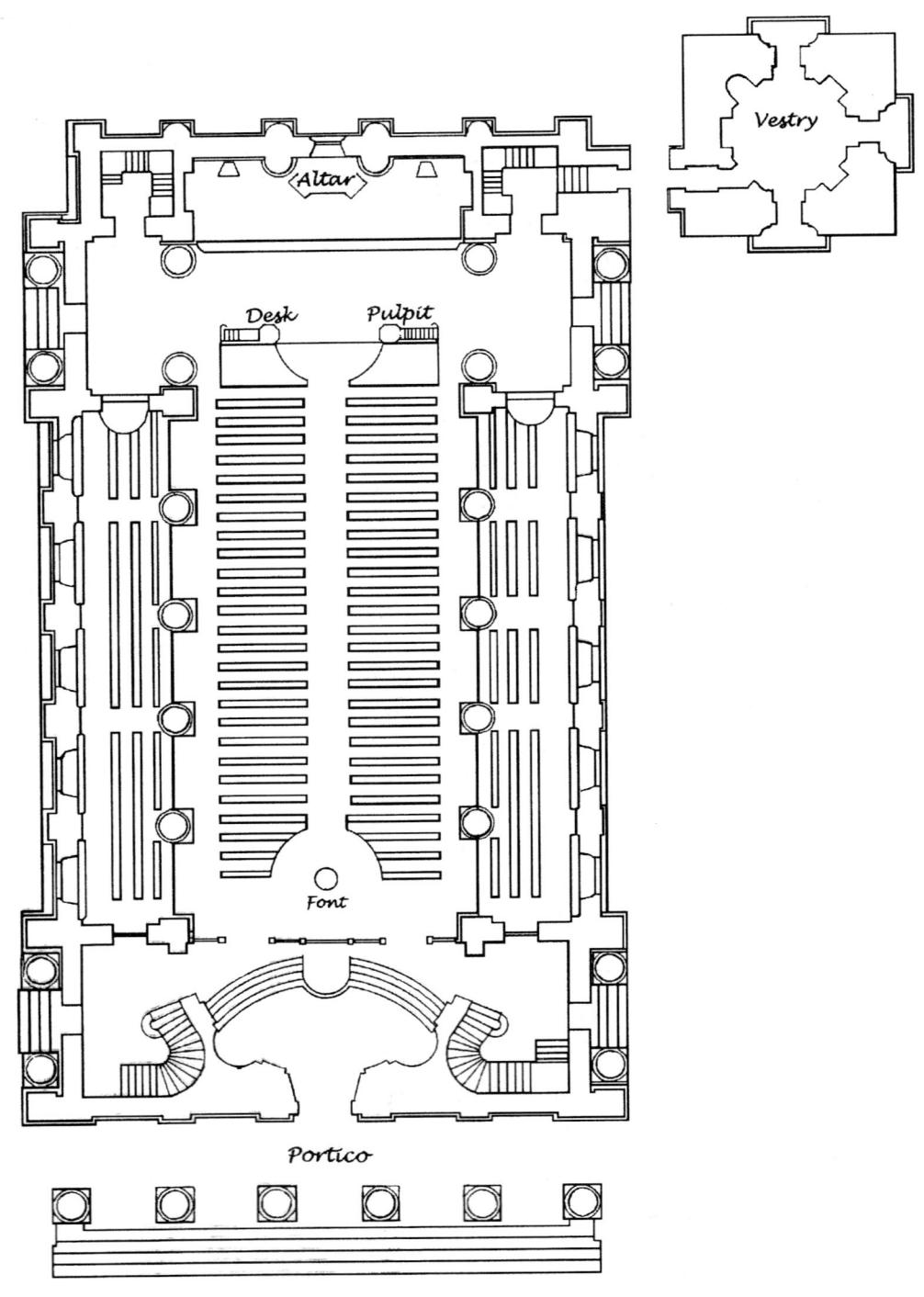

Interior layout as designed by William Scamp in 1842

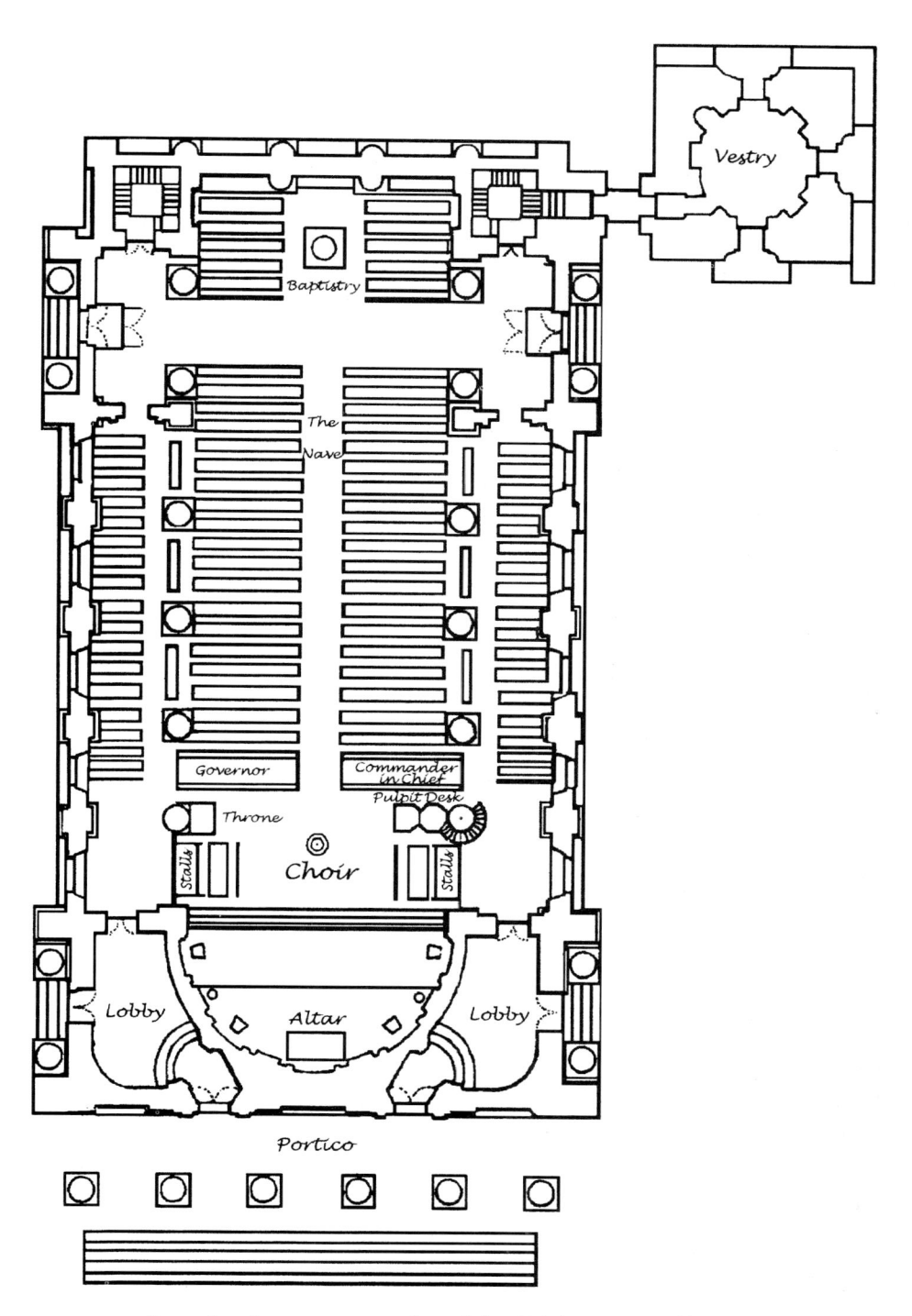

Interior layout as ordered by Bishop Tomlinson

He continues:

"The building now presents the appearance of Stability – I have examined and strengthened every part that appeared to require it and tho' it may appear that a very large sum has been expended for this purpose the Plans will shew that a great quantity of work has necessarily been executed. I believe the Committee are sufficiently aware of the necessity of all that has hitherto been done, and that this work has not been conducted imprudently or executed injudiciously and have great hopes now that the difficulties are nearly at an end of being able to complete the Church to their satisfaction."

On 29th September 1842, there was a fatal accident when a piece of the cornice on the Strada Ponente side of the building fell off and killed three Maltese workmen. Each family of the dead men was given a donation of £5.

Another report sent by Scamp on 28th March 1844, contains his comments on the increased costs incurred, and estimate for completing the Church.[5]

"In a former report it was stated that to rectify the defects in the original construction with the necessary alteration had cost about £2,000 instead of £1,000 as originally estimated to this must be added:

1st. Altering the position of the Tower
2nd. Restoring the Cornice to the South Side of the Church, it having fallen from original imperfect construction.
3rd Alteration in consequence of changing the position of the Altar as suggested by the Bishop of Gibraltar
4th An expense incalculably created by the habitual indolence and incapacity of the workmen much of this might have been avoided had the original design been more in accordance with the customs of this Island.

With respect to altering the position of the Tower I have to observe that for the sake of economy the Tower was originally intended to be attached to the Church at the South side but having an opportunity of making a better arrangement; the plan for placing it as it now is (and detached) was submitted to the Governor and Committee by whom it was approved the Tower is built on the Rock to the depth of 35 feet below the floor of the Church.

I have further to remark that in my opinion the Tower in which should be the Vestry room, Bells, Clock, etc, should always be detached from the Church; the Vestry room especially and the disgraceful practice of settling Parish disputes, and other matters of business within the Walls of the Sacred Edifice should not be permitted and that the Church should stand alone."

The original estimate for building the church was £8,000, but as explained by William Scamp in his reports, considerable unforeseen extra expenses had to be met, and the final figure was around £20,000[6] which Queen Adelaide met from her own resources. Such a large amount left her unable to provide any money for the endowment of the church.

Queen Adelaide showed her appreciation of William Scamp's work by giving him as a present, an inscribed silver-gilt candelabra on 1st March 1845.[7]

Notes

[1] His weather worn tomb can be seen in Msida Bastion cemetery
[2] 'The Life and Letters of Robert Clement Sconce', by his daughter Sarah Susanna Bunbury, published 1861, Cox & Wyman, London. Two Vols.
[3] Held in the Wignacourt Museum, Rabat.
[4] At the same time William Scamp was engaged in building the new Naval Bakery in Vittoriosa. This building now housed the Maritime Museum.
[5] Held in the Wignacourt Museum, Rabat.
[6] In 1999 monetary terms around One Million Pounds
[7] It came up for sale at Phillips Auction House in Scotland, and sold for £8,000 in 1990.

Chapter 6

Consecration

George Tomlinson was consecrated first Bishop of the See of Gibraltar on August 24th 1842 at Westminster Abbey, London. He arrived in Malta at the end of 1842, and was welcomed by a deputation from the island's S.P.C.K.

His degree of jurisdiction over the clergy was unclear. The Chaplain to the Government in Malta, the Reverend Cleugh, was appointed by the Government not the Bishop. Also the Army and Navy Chaplains were not under his authority, but co-operated with him as much as possible.

R. C. Sconce[1] was among the English residents who were impressed by him:

"Our good Bishop" Sconce wrote, in January 1843, *"I have asked him to dine with us, and he is coming to meet a small party the day after tomorrow. We all like him exceedingly. He is apparently just what he ought to be to contend with all the difficulties of his position in such a society, as he will be immersed in.... He preached last Sunday an admirable sermon at our chapel. He neither spouted his sermon nor read it like an essay; but addressed to us what he had to say in the tone in which he would have spoken if the words had arisen from the impulse of the moment. I listened to him willingly, because I saw that he was himself interested in claiming my attention...".*

Dr. Tomlinson decided to reside for six or eight months of each year at Malta or Gibraltar, though mostly at Malta since its central situation gave him more flexibility of transport to other parts of the Diocese, also he was without a house in Gibraltar, but in Malta he had the Auberge d'Aragon at his disposal, which was on the opposite side of the square to St. Paul's, and became known locally as 'Gibraltar Palace'.

One of his first actions was to institute an evening service at the Government Chapel at which all the seats were free.

On Thursday 26th January 1843, he consecrated the British Burial Ground located in the Bastions at Floriana, which had been used since the British arrived on the island, but had recently been enlarged. He was accompanied by the Civil and Naval Chaplains, which caused considerable interest amongst the British residents and Maltese alike.

R.C.Sconce noted:

> "Almost the whole of the English population was present at the consecration. The Bishop perambulated the ground preceded by a verger in purple and followed by ten clergymen in their surplices and scarfs. So many clergymen were certainly never assembled here before. It has happened three times that we have been left for months together with one only to supply all the wants of the 5,000 English which there are generally here including the troops."

On January 31st Dr. Tomlinson held his first confirmation ceremony in Malta, in the Government Chapel which was over-crowded for the occasion. Around 270 people were confirmed, of whom a considerable number were naval officers and seamen.

The Church of St. Paul was still incomplete when Bishop Tomlinson took up his post, and Queen Adelaide gave him the task of supervising its completion, which he undertook but ordered the architect to move the altar to the East End, so reversing the interior design.[2]

The consecration was originally fixed for 1843 as shown by the date on the Communion Plate, which had been specially prepared for presentation on that occasion, but this proved to be impossible. However, towards the close of 1843 the ceremony seemed imminent, and Mr. Sconce wrote in November:

> "You will be glad to hear that our poor church has got over its difficulties, and is to be ready for consecration without fail on St. Paul's Day, the 28th January. The good Queen Adelaide has promptly answered every fresh demand upon her for it, and has desired only that the work may be brought to a satisfactory completion. There was meeting of the people here, in my absence, to subscribe money for an organ and other church furniture, and for paying the organist's salary."

But the consecration was delayed yet again. Governor Bouverie who had been a very popular Governor, and assisted Queen Adelaide's concept since the beginning, had resigned in June 1843 for health reasons. His successor was Sir Patrick Stuart who took the office on 13th July 1843, and has been described as rigid and inflexible in his outlook.

Just a week after the new Governor took office, the Bishop wrote to him:

> "The new church of St. Paul's is now approaching its completion internally and will be ready for consecration in the beginning of December .... It was the intention of the Queen Dowager that the church should be the cathedral for this part of my jurisdiction and according to Her Majesty's wish I have had the interior arranged in such a manner as to adapt it for that purpose and yet at

the same time give it all the accommodation and advantages of a parochial church.[3]"

This led to a dispute between the Bishop and Governor Stuart since the latter objected to it being named a Cathedral, as Gibraltar had already been chosen as the See city.

Lord Howe, Chamberlain to Queen Adelaide wrote to Lord Stanley:[4]

*Marlborough House
March 16, 1844.*

*"My Lord,
It having been made known to Her Majesty the Queen Adelaide that the Church of St. Paul built at Her Majesty's sole expense in the city of Valletta, and intended for the worship of Almighty God, the accommodation of the Protestant inhabitants of the island of Malta, and Her Majesty's Land and Sea forces employed there, is sufficiently completed for consecration. I have the honour, by Queen Adelaide's command to place this edifice in the hands and under the protection of the Queen's Government, with Queen Adelaide's hearty prayers that it may be calculated to effect the object contemplated in its erection."*

The Government responsibility as accepted in 1844 involved the payment from public funds of the stipend of the Chaplain to the Government. The responsibility for other expenses and for repairs was less definite.

The Bishop had written:

"It is certainly not creditable to us that in a city and a garrison like this the English soldiers should for so many years have had nothing but a schoolroom for divine worship . . . . I hope therefore that they will have the Chapel assigned to them as soon as the civil congregation is removed."

It was suggested that when St. Paul's was opened the Government Chapel in the Governor's Palace would be used by soldiers, with any overflow going to St. Paul's. Before the consecration the Governor appealed to the Secretary of State for the Colonies to obtain some financial assistance from the War Office.

However, the War Office did not agree, and proposed instead the use of the Government Chapel with a second service if the number of troops was too great to be accommodated at one.

Before the end of 1844, the dispute over the status of the building, which was now completed, save for the spire which was finished in 1845, was settled and the consecration date fixed. The compromise solution was to describe it as a "Collegiate Church", a term which, in spite of the inclusion of stalls for Canons, was at that time quite meaningless.

The consecration report in The Malta Times,[5] commences thus:

> *"All things having been prepared for the consecration of the new Protestant Collegiate Church of St. Paul: the morning dawn of the 1st November – All Saints day! saw the Royal Standard of England floating from the unfinished cupola of the new Church, as also the Episcopal flag at the Bishop's residence, other flags were flying at the Palace and various Consulates in honor of the day.*
>
> *Shortly after ten, many persons entered the Church and took their seats ... the placing of persons on their appropriate benches was admirably and judiciously performed by Mr. Sparkes and some other assistants. In fact Mr. Sparkes exertions in a variety of ways to forward the good cause is deserving of the highest commendation.*
>
> *At 11 o'clock there could not have been less than 900 persons in the Church, even the very side aisles were filled with chairs. His Lordship, the Bishop of Gibraltar, now began the ceremony of consecration by walking round the outside of the Church reciting the prayers, the Cross carried before him, and followed by his Clergy, H.E. the Governor Sir Patrick Stuart, Admiral Sir Edward Owen, Sir Hector Greig, Colonel Balneavis, Colonel Tylden, Colonel Bayley, Mr. Fletcher, Hon. J. Aspinall, a great number of Civil employees, and Naval and Military Officers.*
>
> *In this order of procession they entered the Church and walked up the centre Aisle to the Communion Table-reciting Psalms and Responses. The Bishop then walked down the Aisle and back again to his seat on a chair in the chancel, on the right hand side of the Communion Table. The Reverend Philip Mules sat on the other on the left."*

Archdeacon Le Mesurier began the morning service[6]. The First Lesson from the Book of Kings Chapter VIII, verses 22 to 62 was read by the Reverend Thomas Gifford Gallwey, Chaplain of HMS *Formidable*, and the Second one from the New Testament, Hebrews X verses 19 to 26, by the Reverend G. P. Badger, the epistle by the Reverend Philip Mules[7], and the gospel by the Archdeacon.

The Bishop ascended the Pulpit and addressed the congregation, taking his Sermon from the Second Chapter of St. Paul's Epistle to the Ephesians, verses 19 to 22 *"Now, therefore, you are no more strangers and foreigners, but fellow citizens with the Saints and of the household of God; etc ..."*

However, The Malta Times says:

> *"We would only mention that when His Lordship remarked on the splendid gift of H.M. Queen Adelaide, in building the Church of St. Paul he was so visibly affected as to be unable for some moments to proceed, his feelings so overcame him that he shed tears and was compelled to omit a portion of his sermon.*

29

After the sermon a collection was made by the following Gentlemen; Captain Cumberland 42nd R.H., Captain Adams 88th, Lieutenant Bedford Royal Navy, and Messrs. Leonard and Sparkes, amounting to £112."

The report in the "The Gentleman's Magazine"[8] included several details regarding donations to the Church:

"The Communion Plate of silver gilt is the gift of Lieut-General Sir H.F.Bouverie, the late Governor. The furniture of the interior, together with the organ, bells, etc. were provided by a subscription at the head of which stands the present Governor, the Hon. Sir P. Stuart, and the principal English inhabitants aided by friends at home. The font, of white Carrara marble is the gift of the late J.W.Bowden Esq. The great Bible was given by the late Countess of Denbigh, the Prayer Book by the Countess of Sheffield, and the books for the Communion were given by the Rev. J. Ryle Wood[9] and the Rev. Philip Mules."

Another observer noted[10]:

"The effect was heightened by the kindness of a number of ladies and gentlemen from amongst the most respectable of the English residents, who sang the chants and psalms in the organ gallery, with much precision, amongst whom were Mrs.W.Frere[11] and her two daughters, who sang Marcello's admired anthem 'O Lord, our Governor', in a manner which evinced the superior taste and science of the singers. The day was one of the finest of that delightful climate, with just enough wind to display the Royal Arms on the Standard which floated in the air from the tower of the church, while the English Ensign, was hoisted over the Governor's Palace, and on the conclusion of the ceremony a Royal Salute was fired from the Castle of St Angelo.

As this is the first edifice built in Malta for the worship of the Divine Being, according to the ritual of the Anglican Church, its conspicuous situation in an open square in the most quiet part of the City of Valletta is a circumstance. Instead of going, as formerly to an obscure chamber on the ground floor of the Palace of the ancient Grand Masters, which suggested to the native people but a poor idea of the religious zeal and feelings of our countrymen, the English Christian will now be seen walking in the open light of day, into an elegant edifice where he may worship his God, and manifest his convictions of the truth of his belief, in the way most conducive to the object of public worship."

Two days later the Bishop performed the first baptism ceremony in the new church, when he baptised the seven-month-old daughter of the architect William

Scamp and his wife Harriet. Appropriately, the baby girl was given the names Adelaide Frances Melita[12].

The spire was duly completed during 1845, when the six bells cast by C. &. G. Mears[13] of Whitechapel, London, were hung in the belfry.

Notes

[1] 'The Life and Letters of Robert Clement Sconce, by his daughter Sarah Susanna Bunbury, published 1861, Cox & Wyman, London. Two Vols.
[2] PRO Kew CO.158/126 Letter 22nd July 1843.
[3] PRO Kew CO.158/126.
[4] PRO Kew CO.158/130.
[5] Tuesday 5th November 1844.
[6] The Rev. John Cleugh, the Government Chaplain was ill, and away from Malta at the time of the consecration.
[7] Chaplain to the Bishop of Gibraltar.
[8] December 1844 page 632.
[9] Chaplain to King William IV and Queen Adelaide.
[10] As reported in the London 'Morning Post'
[11] Mary Frere, nee Gurdon, widow of William Frere. Sister-in-law of John Hookham Frere.
[12] St. Paul's Baptism Register.
[13] This foundry was opened in 1567 and is still in existence today, 1999, having changed ownership many times during this long period. It is one of the two remaining bell foundries in England. It is now the Whitechapel Bell Foundry, 32/34 Whitechapel Road, London, E1 1DY.

Chapter 7

Bishop Tomlinson Era

To be the first English Bishop in Malta was not an easy task. 'Gibraltar Palace' was situated only a few yards from the Roman Catholic Bishop's Palace in Strada Vescovo. Archbishop Caruana was accorded military honours by the British, and since Bishop Tomlinson was not entitled to these, an attempt was made to equalise the position. In a despatch of September 14th 1842, the Secretary of State directed that these honours be discontinued after Archbishop Caruana's death, but these directions, however, were not followed and even in 1858 a Garrison Order was issued stating; *'All guards to turn out to the Archbishop of Malta, and all sentries to carry arms and present arms when the Host passes'*.

Dr. Tomlinson soon found himself in a difficult position, whilst the local Roman Catholic clergy and population resented his presence, the non-conformists were equally ill disposed towards him since they felt that he was not sufficiently anti-Catholic, and such feelings continued for many years. The Methodist Church that opened on the island with much hostility from the local Maltese and clergy had made little headway and it was decided in 1843 to withdraw their Minister because:

> *"Little or no access could be gained to the native Maltese by a Protestant minister, whom they were taught to regard as a dangerous man to be shunned and whose labours were consequently largely confined to the English and Scottish residents and troops."*

Since the money could be put to better use elsewhere, on 26th December 1843 the house, church and premises were sold to the Free Church of Scotland, and the Methodist soldiers and sailors were left in the care of a layman, Mr. J. V. Allan.[1]

The Bishop also had to deal with the complex marriage problem of Mr. Camilleri[2], a Maltese Roman Catholic priest who renounced his Catholic beliefs, and became a Protestant clergyman. He married a Maltese widow, Mrs. Fleri, but she had children by her first husband, a Roman Catholic. This resulted in a series of criminal, legal and civil actions[3] in June 1844. On the other hand even ordinary British soldiers and sailors were switching to the Roman Catholic religion as a convenience in order to marry Maltese girls.

The Reverend John Baillie of Linlithgow, who had been attached to the Malta Presbyterian mission in 1847 wrote a long letter to an Edinburgh journal[4] attacking the Bishop for consecrating the English Burial Ground in Floriana at the beginning of 1843, and The Malta Times[5] commented:

"With all due deference to the Bishop we must in candour acknowledge that it is impossible to peruse that letter without coming to the conclusion that in consecrating the Cemetery he committed a most unjustifiable act. The ground up to the time of his arrival was common property, alike available for Presbyterian as well as Episcopalian. It, of right, belonged as much to the Scotch as the English part of the community, and it was an unjust act virtually to cast them from what was in fact their own. The case is so clear that it would be a mere waste of words to say more about it. Undoubtedly the Bishop has a right to consecrate burying grounds, but let them be his own. What he ought to have done was to have applied for a new piece of Ground and nobody could have blamed him for consecrating it but what excuse can there be for taking the sole possession of the whole of that, a part which had been for half a century the undoubted property of other religions bodies. These things cause great irritation among Protestants who in these days particularly should be united like brothers against the common foe. The Scotch are greater fools than anybody takes them for if they put up quietly with such a barefaced grasping act of intolerant bigotry and injustice."

In 1846 the Governor, Sir Patrick Stuart who was a strong Sabbatarian, when issuing the customary proclamation giving formal permission for the pre-Lent Carnival to be held, he omitted to authorise its celebration on the Sunday.

The people felt that their ancient rights had been interfered with. It was hinted that the Governor had entered into an agreement with Bishop Tomlinson[6] to enforce a rigid observance of the Sabbath, to which the inhabitants of Roman Catholic countries were not accustomed.

Everything passed off well enough on the Saturday, but on the following day, Sunday, large numbers of Maltese from the countryside flocked into Valletta and by about two o'clock a mob of several thousand thronged the principal streets of the city.

Whilst the Governor's proclamation was observed by the people, and no one appeared in masks or any kind of fancy dress, their horses, mules, asses, dogs, and other animals were led about decorated with ribbons, and other forms of ornamentation, as it was interpreted that the Governor's prohibition did not extend to animals. At the same time several young men walked in a solemn procession along the square opposite the Governor's palace dressed in the conventional black suit and white necktie of the Protestant clergymen whilst each held in his hand a book resembling a Bible. It was at once seen that their action was intended as a silent protest of resentment against the supposed interference of the Protestant Bishop with the rights of the people.

Whilst all this was going on the bells of St. Paul's Church were heard summoning the English residents to the usual Sunday afternoon service. Some rabble rousers shouted *"To the Protestant Church! let us pull it down!"* and a crowd ran down Strada Teatro so within a few minutes the building was surrounded. The clergyman decided to proceed with the service in spite of the small number of worshippers within, and the uproar from the large gathering of people without. The noise was such that the congregation could not hear either prayers, or sermon, and at any moment expected the crowd to rush into the church and attack them. However, there was nothing more than shouts, threats, and yelling for about an hour, then the mob moved back in the direction of the Governor's Palace.

It has been suggested that the Reverend Henry Seddall in his account of the disturbances described above, was too alarmist[7], since the official despatch[8] takes a calmer view and merely states that the crowd:

> *"endeavoured to insult the Government, not by masking, but by dressing up some of their number as Protestant Clergymen, and parading them with loud shouts and yelling about the Streets, around the Palace, and near the Protestant Church during divine Service."*

Another slightly controversial matter during Bishop Tomlinson's episcopate was the opening of the "Malta Protestant College"[9] on 3rd February 1846, with the Reverend Samuel Gobat[10] as Vice-Principal, though it did not come under the Bishop's jurisdiction. Apart from providing education for English, German and Swiss children in Malta, and the surrounding countries, it was opened with the object of attracting young men from Middle Eastern countries and educating them in the Anglican tradition. Though it flourished for a time, several difficulties arose and the school was closed down at the end of 1865[11].

The Reverend Cleugh seems to have co-operated quite amicably with the Catholic clergy, as shown by a report in the Malta Mail of Friday 15th January 1847:

> *"Married on the 13th at the residence of Mrs. O'Reilly by the Reverend Father Francis Tonna, Nathaniel Charles Butler, Ordnance Dept, and Charlotte O'Reilly, eldest daughter of the late Bernard O'Reilly, 18th Regiment. Afterwards at St. Paul's Anglican Cathedral by John Cleugh."*

The entry in the marriage register of St. Paul's Church reads:

> *"January 13th BUTLER, Nathaniel Charles, (21+), bachelor, born Marylebone, London, (Ordnance Dept.), son of Charles James & Jane*

The Dowager Queen Adelaide in 1849

Butler, to O'REILLY, Charlotte, (21+), spinster, eldest daughter of the late Bernard O'Reilly, Paymaster, 18th Regiment (Royal Irish), & Mary his wife. Witnesses: H.Balneavis (Major-General), Mary O'Reilly, Thomas Joshua Rutter."

All the English residents and Maltese citizens were saddened to hear news of the death of Queen Adelaide. During her four-month stay during the winter of 1838, she had been seen by thousands of people as she went out and about in an open carriage. Apart from her triumphal entry through the packed streets of Valletta on 4th December as she drove to take up residence at the Governor's Palace, she attended a large number of official and unofficial engagements. During the day, inspecting ships of the Royal Navy moored in the harbour, a Review of Troops on Floriana Parade Ground, visits to the Ospizio and House of Industry in Floriana, the National Library, the studio of the sculptor Ferdinand Dimech, and managed a journey over to Gozo. During the evening, visits to the opera, concerts, as well as numerous soirees, dinners and balls.

The Malta Mail[12] reported:

London. Sunday 2nd December 1849.

This morning at 7 minutes before 2 o'clock Her Majesty the Queen Dowager departed this life at Stanmore Priory to the great grief of Her Majesty and of all the Royal Family, after a painful and protracted illness, which she bore with exemplary patience."

and later in the same issue:

"THE LATE QUEEN DOWAGER: The order for the mourning directs the ladies to wear black bombazines, plain muslin or long lawns linen, crape bonds, shamoy shoes and gloves, and crape fans. The gentlemen black cloth, without buttons on the sleeves and pockets, plain muslin or long lawn cravats and weepers, shamoy shoes and gloves, crape hatbands and swords and buckles."

A serious cause for concern arose in 1850 when the Council of Government introduced the Penal Code of 1850, including articles 'Concerning Offences against the respect due to Religion', describing the Roman Catholic religion as "dominant" and calling for heavier penalties for offences against the Roman Catholic Church than for offences against other religious sects. The matter was referred to London, and after several years the Penal Code was adopted but the whole 'religious' clause was omitted.

Bishop Tomlinson appears to have dealt with the difficulties that arose, and became a well-liked member of the high society. Passing through Malta on his way to the Crimea, Sir George Higginson[13] noted:

"Last night I dined with General Fergusson; it was a military dinner, so rather dull. His cuisine is perfect, which enabled me to find a resource when conversation flagged. The General is evidently the popular man of the place; the Governor's dinners are voted nothing to the General's or the Admiral's.

The latter is also a very popular man – Houston Stewart by name; next in popularity comes the Bishop of Gibraltar, whom every one speaks well of; he resides here entirely."

In 1856 there was another disturbance outside St. Paul's, as reported in the local newspaper[14]:

"On Thursday last, eleven Maltese of the lower order were brought before the Magistrate, Dr. Ceci for committing a breach of the peace on the previous day. It appears that a marriage took place in Queen Adelaide's Church between an English mechanic[15], employed in Mr. Jackson's new steam bakery, and a Maltese widow who keeps a slop shop in Strada San Paolo. The fact of a Roman Catholic being married in a Protestant Church, added to her imitation of English costume, by wearing a bonnet, seemed to excite the ire of the canaille, who accordingly mobbed and insulted the bridal party, by hooting and screeching, as they were quietly proceeding towards their home. The mob consisted of two or three hundred persons of the lowest rabble and the uproar was carried to such a pitch that the interference of a large body of Police became necessary.... The charge was fully proved against ten of the accused who where fined ten shilling each. The fines were all immediately paid."

In June 1861 the Reverend Cleugh reported that he had in his possession the autographed letter of the late Queen Dowager[16] in answer to the address of the British Inhabitants of this Island, thanking her for her gracious bounty in providing funds for the erection of St. Paul's Church. The letter was enclosed in a silver filigree frame and he was requested to continue to take charge of it.

It was felt desirable for St. Paul's to be enclosed by iron railings, and Mr. William Jemison Smith[17], as Secretary of the Church Committee wrote on 11th June 1861 to the Governor, Sir John Gaspard Le Marchant:

"... Messrs. Emmerson & Murgatroyd have most liberally undertaken to supply the railings and gates at working price which they estimate at £260. There would be a further expense for a defence along the top of the walls encircling the Church for painting the railing and other items which may be estimated at £50. The Committee will endeavour to obtain conveyance of the rails, freight free".

After explaining, that the organ debt needed to be settled it meant that additional funds would be needed to purchase the railings, the letter goes on:

"Under the circumstances finding that it will be impossible to carry out the undertaking solely from private contributions the committee trust that His

Excellency will be graciously pleased to take the subject into his most favourable consideration and that His Excellency may find it in his power to authorize a grant of £150 from the public funds of these Islands."

The Chief Secretary replied on 25th June, *"H. E. cannot give a definite answer on their proposal before consulting the Secretary of State"*, but by the end of September £100 was made available by the Government for the various works required at St. Paul's, and the railings were duly ordered.

On many occasions the Committee of St. Paul's was approached with requests for some financial help and generally small amounts of money were granted to aid people in need.

Amongst those recorded are:

October 1861.
"Marchioness of St. George, 8 Piazza Britannica, Floriana.
My dear Mr. Cleugh, Will you excuse my again asking you to assist poor Mrs. Westhrop who Doctor Pisani assures me is well deserving some consideration from the Benevolent. Her disease is chronic, she may live many years, yet in a few hours may be found dead, the heart is also seriously affected, which disables her from earning a penny." The committee sent a donation of 10 shillings, and regretted that they could not do more.

In May 1862, it was decided that 10/-d. per month for four months would be given to Mr. Kennedy, since his wife had been discharged from the Lunatic Asylum, but this payment would stop if she were readmitted.

A year later in May 1863 the Reverend Cleugh reported that application had been made to him for some assistance towards the opening of a hospital in Floriana for soldier's wives and children, and the sum of £5 was contributed from the offertory collection for that project.

A letter was received from Mr. H.O.Wrench, Chaplain to the Forces.

"42 Strada Mezzodi, 14th December 1864.
Sir, I beg to make an appeal to you as chairman of the committee of management of St. Paul's Church for the donation of a portion of the offertory collected there.
The person on whose behalf I make this appeal is Mrs. Lamb, widow of the late Capt. Lamb of the 100th regiment who died here about 2 months ago. Mrs. Lamb had a very dangerous attack of fever at the same time with her husband and is still unable to leave her bed. To add to her troubles, she was prematurely confined on Saturday last, and I believe that £4 is the whole amount of money in her possession.... Mrs. Lamb has 3 children now living, the eldest of which is 12 years old, and the youngest about 2 years.

Capt. Lamb obtained promotion from the ranks and as she was in the same position of life with himself, they had no income beyond his pay. My reason for making this appeal to you is because I believe that a large proportion of the offertory at St. Paul's church is contributed by the Staff and other Officers of the garrison who attend the services of that church.

PS. I may add that Mrs. Lamb is now living in the house of Mr. Shand, Super.Barrack Sergeant and that he and especially Mrs. Shand have been most unremitting in their care and kindness to the poor bereaved widow" It was agreed that a donation of £10 be sent to her.

In March 1865:

"An application from the Rev. Mr. Hillman, Chaplain to the Forces, Cottonera District for a grant from the Offertory Fund to aid in the establishment of a sewing school for married women of the regiments under his charge was considered and it was decided to grant £5 for this purpose."

In November 1861, the behaviour of the Verger Mr. Mattock was brought to their notice, and after some discussion the Committee decided:

"Notwithstanding the highly improper and disgraceful conduct of R. W. Mattock, the Verger, his frequent intoxication and consequent neglect of duties, Resolved:

In consideration of his family and solely from motives of charity he be allowed to retain his position of Verger, but that it be clearly explained to him that this is the last time this indulgence will be extended to him and that the Secretary be directed to deduct from his months salary ten days pay being the time during which he had rendered himself incapable of attending to his duties on the occasions which gave rise to the present consideration of his conduct."

Reverend Cleugh and Archdeacon Le Mesurier called upon Mr. Charles McIver, at his Sliema residence, with a view to getting the iron railings and gates shipped from England freight free, and were successful. In early March a letter was sent to Emmerson & Murgatroyd saying that the rails and gates should be sent by Burns & McIvers Steamers of Liverpool.

At a meeting on 29th April 1862, the Rev. Cleugh read a note from Mr. Riechelmann, the organist, dated the 21st April:

"'Gentlemen, I beg you will kindly take into consideration this my application for an increase of my salary. Since the last four years the living here in Malta, as everybody knows, has become so very expensive, and is still increasing every

day, that it is quite impossible to get on with my present salary. Having been here now about four and a half years I trust you will grant my petition otherwise I shall be compelled to leave this place." but the committee regretted no increase could be given due to present state of church funds.

They also had to deal with the dismissal of the Verger:

"Having been reported and proved that notwithstanding repeated warnings of the committee especially on the 14th November 1861 R. W. Mattock the Verger has of late been for many days in a disgraceful state of intoxication so as to have come under the notice of the Police rendering himself incapable of attending to his duties, and bringing odium upon the Church.

Resolved; That he be dismissed from his offices of Verger and Collector and that his salary and percentages on collections be paid to this date."

A replacement Sergeant Robert Nicholas Beck, late of the 88th Regiment (Connaught Rangers), applied for the situation of Verger and Collector and since his testimonials were found to be highly satisfactory the Committee appointed him from 1st July 1862, and recorded a list of duties that he would be expected to perform:

"To be in attendance at the Church every day from 10 a.m. till Noon, and from 2 p.m. till 4 p.m. (except on those occasions when employed on other duties) for the purpose of superintending and assisting the cleaning of the Church, and also in dusting and arranging the furniture. To be in special attendance on Sunday mornings and evenings and other Great Festivals when there is Divine Service for the purpose of shewing strangers to seats in the Church. On these occasions to be present at least one hour before Divine Service commences to see that everything is in order. Attend to the closing of the Church after service is over, leaving the Key of the door next to the Tower in charge of the Sexton.

To trim and keep clean the lamps and prepare them for evening service when required.

To render any assistance to the Choir at their practice carrying out notices when required and seeing that the gallery is kept clean and the books properly arranged.

Whenever the Sacrament is administered to bring this Sacramental plate from Mr. Cleugh's house and return same as soon as Service is over.

To assisting the ringing of the Church bells when required.

To distribute notices for meeting of the Committee

To render such assistance to Mr. Martin (the Clerk) in the Church as may be required.

To put himself in communication with the Secretary relative to the collections to be made from the Congregation and from Visitors and to carry out his instructions as regards these and any other matters connected with the service of the church.

That his salary be three pounds per month as Verger, commencing from this 1st July 1862, and his remuneration for the collections made from the congregation and visitors be five percent of the amount collected."

Mr. Charles Harper, a leading member of local society, and a magistrate was concerned regarding the bad condition of the Church organ.

Valletta 28th July 1862

Gentlemen, Your organ is much out of order. It requires a general revision and tuning some of the stops are so bad that they cannot be used. A stitch in time may save nine.

I beg to recommend that a small expense be incurred to afford assistance to the Organist to put it in order. He cannot do it alone, one person must sit at the Keyboard, while the other is inside the organ. It will require 4 or 5 visits to complete the operation and I should think 4/- or 5/- each time would be sufficient to pay a person to assist.

I hope you will confer with the Organist, and come to some arrangement with him as the salvation of the Organ requires in my opinion immediate attention.

Having safely received the consignment of iron railings and gates from England, a fulsome letter of appreciation was sent to Burns & McIver, of Liverpool:

August 2nd 1862.

Gentlemen, I write to you at the desire of the Committee for the management of the Fund of the Church of St. Paul's, Valletta. The cases containing the iron railings for the Church consigned to you by Messrs. Emmerson & Murgatroyd have been received, they arrived perfectly safe, without the slightest damage, and are now in course of erection.

The Committee are most anxious you should fully understand their very high appreciation of that liberality, which led you at once to accede to their application, and to your transmitting to them by one of your steamers free of all expenses, these heavy packages. They are quite at a loss how to express their sense of this special favour, the more so when they consider not only the voluntary large sacrifice of freight, and trouble necessarily incurred in the shipment, but the absence of all claim to such extreme generosity.

The Committee will gladly take an early opportunity of making known to the several English residents, who subscribed for the railings the very handsome manner in which you have thus gratuitously assisted them in completing

George Tomlinson D.D., 1794–1863
The First Bishop of Gibraltar
Crayon drawing by George Richmond R.A.

the work; and the Committee doubt not, that they, equally with themselves will always have a pleasure in acknowledging their great obligations, regretting at the same time that the only return they can make is the assurance of their most grateful thanks."

Mr. G.Calleja, the Sexton became too infirm to fulfil his duties, so from 1st of November 1862, a new Sexton, Mr. Alfred Gibson was appointed at a salary of £2. 5. 0d. per month.

Though money was always difficult to come by, at a meeting of the Church Committee, held on the 15th December 1862, Mr. R.C.Legh suggested that the Rev. Cleugh be requested to consider whether it would be possible to adopt the system of weekly collections for the distressed operatives in Lancashire and Cheshire which had met with such success in England, and was supported by Mr. Leonard.

A fortnight later, at the meeting of 29th December 1862, the Reverend Cleugh undertook to communicate with the clergymen of the other churches and chapels on Malta, Mr. Green, Mr. Thompson, Mr. Smith, Mr. Wisely and Mr. Howe, with a view to them joining with the Committee of St. Paul's Church so as to form a General Committee for establishing weekly collections in aid of the distressed Lancashire and Cheshire operatives, and making arrangements for transmitting the contributions to the General Committee in England.

Bishop Tomlinson died in Malta on February 6th 1863[18] and was buried in the Protestant Section of Ta Braxia cemetery, which he had consecrated in June 1857. Areas in this cemetery were available to all religions for the purpose of interment. Recognised Ministers of the various religions could officiate at burials, wear their particular vestments and carry out the service in accordance with their religion.

Notes

[1] The Floriana Story, Eric H. Fawthrop, Malta, 1963.
[2] The Reverend Michael Angelo Camilleri died in Weymouth, England, 10th April 1903. He had been Vicar of Lyford, Berkshire from 1863 to 1897.
[3] Malta Mail 28th June 1844.
[4] 'The Witness' 7th August 1847. Since the Bishop had consecrated the whole of the burying ground, when a young Presbyterian died his family did not want him to be buried there. However, to de-fuse the situation, the Governor, allocated a piece of land nearby for non Church of England burials.
[5] 27th September 1847.
[6] In has been stated in some books that the Bishop was the son-in-law of Governor Stuart, hence their collaboration. However, this is incorrect. George Tomlinson did not marry Louisa Stuart until 21st November 1848.
[7] 'Malta Past and Present', Rev. H.Seddall, London, Chapman & Hall, 1870.
[8] PRO Kew CO.158/134.
[9] For a detailed account of the Malta Protestant College, see an article by Salv. Mallia, in Melita Historica Vol. X No. 3.
[10] Samuel Gobat was a Swiss Lutheran Minister, and had worked for the C.M.S. in Malta. In 1846 he was appointed Bishop of Jerusalem.
[11] The buildings later became St. Ignatius College.
[12] The Malta Mail 21st December 1849.
[13] "Seventy-One Years of a Guardsman's Life", General Sir George Higginson, John Murray, 1916.
[14] Malta Times 7th October 1856.

[15] Robert Turner, from Kirkstall near Leeds, widower, married Maria Carmela Borg, nee Mamo, a widow.
[16] In St. Paul's Archives.
[17] A son in law of Thomas Corlett, having married the third daughter Caroline Corlett.
[18] A stone memorial is in St. Paul's Cathedral, and a memorial window in Holy Trinity Cathedral, Gibraltar.

Chapter 8

Bishop Trower Era

Between the death of Bishop Tomlinson, and the arrival of his successor, the work at St. Paul's Church carried on as usual. The letter from Mr. Harper regarding the condition of the organ had been acted upon, and Thomas J.Robson & Co.[1], had been contacted. They replied:

"Sir, In answer to yours I beg to state that I can send a competent person who can correct and tune again. In sending out from England we charge £1.1.0d. per day and all expenses, this would amount to so much in your job that I fear it could not be entertained. My charge therefore shall be £3.3.0d. per week from when he leaves London till his return and all expenses of whatever kind from leaving London that is living lodging and washing. This would be the best mode for you. You can judge very closely say three or four weeks at most correcting again (if not very bad) The party I send will have no desire to lengthen his stay as he will be wanted back in London.

If this arrangement is not satisfactory I will undertake to correct again (if not in a very bad state) and tune it for £57.0.0d. sterling and the assistance of a man on Island, all expenses on Island living, lodging and washing to be found extra by you. I paying everything else. Time, expenses, travelling, stewards, Inns, incidental expenses, etc.

Signed. Thomas J. Robson.

PS. I feel much indebted for your kind recommendation. We have lately been to Madeira to tune their organ."

Mr. Cleugh proposed that the painting of the Ascension, which it had been hitherto found impossible to sell, and which had been paid for by voluntary subscriptions from the civilian congregation, should be lent to the Civil Government to be hung up on the ward of the Civil Hospital for British Seamen.

This was duly done, and a letter dated 15th July 1863 from Mr. Inglott, Comptroller of the Civil Hospital duly acknowledged the loan:

"The undersigned declared to have received from the Committee of the Protestant Church of St. Paul a large painting with its frames representing

the Transfiguration for the purpose of being temporarily placed in the British Merchant Seamen's Ward in the Central Hospital for the edification of the sick. The undersigned further declares that the above painting is simply lent by the Church Committee to the Hospital with the distinct understanding that the same may be at any time claimed and removed by that body."

When news of Bishop Tomlinson's death was received, a writer in the Colonial Church Chronicle commented:

"In the present religious condition of Italy, and the whole country round the Mediterranean, the appointment of Bishop Tomlinson's successor is a matter of most grave importance. The new prelate will have it in his power to do much good or much evil to the cause of the Church of England and of the Church at large. He should be no Romanizer, no proselytizer, no invalid who would take the post as a mere accommodation; but a man learned, pious, and of pulpit ability, active and zealous, but discreet, possessing a knowledge of the World, familiar with foreign languages, ready always to embrace opportunities of explaining our principles and practices to Christians of other communions, determined to bring the means of grace and religious instruction to the poorest of British subjects in his Jurisdiction whether workmen or sailors."

Such paragons are rare, however desirable, but the man chosen to fill the Bishopric, Dr. Walter John Trower, was very experienced in ecclesiastical matters. From 1848 to 1859 he had been the Bishop of Glasgow, but had to resign from that position due to his wife's ill health.

He arrived in Malta towards the end of 1863, and very soon made application to the Society for Promoting Christian Knowledge, (S.P.C.K.), for a grant of prayer books for the purpose of holding services on board Royal Navy or Merchant ships which did not have a Chaplain, and also for use by the prisoners in the civil prison at Corradino.

Meanwhile the London Office of the P. & O. Shipping Company, confirmed that they would grant a 2nd class passage, free of charge, to Malta and back for the employee that Mr. Robson had arranged to send out to repair the organ. In fact it was his brother, who arrived in June 1864, and after an initial inspection estimated that the work would take six weeks. Mr. Leonard had arranged a room for him at Dunsford's Hotel with four meals a day at a rate of 4 shillings per day, but Mr. Robson requested that a small extra sum be allowed for him:

"... to take beer which he has been used to take with his dinner, and for a glass of brandy and water at night, which are not included in the arrangement with the Hotel and which he considers from long habit he could not do without

risking his health the work of the organ at present being heavy he is taking out all the pipes and some of the mechanical portions, and provoking thirst which he fears to quench with water."

The Committee was sympathetic to Mr. Robson's 'health' fears, and agreed that a sum of between 1 shilling and 1 shilling and sixpence per day be given to him. After the work was completed the Sexton, Alfred Gibson, asked for some compensation for his assistance to Mr. Robson with the repairs, and he was given a payment of 15 shillings. However:

"It having been reported to the Committee that Alfred Gibson has been employed in distributing the New Testament in Hebrew to the Jews (who have recently come from Barbary), without the knowledge of the Committee, the Committee called him before them and denied him in future from distributing any books or tracts to the Public without having previously obtained the sanction of the Committee."

A couple of months later Mr. Gibson, gave notice that he wished to resign from the situation from 1st January 1865, which was accepted.

A major improvement in the Church amenities was considered during July 1864. The Reverend Cleugh invited Mr. Fowles of the Malta and Mediterranean Gas Company[2], to examine St. Paul's and give his advice regarding the installation of gas lighting. Finding the idea feasible, it was decided to go ahead with trials and accordingly it was resolved:

"that the Malta and Mediterranean Gas Company be authorized to lay down the tubing agreeable to the plan suggested by Mr. Fowles say for the nave, aisles, organ gallery, staircases, and that Col. Montague and Mr. Leonard be requested to superintend the execution of the work."

The following March the Bishop of Gibraltar convened a meeting on Tuesday the 21st, of the congregation of St. Paul's Church to consider the question of lighting the church and after much discussion it was decided that it would be desirable for the church should be lit by gas. Not only did the talk about this topic continue for some considerable period of time, but also the project took over two and a half years before the final decision was made.

By September[3] it was decided that the fittings should be ordered from the catalogue of J.Hardman & Co. of Birmingham, and a very detailed letter describing the interior of the church, ideas for gas installation, and several questions, was written to them accordingly:

8th September 1865
"Gentlemen, As chairman of the committee of the Collegiate Church of St. Paul's, Valletta, I am instructed to communicate with you relative to gas

fittings which we wish to have erected in the above named Church with as little delay as possible.

... the committee having before them the new catalogue of Designs for Gas Standards ... and one viz: No.14 was selected. It is between these (Columns) that we propose to place a standard as marked in red in the plan, that is 4 standards on each side, 2 other standards will also be required to be placed in front of the Communion Railing, as also marked in red.

From the loftiness of the church and more especially to prevent the heat of the gas inconveniencing the sitters beneath the standards, these standards must be at a tolerable elevation. That elevation is a point to be well considered. The Committee leave it to your judgement, tho' after the trial made last year in lighting the Church with temporary fittings ... the height of the standards from the ground to the top of the Corona should not be less than 9 feet 9 inches.

Our idea is this, which we beg you to bear in mind, that the pattern of the Corona and of that part which supports the Corona should be Grecian in character to be in keeping with the church ornaments."

On 26th October 1865 J.Hardman of Birmingham wrote to Malta, submitting a quotation for the gas standards as requested, but by letter on 7th December 1865 Archdeacon Cleugh thanked them for their quotation but indicated that the church funds at the moment were not sufficient to go ahead and place an order.

A further six months went by before Hardman & Company were contacted again, and on 3rd April 1866, it was decided to request them to send out just one of the proposed standards to see if any alterations may be necessary before shipping out the others.

This sample standard duly arrived and was installed in the church so a special gathering of the Church Committee was called *"To meet on November 1st at 6 o'clock to have said standard lighted, in order to judge of its effect, and see if any alterations would be necessary."*

Archdeacon John Cleugh, Colonel Mitford, Mr. Thompson, and Mr. William Jemison Smith were present in St. Paul's that evening and after seeing the standard lit, unanimously agreed that the whole consignment should now be sent over to Malta for installation.

Up until 1864 the interior walls of St. Paul's were bare. In the September of that year the Archdeacon Le Mesurier died, and his sister approached the Reverend Cleugh with a request that she could arrange for a brass tablet to be put up in his memory. It was felt that a marble tablet would be more in keeping with the building with which she agreed.

The Bishop contacted the Governor, Sir Henry Storks, who had only taken up his post in November, who replied:

17th December 1864
"My dear Lord Bishop, I have had the pleasure of receiving your Lordship's letter of the 16th inst. and its enclosure herewith returned.

I concur in the view you take of the admission generally into the Church of St. Paul of Memorials of the description, which the sister of the late Arch Deacon Le Mesurier wishes to erect to her lamented and most excellent brother. But in the case you refer to such as ecclesiastics officially connected with the Church I think an exception should be made and I can see no objection to Miss Le Mesurier placing the tablet as she proposes, provided the design be sent out for approval and the place where it is to be erected pointed out.

In the case of the late Bishop I would gladly see some memorial to his memory, and if at any time a local movement be made with this object I would contribute my mite for I believe that both Bishop Tomlinson and ArchDeacon Le Mesurier labored with true zeal and great ernestness in arduous times and under difficult circumstances to improve the moral and religious condition of their flock."

The question of mixed marriages between Roman Catholics and Non-Catholics, which had already arisen during Bishop Tomlinson's time, re-surfaced. On 8th December 1864 the Reverend John Cleugh had performed a marriage in St. Paul's between Lieutenant John Rutter, of the Royal Malta Fencibles, and Margaret Giappone, both bride and groom being born in Malta, and by birth Roman Catholics. Lieutenant Rutter however had declared himself a Protestant, so convincing the Reverend Cleugh to permit the wedding.

It appears that Lieutenant Rutter was facing a breach of promise suit, and fearing that there would be a delay in his marriage to Miss Giappone, deliberately declared himself a Protestant, as a way of proceeding with the wedding. It was also known that in several instances Protestants had declared themselves Roman Catholics so as to avoid any delay in marrying Maltese girls. To prevent such abuses in future, Bishop Trower wrote to all clergymen within the Gibraltar Diocese:

"A circular has been addressed to his clergy by the Archbishop of Malta in reference to the common case of a Protestant wishing to marry a member of the Roman Catholic Church and abjuring his religion on finding that unless he becomes a member of that Church he cannot be married according to its rites without a dispensation from the Head of the Church of Rome. In such a case there is obviously too much reason to think that the abjuration has

not arisen from conscientious conviction, but merely from the desire to secure the ministration of a Roman Catholic priest for the marriage rite. And the Archbishop of Malta has directed his clergy to refuse (in such a case) the solemnization of holy matrimony until the person professing to abjure Protestantism has continued for six months a member of the Roman Catholic Church. The wisdom and justice of this direction are apparent.

And I hereby counsel and direct you (as far as the law authorises me to do so) to act on the principle thus asserted by the Archbishop of Malta, in the parallel case of a Roman Catholic professing to abjure his Church and declaring himself a Protestant, when seeking the solemnization of holy matrimony by an Anglo-Catholic clergyman. I recommend and direct you in such a case (as far as the law authorizes me to do so) to suspend or withhold the celebration of the marriage service until the person seeking its performance has continued for six months a member of the United Church of England and Ireland.

W. GIBRALTAR. Gibraltar Palace, Valletta, January 14th 1865.

An attempt to obtain a definite legal ruling from the British Government in the matter, however, proved unsuccessful.

The village of Sliema had been growing in size and was popular with English residents, largely married Army and Navy officers and their families, who found it a more desirable area to live than in Valletta. To meet their religious needs a Sunday evening service had been held in the schoolroom of the Malta Protestant College[4], in closeby St. Julians, but the College closed in 1865. This meant that they would have to travel to St. Paul's enduring uncomfortable conditions in summer due to the heat, and a hazardous crossing of Marsamuscetto harbour by boat in the winter months.

Accordingly, early in 1866, Bishop Trower issued an appeal for £4,000 to build and endow a Church and parsonage in Sliema, and opened the subscription list by giving £1,000 himself. His initiative was successful and by the 20th September the foundation stone of a new church in Rudolph Street, Sliema, was laid by the Acting Governor of Malta, Major-General Sir William John Ridley. The church, a beautiful little building in the early English style, was designed by G. M. Hill, of London, and constructed under the supervision of Webster Paulson, a civil engineer later connected with the Public Works Department.

Named Holy Trinity, Dr. Trower consecrated it on Easter Tuesday, 23rd April 1867, but simultaneously announced that he had decided to resign, since he felt that he was no longer young enough or active enough to travel as much as the needs of the Diocese required.

At the end of the year his successor was announced as the Hon. Charles Amyand Harris, Archdeacon of Wiltshire.

Notes

[1] Their premises were at 101 St. Martins Lane, London, W.C.

[2] Started as a private concern but converted in 1861 into a limited liability company with captial of £75,000. The Gas Works was located in Marsa, from where mains ran as far as St. Julians, Birchicara, Qormi and Tarxien.

[3] During the second half of 1865, there was a cholera outbreak, so church attendance and meetings were affected.

[4] In 1872 the property was bought by two Maltese, and in November 1877 opened as St. Ignatius College.

Chapter 9

Government Chaplain's Post Abolished

St. Paul's Church and the English residents of Malta benefited from the presence of Bishops Tomlinson and Trower on Malta for long periods, but future Bishops did not follow their example. Throughout the five-year period of his episcopate Bishop Harris only spent a total of about six months in Malta.[1] He therefore had little involvement with the day-to-day life of St. Paul's church as the records of his visits clearly show, but nevertheless some of his comments are interesting:

"I must now pass to Malta which I reached on the 8th of June (1868), remaining there till the 23rd, most royally entertained by the Governor, Sir Patrick Grant, at his Palace.... At Malta as at Gibraltar, strategic generally prevail over ecclesiastical considerations; the clergy with one exception, are military, naval, or civil chaplains. The church of St Paul's, with its unaccountable prefix of 'Collegiate' is simply a Government chapel under the ministration of the civil chaplain, and the Bishop's 'coercive' jurisdiction is confined to one individual the incumbent, or curate, of Holy Trinity, Sliema, a beautiful little church, built by my predecessor, Bishop Trower".

Later the same year:

"Of Valetta it is not needful to give a description. If, as to landscape, Naples be 'pezzo di cielo caduto in terra' Valetta as to society, is 'a piece of Belgrave-Square fallen into the Mediterranean', so unintermitting are its dinners, dances, 'kettledrums', and the like.

A word, however, as to its delicious winter climate. Up to the day of my leaving it, January 4th, the thermometer in my room without a fire had never sunk below 62 degrees. Outside, almost perpetual sunshine with fresh westerly breezes, and a temperature ranging between 58 degrees and 67 degrees. The chief materials for our Christmas church decorations, roses and the beautiful scarlet-tipped Poinsettia, which at Valletta becomes almost a tree."

During his second tour he stayed from 11th February 1870 until 30th March:

"Malta", he wrote, "...needs no notes beyond the satisfactory one of my finding 'All's well'. There is now weekly celebration of the Holy Communion at

St. Paul's, the Barracca Chapel, and at Holy Trinity, Sliema; daily prayer at the two latter; and on Wednesday, Friday, and all Holydays, at the first."

On St. Mathias's day, he confirmed 125 candidates, and on Sunday 13th March ordained William Bevill Browne, *"a very promising young deacon, who will assist one of the military chaplains".*

He returned again on 3rd February 1871, on his third tour, and recorded:

"Seven weeks passed away in the ever pleasant, though, somewhat secular atmosphere of Valetta. The most pleasing ecclesiastical event was the Confirmation of 102 candidates, of whom the larger portion were seamen. On March 25th I left Malta."

His final visit commenced on Easter Monday 1872 and ended on 6th June:

"Seven weeks at Malta furnished, as usual, but few subjects of ecclesiastical or religious interest. The most pleasing episcopal act I had to perform was the confirmation of 125 candidates from the Fleet. I cannot speak too highly of the quiet reverence with which these young men approached the rite, indicating as it did the careful and earnest preparation they had received at the hands of their chaplains. I held two other confirmations for military and civilian candidates, numbering sixty-six of both sexes. For once I quitted Malta without regret, having fallen into the grip of its most depressing fever, which from some unexplained cause had become epidemic, and had seized most impartially on fleet, army and native population."

In the meantime the Church Committee had received an approach from the Reverend M. C. O'Dell, and met on 1st May 1872, to give it their consideration.

"Sir, I have the honor to report on the information of Hon. Excellency, the General Commander that the case of the 52nd Light Infantry being stationed in Valletta, the small size of the Baracca Chapel will not admit of their accommodation at divine service at the same time with the Royal Artillery and as the Florian Troops now fill the Chapel at the time they attend, it will be necessary to have three parade services, rendering the risk of exposure to the sun during the summer considerable, for whatever troops attend the later service.

Under these circumstances I recommend that application be made for permission for the troops in Valletta to be allowed to attend at 9 a.m. at St. Paul's church, the troops in Florian continuing to attend the Baracca Chapel. The Chaplain who has to officiate to the Valletta troops being then relieved of the 3rd parade service which would have fallen on him had the troops attended at the Baracca might in consideration give assistance to the incumbent of St. Paul's at the Civil service at 11 a.m. It being clearly understood that the Military Chaplain is to be solely responsible for the ... of the military service in according with military regulations.

A fatigue party, viz: Corporal and 6 men could be sent on Saturdays to give assistance to the Church attendants in preparing the church for service, and a similar party can remain after the service to remove any dust or left by the troops in the sitting."

The Committee accepted this proposal with some minor reservations, and a letter sent to the Chief Secretary's Office accordingly.

Bishop Harris never fully recovered from the Malta fever he contracted during the 1872 visit, and ill health led to his resignation on October 11th 1873.[2] His successor, Charles Waldegrave Sandford, was appointed by Royal Mandate, as it had been decided in 1872 to cease appointing Colonial Bishops by Letters Patent.

Bishop Sandford was Bishop of Gibraltar for almost thirty years. He settled at Cannes, in the South of France, rather than Malta, but made sixteen visits to the island during his term of office.

Much of his time was taken up with the complicated legal situation regarding the ownership and responsibilities of various parties in relation to St. Paul's Church and Holy Trinity, Sliema, due to the different manner in which they were originally established. However, after much discussion the matter was resolved by setting up the Anglican Church Commission.[3] It consisted of five members; the Bishop of Gibraltar was a permanent member, with four others appointed by the Crown.

At the first meeting held on 21st February 1880, the other members were, Sir Victor Houlton Chief Secretary to the Government, Archdeacon John Cleugh, the Reverend E. A. Hardy Chaplain to the Government, and Mr. H. L. Gale. This Commission with changing membership convened on an irregular basis, often with several years between meetings, and continued until 1983, when a motion to terminate the Commission was passed in view of Act XXXIX of 1972 The Anglican Church (Property) Ordnance.

The Commission spent the first twenty years of its existence trying to regularise the legal position of St. Paul's and Holy Trinity, Sliema, and its own authority since various building and re-building schemes were put forward. They also had to approve or turn down applications for the erection of memorial tablets in both churches. There was also the ever-present problem of finance, both for the Chaplain's stipends and the maintenance of the fabric of the buildings.

The problem did not become acute in the early days of the Commission, however, as the Church's finances were in a satisfactory state; the Chaplain's stipend was assured by the Government and an annual offertory of about £500 made possible the employment of Assistant Chaplains for St. Paul's, as well as the incumbent of Holy Trinity.

Regarding events at St. Paul's itself, the most significant happening in 1877 was the resignation of Archdeacon Cleugh as Chaplain to the Government, now 86 years old, after an outstanding service of fifty-three years to the English community. He died four years later on 25th March 1881, and was buried in Ta Braxia cemetery. His place at St. Paul's was taken by the Reverend Henry White, but he left after one year, and the Reverend Edward Ambrose Hardy arrived in October 1878 to be the Chaplain to the Government.

In the middle of 1877 Mr. Gale reported that the organ needed repairing since thirteen years had elapsed since it was last restored, and he wrote to Robson & Co. A reply came from Gray & Davison of London, saying that they had taken over the business of Robson & Sons, and were arranging to send out one of their employees, Mr. Monk, to clean and make whatever repairs were necessary. He arrived on 4th August on board the P.& O. steamer *'Khedive'*.

A Memo accompanying the Church Accounts for 1881 says:

> *"In presenting the Accounts for the past year, the attention of the Congregation is necessarily called to the adverse balance of £34.10.5d. Our necessary expenses for the present year, including our debt, are estimated at £470.*
>
> *It will be remembered that a large proportion of our expenses are incurred on behalf of the British Mercantile Seamen in the Civil Hospital and in the Civil Prison. During the past year there have been 244 British Seamen in the Hospital and 55 in the Prison. Spiritual ministrations have been provided for these in the form of a service four days in the week at the Hospital, and once a week at the Prison, besides such other visits and help as the circumstances seemed to render advisable or necessary. The numbers show a slight increase of Patients in the Hospital and a considerable decrease of Prisoners in the Prison.*
>
> *It will also be remembered that it was proposed last year to make some alterations in the Church including the removal of the Organ to the East end at an estimated cost of £350. This proposal was however postponed in consequence of the lamented death of the Venerable Archdeacon Cleugh."*

Mr. Carl Franz Riechelmann, who had been the organist for about twenty three years tendered his resignation from the end of 1881, to take up an engagement in London[4], minutes say *"with a view of bringing his wife before the public in London as a singer."*

In April a Mr. George Havelock[5] of Basingstoke, Hampshire, applied for the post and was accepted. It is not known exactly when or why he left St. Paul's but in 1885 the Reverend Hardy felt it advisable to have a schoolmaster and organist combined, and sent a letter offering the position to Mr. Walter Stanley Robinson[6] of Carlisle, who accepted. He was 27 years old, and upon arriving in Malta, established the Collegiate School for boys and girls.

There was discussion and confusion for many years regarding the legality of marriages by non-Catholics which had taken place in Malta, so in 1889 General Sir Lintorn Simmons[7] was sent as the British Envoy to Pope Leo XIII at the Vatican to discuss this and other religious questions. The validity of completely non-Catholic and mixed Catholic/non-Catholic marriages in Malta was finally agreed; but in the matter of 'conversions' due merely to a desire to avoid delay in getting married, it was decided that no legislation could usefully be introduced into what was primarily a matter of personal conscience.

On April 11th 1894, a debate with far-reaching consequences for the Church of St. Paul took place in the Malta Council of Government, when Monsignor Mifsud put forward the motion:

> *"It is the opinion of this Council that a humble address be made to His Excellency the Governor praying that he may be pleased to recommend to the Imperial Government that the sum of £551.15.0d. allotted to the Chaplain of the Established Church of England be removed from the Civil List."*

It was unjust, he declared, that a Roman Catholic population should be called upon to support the priest of another religion from the revenues, particularly as there was no parallel post for a Roman Catholic priest.

The Governor General Fremantle transmitted the resolution to the Secretary of State in London, Lord Ripon, who replied that *"when Archdeacon Hardy vacates the office of Chaplain to the Government of Malta the question of its abolition shall be considered."*

Archdeacon Hardy made the next move. At the end of 1894 feeling that *"the Chaplaincy cannot much longer survive the agitation of the Maltese based upon the contention that a purely Roman Catholic community ought not to be compelled to provide a stipend for a Protestant Chaplain"* and in the knowledge that it almost certainly would be abolished on his death or sudden retirement, he submitted to the Governor that it would be to the benefit of the Church of England if he retired in the near future, leaving time for the authorities of St. Paul's to make arrangements to meet the altered circumstances. He did this with the approval of Bishop Sandford, though both were most emphatic that the rights of the civilian and naval worshippers should be safeguarded in accordance with Queen Adelaide's original intentions.

At the time Mr. Hardy commented in a letter to the Colonial Office:

"The congregation of St. Paul's is composed almost entirely of 'well to do' people, Officers and their families and visitors for the winter season, and there is no reason for supposing otherwise than that they will, if required, provide as liberally for the Clergymen in Malta as is the case elsewhere."

Regretfully this statement proved to be wildly over-optimistic. When the Government stopped paying the Chaplain's stipend, the financial headache of obtaining adequate funding for St. Paul's started, and has continued ever since.

Notes

[1] Bishop Harris preferred to concentrate his efforts on covering the whole area of his jurisdiction. He covered some 49,000 miles over the scattered Diocese, and visited many chaplaincies his predecessors had never seen.

[2] He died in England on 15th March 1874.

[3] Many original records of the Anglican Church Commission are now lodged with the Guildhall Library, London.

[4] Born 1832, near Hamburg, Germany. He returned to Malta from London and became organist at the Presbyterian church.

[5] Before leaving England on 30th April 1881 he married Elizabeth Clara Daisy Unwin.

[6] He spent the rest of his life in Malta. His wife Janet died aged 35, in 1894. He died 15th August 1938, aged 80. Both buried in the same grave at Ta Braxia cemetery.

[7] He had been Governor of Malta from 1884 to 1888.

Chapter 10

Anglican Church Commission

The chaplaincy was finally abolished on 31st December 1895, but in the months before then there was considerable anxiety amongst the civilian residents that St. Paul's would be handed over to the Military authorities, but if they wished to avoid this happening they would have to raise sufficient money to meet the cost of maintaining a Civil Chaplain.

The minutes of a meeting of interested parties held on Tuesday 21st May 1895 clearly show what needed to be done to keep the church in civilian hands, in accordance with the wishes of Queen Adelaide. The full text is given in Appendix 2.

Clause No. 8 reads:

> "That a fund for the endowment of the Chaplaincy be at once initiated and that H.E. the Governor, and Admiral Commander in Chief and the Bishop be invited to be Patrons of a Committee to be nominated by this conference to open such Fund to secure contributors and to receive the Donations that may be made to it, and that the Patron of the Chaplaincy shall always be the Bishop."

Admiral Sir Michael Culme Seymour, the Commander-in-Chief Mediterranean Fleet, approved the raising of an endowment fund, but Governor Fremantle was somewhat dubious, and he wrote to Colonel Wood:

> *S. Antonio – 24th May 1895.*
>
> "... *Personally I do not see any reasonable prospect of raising a fund of say £10,000 for the eventual endowment of the church, unless something quite unforeseen were to occur and I therefore think it would have been better to have negotiated with the S. of S. for War in order that if possible one of the Military chaplains should have been appointed (under proper safeguards) to perform the duties which have hitherto devolved, so far as St. Paul's is concerned, upon the Chaplain to Government.*
>
> *The majority of the congregation undoubtedly appear to think otherwise and evince an objection to any course which might tend directly or indirectly to place the church under the control of the War Secretary.*"

Due to his opinion he found it embarrassing to become a Patron as called for by clause No.8 but it was considered of vital importance that the support of the Governor should be secured. General Fremantle was approached by Colonel Wood, who explained that the congregation did not so much object to a Military Chaplain being in charge of St. Paul's but that they thought it desirable in the interests of the Anglican Church to have a church in Valletta independent of any Public Authority, whether Military or Naval. His Excellency understood this position and became a Patron of the Committee.

Bishop Sandford having considered the proposals put forward by the residents, wrote:

Bishopsbourne, Cannes, France. June 3rd 1895

"My dear Archdeacon Hardy, The settlement of affairs concerning the Civilian Chaplaincy and the Church of St. Paul, Malta, as set forth in the paper you have sent me has my approval and I earnestly commend it to English Church people for their support."

Help from friends in England was sought, and on the 20th of August a question was raised in the House of Commons, Sir Henry Fletcher[1] asked the Secretary of State for the Colonies:

"If it were intended to make any alterations in the arrangements connected with the Church of St. Paul's, Valetta, built by the late Queen Dowager Adelaide for the use of the Anglican community in Malta, which have existed for the last 50 years; could the correspondence on this subject be laid upon the table of the House, and was there any truth in the report that this Church as thus given by the late Queen Dowager was now to be converted into a military chapel."

Mr. Joseph Chamberlain replied:

"The church of St. Paul, Valletta, which was built at the expense of the late Queen Adelaide for the use of the Protestant inhabitants of Malta and her Majesty's land and sea forces employed there, has hitherto been served by the Chaplain to the Government. Last year in answer to an address from the Council of Government of Malta praying for the abolition of the salary of the Chaplain, the late Secretary of State said that when the office became vacant the question of its abolition would be considered, and subsequently he approved a proposal made by the Governor with the concurrence of the present Chaplain and of the Bishop of Gibraltar that the present Chaplain should retire on a pension, and that the office should thereupon be abolished, provided that arrangements were made for protecting the interests of the non-military portion of the congregation of St. Paul's Church. The question of the

arrangements to be made for the purpose on the abolition of the Chaplaincy are still under consideration. When the correspondence is complete, I will consider whether it can be produced. The answer to the third question is in the negative."

By the autumn of 1895 the total amounts guaranteed towards the stipend of a Civilian Chaplain were £267.10.0d. for each of the first two years and £228.0.0d for the third, and the Reverend Arthur Babington Cartwright took over the chaplaincy of St. Paul's from January 1st 1896.

The problem now was to raise a fund for the permanent endowment of the living. A start had been made by Mr. Hardman, as the following letter shows:

180 Strada Cristofero – 27th May 1895.

"At the penultimate sitting of the Commission it was decided that owing to certain difficulties which had arisen in connection with the building of a School House for St. Paul's Church, which my wife and I had contemplated erecting, the work should be postponed, and as it would now appear that the approaching abolition of the Government Chaplaincy renders the project undesirable we have decided to offer the estimated cost of such abandoned proposal (One thousand pounds Stg.) towards a Fund to be raised for the endowment of a Civilian Chaplaincy, for the said Church, provided that in the course of three years from this date other nine thousand pounds stg. for that purpose are contributed. Failing this scheme of endowment, we shall devote this sum of one thousand pounds in God's service as we may be best advised."

The appeal for £10,000 to *"Residents and Visitors in Malta to assist us both by their own Contributions and by gaining, for us the support of their friends"* was issued with Mr. Gale, the churchwarden as the Treasurer for this appeal.

At about the same time an appeal was issued in London by a Committee, which included Sir Victor Houlton as its Treasurer.

ST. PAUL'S, VALLETTA, MALTA – ENDOWMENT FUND

"On the 31st December 1895, the Chaplaincy to the Government of Malta, which had existed from 1802 was abolished; and the provision for the services at St. Paul's Church, Valletta, instead of being a charge upon the revenues of the Island, has to be supplied by private subscriptions, and from an offertory fund which during the last ten years has on the average not exceeded £300 a year, of which half is absorbed by the necessary expenses of the Church."

The letter then went on to give some details of St. Paul's foundation at Queen Adelaide's expense, and some history of the following years.

Unfortunately, the London Committee did not obtain a very generous response to this appeal, and a meeting was held at the Mansion House on June 28th 1898, in an attempt to arouse more interest. The Lord Mayor presided and the principal speaker was Sir Victor Houlton, who outlined the history and needs of St. Paul's. During the next year the London Committee continued to seek funds, press advertising proved of little value, but hand-written letters enclosing printed appeals proved more satisfactory, and 15,000 of these were sent out. The result was a net profit, after all expenses had been paid, of £772.14.8d. at the end of the year; the final total was £1,363.10.0d. but this was still very inadequate and a further appeal letter was sent to the Editor of 'The Times' in London on July 14th 1899.

In his Pastoral Letter of 1898, Bishop Sandford described the position of St. Paul's thus:

"We are there in the presence of a Church and people who regard us with watchful and not very friendly eyes. We have always abstained from interfering in the affairs of the native Church; but, while we rightly continue to pursue this policy, we feel that every effort should be made by us to uphold the position which belongs to our own. We ought to provide that the edifices in which we worship and the clergy who officiate in them, should be worthy representatives of our country our religion, and our communion.... The English civilian population ... require the ministrations of a clergyman who would settle permanently among them, and thus acquire an interest in them and their families, not being changed like the military chaplains every three years. If for lack of funds we should be unable to maintain a permanent civilian chaplain, our Church's influence would inevitably languish; much good work which it now conducts would drift away from us, and fall into other hands."

He continued: *"When we consider, that (the revenues of Malta) during the last 40 years have increased from £150,000 to £300,000 annually,...it can hardly be thought unreasonable that...this small sum of £500 should be annually granted from the revenues for the support of our Church."*

But there was no chance of the payment being resumed, and the War Office, though willing that troops should attend St Paul's when convenient, declined to give any financial aid to the Church.

On August 24th 1899 Sir Victor Houlton, Chief Secretary to the Government of Malta from 1855 to 1883, and a staunch supporter of St. Paul's died in London. He had worked tirelessly on behalf of the Church, and it was mainly through his efforts that money was raised in the London appeal.

In his will, drawn up on 28th July 1899, only a month before his death, Sir Victor left the sum of £1,000 for the endowment of St. Paul's:

"Provided that at the date of my death such Church shall in no way be connected with or under the management or control of the War Office. Authorities in London or of the Military Authorities in the island of Malta, and that the services of such Church shall at the date of my death be exclusively conducted by a Civilian Clergyman nominated for that purpose by the Bishop in whose See such Church shall be at the time of my death and provided also that such services shall not then be conducted by any Chaplain or Military or other Clergy nominated by or under the control War Office Authorities in London or the Military Authorities is the said Island of Malta."

The conditions being fulfilled, the £1,000 was paid by his Executors and invested in the Scinde, Punjab and Delhi Railway stock, as was £1,278 of the amount collected by the London Committee.

On April 2nd 1901, though the original conditions he had stipulated had not been fulfilled, Mr. Hardman and his wife Aloisa Annetta Hardman[2], gave the sum of £2,000 to the Society for the Propagation of the Gospel, to be held in trust as an endowment for St. Paul's, the interest to be paid to the Senior Church-warden or the Chaplain:

"Provided always that if at any time hereafter the said Church shall be taken over by the War Office or any other department of H.M. Government or the Governor of Malta, and if the services therein should at any time be conducted by a Military or Naval or any other Government Chaplain either Imperial or Local and provided that if at any time hereafter the Churchwardens, or Authorities of the said Anglican Collegiate Church of St. Paul shall fail to transmit to the said Society for the Propagation of the Gospel in Foreign Parts a copy of its annual statement of accounts showing the dividends or interest from the said Capital received by them to appear therein and to be called in that statement "THE HARDMAN TRUST", the said Capital sum of two thousand pounds (£2,000) and the Dividends and Interest thereof shall revert to the said Society as absolute owner thereof to be applied to any other purpose as in its discretion the said Society may think fit to direct."

The total income from both the Houlton and Hardman endowments was less than £140 per annum, and therefore the financial position of St. Paul's church continued to be exceedingly precarious.

Notes

[1] The Member of Parliament for Lewes, Sussex.
[2] She was born in Malta, the sixth daughter of Thomas Corlett. She was the widow of Joseph Whitaker when she married William Hardman on 17th September 1885. Her distinctive white marble grave is in Ta Braxia cemetery.

Chapter 11

Bishop Sandford's Visits

Without interfering with his pastoral duties with St. Paul's Bishop Sandford was concerned regarding the needs and difficulties of sailors, and he commended the work of the Missions to Seamen Society. This Society had maintained a Scripture Reader at Malta for a number of years, and the Reverend E. A. Hardy of St. Paul's acted as its Chaplain. More than 100,000 British sailors annually visited Malta, and though many of the ships only stayed for a few hours to take on coal, others were there long enough for their crews to be looked after by a 'Seamen's Chaplain'.

He spoke in 1878 at a meeting of the Church of England Temperance Society, held in the military gymnasium, at which he expressed grave concern at the casual way in which licences to sell wines and spirits were issued – at a cost of £4 a year in Valletta, and 4/-d. in other parts of Malta. There were nearly four hundred drinking-shops in Valletta – more than one to every four houses.

His work in this area was particularly appreciated by the senior Naval officers, and on occasions found them solid friends of the church. Admiral Inglefield, who left Malta in 1876, for example, had not only shown great interest in the welfare of sailors', and had turned the one-time sail-loft used as a Dockyard Chapel, into a *"comely place of worship."*

He shared in the mourning for Admiral Sir George Tryon and the officers and men of HMS *Victoria*[1] who were lost when the ship sank off Tripoli on the 23rd June 1893 following a collision with HMS *Camperdown*. Two of the twenty-nine candidates confirmed by the Bishop in the Dockyard Chapel in May were children of the Reverend Samuel Sheppard Oakley Morris, the Chaplain of HMS *Victoria* who was lost in the disaster.

During his term as Bishop of Gibraltar, Bishop Sandford consecrated several cemeteries. An addition to Bighi Naval Cemetery on the 8th May 1893; the new cemetery[2] at Imtarfa on the January tour; in February 1901 the Royal Naval Cemetery[3] situated near Kalkara, and the Church of England portion of the military cemetery on the island of Gozo, on Monday 28th February. Also in 1894, on Thursday 13th December in a brief ceremony he dedicated the Chapel in the grounds of Ta Braxia Cemetery. It had been built by Lord

Stanmore in memory of his wife[4] who was buried on the spot. The Governor and his Staff, the Chaplains to the Forces, and other British residents were present that afternoon, with Captain Gordon representing his uncle Lord Stanmore.

As required by clause No.10 of the Resolution passed on 21st May 1895 a meeting in the Vestry on 19th January 1897, to elect churchwardens, chose Mr. Hardman and Mr. Gale to represent the civilians, Mr. H. G. Chapple R.N. and Fleet Paymaster Mr. J. K. Mosse for the Royal Navy, Colonel Elliott Wood and Captain Frederic Gordon, Infantry Brigade Major, for the military.

The Governor, Sir Arthur Fremantle requested on October 27th 1898 that seating arrangements be made at the 11 a.m. service on Sunday morning at St. Paul's for men of the Sherwood Foresters then quartered at the nearby at Fort St. Elmo Barracks. Accordingly, spaces for 420 men were provided by using the galleries, the side aisles, and the first six benches in the nave.

Fremantle relinquished his Governorship at the end of December 1898, and was succeeded by Lieutenant-General Sir Francis Grenfell, who took the oath of office on 6th January 1899.

Later that month, whether as a result of the change in Governor or not, Archdeacon Cartwright was told that in future the Sherwood Foresters would only attend the 11 o'clock services on alternate Sundays and that on other Sundays two companies of the Border regiment, plus Royal Artillery, and Royal Engineers would be at the church.

Due to the continuing financial difficulties, in January 1899 the churchwardens wrote to the organist Mr. Robinson saying that they must cut his salary from £100 to £60 per annum. Though a significant reduction, he agreed on the understanding that he was not expected to pay the choirboys, and a suitable settlement for the choirboys was found.

At the Annual Meeting held on 17th January 1900, Mr. Gale and Mr. Hardman were re-elected as churchwardens for the civilians, but due to naval and military movements, new churchwardens were needed to represent them. Those chosen were Admiral Sir John Fisher and Commander Ricketts for the Royal Navy, Major-General D.O'Callaghan and Colonel Cameron, C.R.E. for the military. Sidesmen elected were, Major Boyd, Bertram Raves, Alfred Twelves, Henry Twelves, Mr. Starkey, Mr. Kimm, Captain Dyke R.N., Fleet Surgeon May R.N.

But Bishop Sandford also had to face the problem of finding a suitable chaplain for St. Paul's, since the Reverend Cartwright had left Malta early in 1901.

"In response to an enquiry from Mr. Hardman (in February), the Bishop informed him that the new Chaplain who he hoped would arrive here about

> *Easter, would remain for one year certain and would give three months notice if he intended to resign. Then the question of his stipend was discussed when on the proposal of Col. Cameron, seconded by Mr. Hardman it was unanimously agreed that in addition to three hundred pounds (£300), per annum half the balance at the end of each year should be handed over to him provided the amount did not exceed £50."*

Archdeacon Cartwright was followed by the Reverend F. Bullock Webster, who agreed to stay until September at the latest unless he decided to accept the post permanently. But he did not continue, and the Reverend Franklyn de Winton Lushington took over the chaplaincy in 1901.

The following year the AGM was held on 8th February 1902. Mr. Gale proposed and Mr. Hardman seconded a motion that:

> *"A unanimous vote of thanks be accorded to the Admiral, Commander in Chief Sir John Fisher, for his assistance by sending seamen to the Sunday morning service and in other ways rendering valuable aid to the church, also to Lady Fisher on the proposal of Mr. Hardman and seconded by Mr. Starkey for her kindness in continuing the Ladies Committee, who had collected £79.15.6d. in aid of the Church funds."*

At the same meeting the Churchwardens for the forthcoming year were elected:

For the Royal Navy: Admiral Watson and Admiral Hughes Hallett
For the Army: General O'Callaghan and Colonel Cameron
For the Civilians: Mr. Gale and Mr. Hardman.
Sidesmen: Major Boyd, Mr. B. Raves, Mr. Alfred Twelves, Mr. Henry Twelves, Mr. Starkey, Mr. Thomas Corlett Smith[5], Mr. Lockwood

In April 1902 the caretaker, Saverio Muscat, was unable to continue his duties due to prolonged illness, and he was retired and provided with a pension of 1 shilling per day throughout his life, but to cease on his death. He had served St. Paul's for many years, as Sexton, Bellringer, and Verger. He in fact lived until 5th July 1909. Colonel Stringer of the 3rd Battalion Garrison Regiment was approached with the view to getting a steady soldier to take over as caretaker of the church.

Notes

[1] HMS *Victoria* and HMS *Camperdown* were cruising parallel with each other when Admiral Tryon gave an order which meant that both vessels turned inwards towards each other.

Nobody queried this order, so it was obeyed with catastrophic results. The Victoria was rammed and sank within ten minutes with great loss of life, including Admiral Tryon.

[2] Now under the supervision of the Commonwealth War Graves Commission.

[3] Now under the supervision of the Commonwealth War Graves Commission.

[4] Rachael Emily Hamilton Gordon, died 28th January 1889, aged 60 years. Before becoming Lord Stanmore, her husband was Hon. Sir Arthur Hamilton Gordon.

[5] Son of William Jemison Smith, who had been Sec. to the Church committee.

Chapter 12

St. Paul's v Barracca Church – First Round

With the departure of the Reverend Lushington[1], the churchwardens were convinced that they needed a period of stability, and in reply to a question put by Mr. Hardman at a meeting on 7th March 1903, the new arrival, the Reverend Daniel Collyer was pleased to say that he had accepted the Chaplaincy permanently.[2]

At the close of 1903, Mr. Gale was suffering from ill health, making it increasingly difficult for him to carry out his duties as Secretary and Treasurer to the Church committee, so after thirty years service he decided it was time to resign.

Bishop Sandford was unwilling to continue in a post he was no longer able to serve as adequately as he felt necessary, and intimated his intention of retiring early in 1904; but he died at Cannes, on December 8th 1903, shortly after the choice of William Edward Collins had been made as his successor. Dr. Collins was enthroned at Gibraltar on February 7th and installed in his "second Cathedral" at Malta in March. A systematic series of tours, such as Bishop Sandford had undertaken, was not possible for him physically since he was a semi-invalid.

In February 1904 at the Annual Meeting of St. Paul's, Mr. Hardman retired as a churchwarden after many years service, but agreed to act as a sidesman, and Mr. Henry Twelves[3] was elected as his replacement, to represent the civilian worshippers.

There was at this time no permanent residence for the Chaplain. During the early years of the twentieth century a dwelling known as 'The Cloisters' was used; improvements were made to it during the chaplaincy of Archdeacon Collyer, but the finances of St. Paul's were so very precarious at this time, that he made a loan of £55 for the work to be done.

He led a discussion on the advisability of transforming the present quarters of the caretaker, which were situated under the church adjoining the crypt, into a dwelling house for the use of the Chaplain. Such discussions continued for more than twenty years before living accommodation for the Chaplain finally was provided in 1928.

A large meeting attended by the Churchwardens and members of the congregation took place on the 14th November. The full committee composed of Archdeacon Collyer, Captain The Hon. S. Colville, R.N., Mr. William Hardman, Mr. Alfred Twelves, Captain Worcester R.N.R., Eng. Captain Edwards, R.N., Mr. Henry Twelves, J. W. Starkey, Ernest Geoghegan, Mr. Reid, Mr. Anderson, Lieutenant and Mrs. Dyson, Thomas C.Smith, Mr. W. S. Robinson, organist, Mr. Baker, Mr. Wright, Mr. Moore R.G.A., were present.

The reason for such a large gathering was that the Military Authorities wished to take part of the collection in the Church on Sunday 23rd October and probably once a month for Military charities or purposes and the Archdeacon requested his member's thoughts on the matter. The full letter from the Senior Chaplain to the Forces was read out.

Additional disheartening news was provided by Captain Colville who informed the meeting that he feared very shortly the Naval contingent would cease to attend service at St. Paul's as a Naval Chaplain had been appointed, and would take services, for the crews of the smaller ships, on **HMS** *Leander*. This was unanimously regretted since it would mean a loss to the church funds of the annual contribution paid by the Royal Navy for the sailors attending the church.

It was unanimously resolved that in future, the civil choir with organ accompaniment, would take part in morning services, replacing the military band, and the secretary wrote to the Senior Chaplain of the Forces and the Officer Commanding the regiment at St. Elmo of this resolution.

Bishop Collins was only in Malta for three short visits on his 1905[4] tour, but during the first one he performed the consecration ceremony at the Pieta Military Cemetery[5], on 24th February.

At the Annual Meeting held each year at which two churchwardens were elected to represent the Navy, Army and Civilians, the 1905 participants elected the Hon. Capt. Colville and Eng. Capt. Edwards for the Royal Navy, Colonel Sill, C.R.E. and Colonel Bushe, R.G.A. for the Army, and Henry Twelves with John W. Starkey[6] for the civilians.

Early in 1905 Mr. Goll of Lucerne came to St. Paul's to inspect the organ, and later submitted an estimate for the repairs and improvements, which he considered necessary. On the 1st May a meeting was held at which Mr. Robinson, the organist was able to give his response to Mr. Goll's plans. After hearing Mr. Robinson's opinion, it was agreed to accept the proposed improvements, which included using electric power for blowing the organ.

Archdeacon Collyer felt that a suitable memorial should be erected in St. Paul's in memory of Mr. Gale, who had been a devoted worker for the church for so many years. At a similar time Mrs. Gordon Paterson requested permission to place a tablet in the church in memory of her 18-year-old son[7] who had died in January 1905. Both were approved and their location on the church wall was decided.

Some slight improvement in the financial position came in 1905 when, a grant of £100 per annum was obtained from the military authorities in return for the use of St. Paul's by certain troops and for military duties undertaken by the Chaplain and it was agreed by the Bishop and the churchwardens that 50% of this should be devoted to a fabric fund, the remainder being added to the stipend of the Chaplain.

In the letter approving this arrangement, the churchwardens requested that a fit man should be appointed to replace the Reverend Collyer who had resigned in September 1905 after only two years, to take up a living in England. They asked that adequate safeguards be taken to prevent undue absences or hasty resignations. At that time it was reckoned that there was an English colony of around 20,000 persons living on Malta.

The Bishop appointed the Reverend Charles George Gull, who had been the Headmaster at the Grocer's Company School since 1882, at first temporarily, but later as the permanent Chaplain of St. Paul's.

Two new churchwardens needed to be elected for the Royal Navy in 1906, since during the year both the Hon. Captain Colville and Eng.Captain Edwards had departed from Malta, and accordingly Fleet Surgeon Lomas R.N., at Bighi, and Commander F. Pierce, of HMS *Egmont* were chosen.

On the basis of a memorandum from the Reverend Gull and Mr. Henry Twelves, the Senior Churchwarden, the Anglican Church Commission on May 23rd sent a letter to the Secretary of State, Lord Elgin, asking that the Government should accept responsibility for repairs to the fabric of St. Paul's and provide a house for the Chaplain. Though they submitted valid reasons for such help, this Petition met with an uncompromising refusal.

During the latter part of the year Mr. Gull made fresh efforts to obtain a fixed remuneration for the prison and hospital duties that he undertook. He rejected the idea of a fee per visit, and was prepared to continue them gratis rather than accept an unjust settlement, which eventually led to an annual payment of £50. A reduction in the number of troops stationed in Valletta caused the £100 grant that had been so warmly welcomed the previous year to be withdrawn, so the church had a deficit of £93 at the opening of 1907.

The churchwardens, in a memorandum to the Bishop, outlined their financial problems, and suggested as a possible solution the obtaining of a larger grant for the Chaplain's civil duties; the use of St. Paul's by troops, with a capitation allowance for the Chaplain's ministry to them; or an addition to the Endowment from official sources.

Consequently a letter dated 1st June 1907 was sent to the General Officer Commanding, i/c Administration, Malta, setting out the view that there was no longer sufficient justification for two Valletta churches, and that the obvious inferiority of the Barracca Church, which had never been consecrated, left no doubt that St. Paul's should be retained as the centre of Anglican worship; the Barracca could be turned into a military club and its fittings used to equip a military church for one of the outlying barracks to which many of the troops formerly in Valletta had moved.

The Reverend Arthur Augustus Lynn Gedge[8], Senior Military Chaplain, in commenting on this proposal, was emphatic that Sunday services for the troops should be taken by the same clergy who ministered to them at other times. If it were necessary to close the Barracca, he thought that St. Paul's should be placed under the Senior Military Chaplain, who could be issued with the Bishop of Gibraltar's licence, and have a civil clergyman assisting him.

Alternatively, if both churches were kept open certain troops could attend St. Paul's, the Chaplain thereof undertaking certain clearly specified duties in return for a capitation allowance. Major-General H. Barron, in forwarding the correspondence to the War Office, said that the former plan might save the work of one chaplain; the latter was a reversion to the scheme in force a few years before and the expense involved was no longer justified as the number of troops in the Valletta area was now much smaller[9].

The Reverend Walter Charles Haines, the Reverend Gedge's successor as S.C.F., endorsed his predecessor's remarks, adding that it was undesirable that a clergyman should minister to troops but not be under military control. He suggested that the Chaplain of Holy Trinity should serve the civil worshippers. The War Office decision, sent on April 27th 1908, was that they could see no benefit for the troops in Malta and so the scheme was dropped.

The Reverend Gull resigned as Chaplain of St. Paul's as from 31st December 1907, and in an attempt to improve the conditions for the Malta chaplaincy, Bishop Collins arranged in February 1908 that the Chaplain's stipend should consist of the income from the Endowment, the Government allowance, living quarters, plus 25% of the surplus of income over expenditure, which would be increased to 75% after 31st December 1911.

The Reverend William Evered[10] was appointed as Chaplain on these terms in 1908, but unfortunately he suffered ill health and was unable to fulfil his Chaplaincy duties adequately, being absent for long spells. He tendered his resignation in early 1910, and was followed by a series of locum tenentes.

At the AGM on 15th April 1909, the churchwardens elected were, for the Navy, Admiral Curzon Howe, and Lieut. Arnaud, for the Army, Colonel

Patten A.P.D. and a vacancy, for the civilians J. W. Starkey Hon. Treasurer, E. G. Geoghegan, Hon. Secretary.

Mr. Robinson the organist submitted his resignation from the end of July 1909, after twenty-four years at St. Paul's, and it was agreed that he should be elected Honorary Organist of the Cathedral. A replacement organist was sought, and Mr. O. J. Hurst accepted the position.

Bishop Collins had gone to Sicily to give what aid he could to the stricken city of Messina at the end of 1908, following a terrible earthquake in which it was estimated that around 100,000 people had perished, and remained there for several weeks. He caught a throat infection and was prevented from visiting Malta during 1909.

Consequently at a meeting of St. Paul's congregation held on April 11th 1910, it was decided that a four man committee, consisting of the two Churchwardens, plus Captain Worcester and Mr. Alfred Twelves, should draw up a report on the present condition of the church and send it to the Bishop for his information.

It is not surprising, as many letters show, that the lay church officials tended to feel themselves far more important than the many temporary chaplains, since they were totally committed to the well being of St. Paul's and its future. The lack of a satisfactory Chaplain was unsettling the worshippers, so it was felt that the Bishop of Gibraltar should be asked whether he could see any possibility of improving the situation.

The facts were set out in a letter dated 19th April 1910 addressed to Bishop Collins:

"During the period from 2nd June 1907 when the Reverend Gull left the island to 10th April 1910 the church services were conducted by the permanent chaplain on 44 Sundays out of a total of 153 – the services of the remaining Sundays being conducted by a locum tenens on 67 Sundays; by the chaplain of Holy Trinity, either alone or with the assistance of naval or military chaplains on 24 Sundays; by the chaplain of Holy Trinity with the assistance of laymen on 6 Sundays; by laymen (both services) on 2 Sundays, by laymen and naval or military chaplains on 6 Sundays and by naval or military chaplains on 4 Sundays. 16 of the above services were conducted by churchwardens or by the organist in the absence of any available chaplain.

The effect of this unsettled state of affairs has been that the congregation has greatly fallen off in numbers and that the residents and visitors are losing all interest in the welfare of the church

In conclusion I am desired to say that in the opinion of the congregation, unless promptly remedied this most unfortunate state of affairs must ultimately result in the closing of the church a disaster which would cause infinite harm to the Protestant community of Malta and occurring in the midst of a rigid Roman Catholic population could only reflect discredit on us as members of the Church of England....

I am therefore desired to ask with all due respect that your Lordship may be pleased to inform us whether you are prepared to appoint a permanent chaplain who shall be acceptable to us as a congregation, who will be prepared to make his home among us, and if you will allow us a voice in the matter of whom you may propose to select.

Letter was signed by Leslie Rundle, as Chairman of the Church Meeting, but at that time he was also the Governor of Malta so St. Paul's could not have had a stronger champion.

The Bishop acted quickly and by the 22nd June 1910, had appointed the Reverend Arthur Fowler Newton M.A., formerly a Minor Canon of Ely Cathedral, and currently serving at Odessa, to the Chaplaincy of St. Paul's. However, this appointment was made without any consultation with St. Paul's congregation so they decided to tell him that they were:

"...reluctantly obliged to inform him that the congregation were not prepared to form any guarantee fund for the stipend of the Chaplain; and further to ask his Lordship if he would kindly inform the churchwardens on what terms he has engaged the services of the Rev. A. F. Newton."

Apart from the regular worshippers at St. Paul's the tone of his reply to the letter of the 19th sent to the Governor, was not very conciliatory. After a further exchange of letters a certain coolness developed between the two men. This coolness turned to positive hostility when Bishop Collins protested to Sir Leslie that the return sent to the British Government showing the ecclesiastical grants considerably understated the amount paid to the Roman Catholics in Malta.

From the minutes of a meeting held on 18th April 1910, it would seem that some of the locum tenens manner in conducting the church services had not suited all members of the congregation.

Mr. Robinson proposed but Mr. Geoghegan negatived that the following portion of the committee's report be deleted:

"Members of the Church of England who desire High Church doctrine find their wants adequately met elsewhere, and some of the influential members of St. Paul's Church have already intimated that the continuance of their subscriptions and attendance at St. Paul's Church depends upon the Protestant character of the service, also in the past the attendance's of the worshippers have been adversely influenced by the proclivities of the Chaplain, since the feelings of the congregation have for many years past been and still are strongly Protestant.

St. Paul's was the venue for a Memorial Service on Friday 20th May 1910, the day of the funeral of the late King Edward VII, at which clergymen of many denominations took part, and the congregation was made up of members from many faiths. The memorandum reads:

> *"The first portion of the Burial service was read by the Reverend Edward Cawood, Acting Chaplain of the Cathedral, the lesson by Reverend Morrison (Presbyterian), an address was given by the Bishop of Western Australia and the rest of the service was read by the Reverend J. Blackborne, Senior Forces Chaplain, and Reverend J. Icely, Royal Navy. Representatives of Holy Trinity Sliema, Presbyterian Church, Wesleyan Church, Army Scripture Readers and Salvation Army attended."*

Though a very sick man the Bishop spent the last two months of 1910 in Malta. On this visit apart from consecrating the Garrison Church of St. Luke, at Tigne Barracks, the home of the Royal Artillery, on 27th November 1910, he made a major policy decision that enhanced the role of St. Paul's.

During this visit he met a long time worshipper and friend of St. Paul's Mrs. Hardman, and was grateful for her help in attempting to ease the continual financial plight of the church. He noted:

> *"...Mrs. Hardman has been wishing for some time to give a gift to St. Paul's Cathedral in memory of her late husband[11] and ultimately decided that it should take the form of an endowment in augmentation of the Chaplains stipend she has now sent directions to her bankers in England to transfer £2400 2½% Consols to the Gibraltar Diocesan Fund to form the "William Hardman Memorial Trust."*

Notes

[1] He became Headmaster of Elstree College, Herts., 1903–1911.
[2] He had spent the previous ten years serving at Cannes in the South of France.
[3] Mr. Henry Twelves was a Wine & Spirit Merchant.
[4] Only four days during his 1904 tour.
[5] Now under the supervision of the Commonwealth War Graves Commission.
[6] He was General Manager of the Malta & Mediterranean Gas Co.Ltd.
[7] Midshipman John L.Gordon Paterson, of HMS Bacchante.
[8] He had served in Egypt 1894–1895, at Shorncliffe 1897–1899 and 1900–1903, in Natal 1899–1900 and was awarded the South African Medal with three clasps, and Mentioned in Despatches.
[9] The men were now housed in the new St. George's Barracks at Pembroke Camp.
[10] For twenty-one years he worked in the West Indies, and had only been back in England for one year when he took the Malta post.
[11] Born in Liverpool, William Hardman died in London 22nd November 1907.

Chapter 13

Collegiate Status Established

For almost two years Bishop Collins had been unable to visit Malta due to ill health, but he had spent a considerable amount of time with the aid of his Chaplain, the Reverend Algernon Leslie Brown, on preparing a body of Statutes to make St. Paul's a 'Collegiate' Church in fact and not only in the name, which it had borne since 1844. He wrote:

> *"One effect will be to make Malta a centre of our Church life again, for by the Statutes every member of the College has to be duly admitted on the spot, and contracts a real and permanent link with St Paul's at Valletta. Ultimately, the provision of such a centre may have other effects. The vexed question of the episcopal oversight of our people in and about Europe may some day be met by a redistribution of regions, and a division by a line running north and south instead of east and west. In such a case, there would be already two strong centres of English Church life available, both within the British Empire, at Gibraltar and Malta."*

To gain support for such a move, Chaplain Newton arranged a special meeting to be held on the 18th December 1910, at which he explained the Bishop's thoughts and as a result:

> *"The vestry hereby express their willingness to co-operate in the use of the cathedral church by a Collegiate Body in which the Chaplain as Chancellor and Senior Canon, is the chief authority under the Bishop, so far as it concerns them"*

Before the service on 1st January 1911 these Statutes were promulgated and a Collegiate body formally inaugurated, with safeguards of the rights of the Vestry and congregation. It was to consist of the Dean (the Bishop of Gibraltar for the time being); the Chancellor or Senior Canon, who being the Chaplain of St. Paul's must be resident; four other Canons, who, though not necessarily resident, must be actively working in or for the Diocese; and four lay members. The Chancellor's duties included installing each Bishop as Dean after his enthronement in St. Paul's, and presiding over the Chapter in the Bishop's absence.

On the same day the first Inauguration Ceremony was held, the Reverend Arthur Fowler Newton was installed as Chancellor of St. Paul's and Senior Canon, and the Reverend Henry Jenkins Shaw[1], of Holy Trinity Sliema was made a Canon of St. Paul's. A further installation took place on the 25th January, when the Reverend Francis Cowley Whitehouse, Chaplain to His Majesty's Embassy at Constantinople, became a Canon of St. Paul's.

Feeling that his influence had at last led to some discernible improvement in the stature of St. Paul's, the Bishop left Malta for Sicily early in 1911 but died at sea shortly after whilst en route to Smyrna.[2] The man appointed to the Bishopric in his stead, was Dr. Henry Joseph Corbett Knight, who had been the Principal of the Clergy Training College at Cambridge since 1901.

In October 1911, Canon Newton, first Chancellor of St Paul's, wrote a summary of his first year's work to Bishop Knight. In spite of the Governor's continued disfavour, shown in such petty restrictions such as forcing officers attending St. Paul's to wear uniform, there had been some progress. But after another eight months, he wrote that the improvement had only proved to be temporary, and that the present congregation of around 70 persons was insufficient to justify St. Paul's continuing as a civil church, and gave the opinion that the attendance of the Governor, Sir Leslie Rundle, and troops might help to improve the situation.

A few days later Bishop Knight had an interview with Sir Leslie about the position of St. Paul's. The Governor suggested either its transfer to a Military Chancellor with civilian assistant, a proposal which the Bishop felt would be as unacceptable to the Chaplain-General as it was to him or the use of the building by troops at specified times with due safeguards of the rights of the civil worshippers. Both agreed that no temporary expedient would be adequate, bearing in mind that St. Paul's was the principal Anglican place of worship in Malta. Some formula for the unification of church life was most desirable, but no concrete plan emerged and things continued as before.

To keep up with the times, the Church Committee at their meeting on 20th April 1911, resolved to obtain an estimate for lighting the church by electricity in place of gas, but to use the existing gas standards if possible. By June a trial had been arranged, and on the 27th *"The members proceeded to the church and inspected two standards, one fitted with incandescent electric lamps, the other with patent incandescent gas burners...."*

The members then adjourned to the library and resumed their discussion. Mr. Starkey, one of the Churchwardens, on behalf of the Malta and Mediterranean Gas Company offered to reduce his original tender from £89 to £70, against the Government Electric Light tender of £60. After much discussion when put to the vote the members voted 4 to 1 in favour of electricity.

At noon on Sunday 25th February 1912 a simple ceremony took place at the Governor's Palace, attended by the Chancellor and Churchwardens of St. Paul's. It concerned the silver trowel used by Queen Adelaide to lay the foundation stone of the church, which she had taken back to England, where it had remained until now amongst the Sovereign's possessions. King George V returned it to Malta with a letter saying that he wished it to be handed over to the responsible officials of the church for safe keeping, and this was duly done.

On the topside of the trowel is the inscription: On the underside:

THIS TROWEL
WAS USED BY
HER MAJESTY ADELAIDE
QUEEN DOWAGER OF ENGLAND
IN LAYING THE FOUNDATION STONE OF
ST. PAUL'S CHURCH IN VALLETTA
AND HUMBLY OFFERED TO HER MAJESTY
AFTER THE CEREMONY AS A MEMORIAL OF THAT
MEMORABLE OCCASION.

LAUS DEO
HIC LAPIS ÆDIS SACRÆ
SANCTI PAULI FUNDAMENTUM
PROPRIÂ EXCELLENTISSIMÆ
ET PIENTISSIMÆ ADELAIDIS
REGINÆ VIDUÆ NOBILIS
MANU POSITUS EST DIE
20 MARTI A.D. 1839 CUJUS
ET PIETATE ET SUMPTU HOC
TEMPLUM IN USUM ECCLESIÆ
ANGLICANÆ ÆDIFICATUM EST.

A few months later Canon Newton informed the churchwardens that the Pectoral Cross of the late Bishop Collins had been presented to the Church by the Archbishop of Canterbury, and that it had now been mounted on the small silver chalice used in the Government Chapel since 1809.

In view of his feelings that St. Paul's faced an uncertain future, it was no surprise that Canon Newton decided to resign later in the year. Bishop Knight had very great difficulty in finding a successor. Dr. Barnes, a personal friend of the Bishop, spent the winter of 1912–13 at St. Paul's whilst the search for a suitable man continued. The churchwardens insisted that any newcomer must have private means, which limited the possible candidates.

Eventually the Reverend Frederick Davies Brock, who had spent the last thirty-one years as the incumbent in the small village of Kirklevington[3], was appointed. He was now rather elderly and infirm, so his appointment was unfortunate since St. Paul's really needed a younger man who could expand its life and activities. The churchwardens protested that they had no say in his selection, but Bishop Knight felt this was unjust since the field of choice was extremely small, and he had followed their requirements as far as possible.

There was still no private residence for the Chaplain of St. Paul's, and no less than fourteen clergymen filled the post for varying periods in the first decade of the twentieth century. The outbreak of the Great War in August 1914 brought new problems. Travelling difficulties were enormously increased, and the shortage of clergymen became acute. The work of the all clergy on the island was greatly expanded by the war for Malta became a hospital base for British and Commonwealth troops from Gallipoli and Salonika. With over 120,000 casualties being cared for, Malta gained itself the name *'The Nurse of the Mediterranean'*, since there were 28 hospitals and convalescent centres located throughout the islands.

Though the spiritual welfare of these men was largely in the hands of their own chaplains, the civilian residents helped with practical matters. A Soldiers' and Sailors' Home was organised in the Gymnasium at Valletta by the Church of England, and the ladies of St. Paul's provided tea every Sunday afternoon for the wounded.

At the close of 1915 the organist Mr. Hurst, who had been at St. Paul's since August 1909 submitted his resignation, and Mr. W. S. Robinson was invited to resume the post he had originally filled in 1885.

Notes

[1] Who had returned as Chaplain at Holy Trinity in 1905 after two years at Costebelle.
[2] He died 24th March 1911, at the young age of 44 years.
[3] About ten miles south of Middlesbrough.

Chapter 14

St. Paul's v Barracca Church – Second Round

In January 1916 Lord Methuen, General Rundle's successor as Governor of Malta wrote to Bishop Knight that he thought Canon Brock was quite unsuitable for St. Paul's. The troops used the Barracca church, which was *'rather poor'* and he felt is would be better for them to use St. Paul's which in its present state was *'like a watch with a fine case and poor works'*. He said that there was not room for two Anglican Churches in Valletta and considered that Queen Adelaide's letter of donation gave the military authorities rights in the use of St. Paul's.

In his reply the Bishop pointed out that there was no possibility of changing the Chaplain whilst the war was on, so it was advisable to defer any decision as to the church's future, but added that St. Paul's with the right man in charge could become the centre for all the Anglican church life of Malta.

Lord Methuen clearly was unhappy with the manner in which St. Paul's was operating, and again wrote to Bishop Knight requesting the removal of Canon Brock. The Bishop explained that many of the younger clergy were serving in H.M. Forces, and that he could not easily find a replacement. In addition he had obligations to Canon Brock who had served throughout the war under difficult conditions.

Bishop Knight had been unable to reach Malta during the war, so his only contact with the Governor, and the clergy, was by letter. He did not set foot on Malta until November 1918, after a five-year interval, when he arrived on the 4th November just a week before the Armistice was signed. He attended the Service of Thanksgiving on November 13th, at St. Paul's at which the sermon was preached by the Bishop of London, who was in Malta for forty-eight hours en route home from Salonika.

Having been absent for such a long time the Bishop was keen during this visit to meet and discuss with many people directly concerned with the state of St. Paul's. He received a conflicting number of opinions, which can be summarised as follows:

The Governor, Lord Methuen thought it would be best to transfer St. Paul's to the control of the Senior Military Chaplain. It would be wrong for soldiers to be under their own Chaplains during the week but at services conducted by a Civil clergyman on Sundays. This latter view was endorsed by the Archbishop of Canterbury.

The Reverend E. Edmonds-Smith, Chaplain to the Forces, said that any services held at St. Paul's only for troops must be completely under Military control, and he considered that such exclusive services would tend to deplete the congregation at the civilian services. He also stated that if there was to be joint use of St. Paul's, then Military chaplains should have complete control of parade services and retain the collections.

Mr. Henry Twelves, the Senior Churchwarden agreed that the normal services would suffer if some of the military did not attend and as a personal view favoured a united service.

Major-General Hunter Blair, broadly agreed with the Reverend Edmonds-Smith but urged caution and felt that the development of co-operation between the Forces and Civil clergy was a matter of immediate importance.

Though all said that the views of the Royal Navy should also be considered, there is no trace of the naval authorities being contacted, but since the Royal Navy used the Dockyard Chapel the affairs at St. Paul's did not affect them too much.

Bishop Knight was sure that a joint rule of St. Paul's would never work, and said so. Most of the Endowment of St. Paul's was conditional upon the retention of a Civil chaplain, and having taken account of all the opinions given to him decided against the transfer of St. Paul's to the Military and the matter was once again dropped.

He told the Archbishop of Canterbury on 31st May he was convinced that St. Paul's should remain under a Civil chaplain, and with the right man the much needed parochial work could be undertaken and he was in favour of a church service *"fuller, less hurried, more reposeful"* than a parade service for the Military. He also hinted that a change of chaplain could be made at the end of the year.

At least the date of Canon Brock's retirement was decided upon, and the Reverend Archibald Hugh Conway Fargus, was appointed as the new chaplain, with Reverend E. A. Ommaney as locum tenens until Fargus's arrival in the autumn of 1919.

Lord Plumer succeeded Lord Methuen as Governor of Malta during 1919, shortly before the departure of Canon Brock. When the Bishop approached him before launching an appeal for funds in order to build a residence for the St. Paul's Chancellor, Lord Plumer expressed the view that a civil clergyman was not justified due to the small number of civilian inhabitants attending Sunday services. As a temporary help to the church he instituted a parade service at St. Paul's every other Sunday.

Unfortunately, the question of St. Paul's destiny came at a time when a dispute arose with the Reverend Ommaney over the Peace Thanksgiving Service of 6th July 1919. The Non-Conformist Chaplains had stayed away from St. Paul's in protest at not being allowed to take part in the service. The Governor felt their grievance was justified whereas Bishop Knight supported the stand taken by the Reverend Ommaney, and said that since the Government did nothing to maintain St. Paul's then they could not dictate policy to him.

After more consideration Lord Plumer came to the conclusion that he should approve the transfer of St. Paul's to the military authorities, and asked the Bishop to visit Malta for discussions. In reply Bishop Knight said that he could not see much value in visiting Malta until Canon Fargus had settled in, as there had been no change in the situation. He added: *"I have a trust to guard and to use.... I do not think a few years of difficulties justify an impulsive surrender which I am of opinion a later generation would bitterly regret."* So the matter was left unresolved when Bishop Knight died in England on 27th November 1920[1].

Whilst this debate was taking place, St. Paul's was the scene of one of the grandest weddings ever held there, when on 27th January 1920 the Governor's youngest daughter, Marjorie Constance Plumer married Major William Halliday Brooke,[2] his Aide-de-Camp. Well before the fixed time of 2.30 p.m. the church was filled to capacity with high ranking officers from all the British services, members of Maltese nobility and leading political, foreign and civil service communities. The bride left the Palace with her father, and was driven through crowd-packed streets which were lined by Boy Scouts to St. Paul's. Upon their arrival a Guard of Honour provided by the 1st Loyal North Lancashire Regiment presented arms.

Other members of the wedding party were two young pages Master Fisher and Master Monteith, the bride's sister Mrs. Anthony Orpen as Matron of Honour, and Lieutenant J. G. Sandie M.C., of the Loyal North Lancashire Regiment as Best Man.

The service was conducted by Canon Fargus, assisted by the Reverend F. J. Walker, S.C.F., and the Reverend A. C. Moreton. After the ceremony as the bride and groom left the church they passed beneath an arch of swords formed all the way down the aisle.

A reception was held at the Palace and attended by a large number of distinguished guests, including the Archbishop Dom Marius Caruana, and the Chief Justice of Malta Professor M. A. Refalo. Amongst the vast array of wedding gifts was one on behalf of the Maltese people, which consisted of three large bowls on an ebony stand, richly ornamented with gold coins of the Order of St. John of Jerusalem, Maltese Crosses and English Roses, suitably inscribed.

The new Bishop of Gibraltar, John Harold Greig, paid the first of his six visits to Malta in April 1921 and seems to have struck up a good relationship with Lord Plumer from the outset, as shown:

> *"Though the wind and the sea were as hostile as when St. Paul paid his first visit, nothing could have been happier than the ten days I spent in Malta. Canon Shaw at Sliema, Canon Fargus at Valletta, the Chaplains of the Forces, and last but the very reverse of least, Lord and Lady Plumer did all they possibly could, and all that any Bishop could desire, to welcome and help in me."*

In the post war years there was much political agitation by the Maltese, which led to the granting of Self-Government in 1921.[3] Such an important change in relationship of England and Malta clearly took up much of the Governor's time, and in comparison the future of St. Paul's was a very minor matter indeed.

Canon Fargus proved to be unsuitable at St. Paul's and in 1922 the Bishop appointed an ex-Naval Chaplain, the Reverend Arthur Cyprian Moreton to replace him. It seems that both Bishop Greig and Governor Plumer were unenthusiastic about the appointment of Canon Moreton, but he proved them both wrong since under his guidance the church made steady progress.

However, he could see that St. Paul's would not be able to maintain itself independently in the future, the view shared by Lord Plumer, and on 10th May 1923 Moreton proposed that the chaplaincies of St. Paul's and Holy Trinity Sliema should be combined, and that although the Bishop of Gibraltar should retain nominal ownership of St. Paul's, it should be used by the Army as the Garrison Church in place of the Barracca church which could then be closed.

The Bishop was hesitant and said that when Canon Shaw retired it would be best for Canon Moreton to take over Holy Trinity. It seems that he had never been very hopeful of the long-term prospects of Malta, and had not bothered to be enthroned there on becoming Bishop.

To keep up the momentum for change Lord Plumer called a Conference at the Palace on 25th January 1924, attended by the Governor, the Bishop, Canon Moreton, and the Reverend Francis Joseph Walker, the Senior Chaplain to the Forces. As shown by his notes at this meeting even the Bishop could see that the Barracca Church had: *"the air of a church that people use and care for; and in this alas! very different from St. Paul's which altho' architecturally grand is cold and bare and forbidding and lacks the atmosphere of worship and affection as much as the Barracca possesses it."*

The fall in the English population however made two churches in Valletta unnecessary, and at the Governor's initiative, a parade service was held at the Cathedral, but when it was suggested that all the services held in the Barracca church should also be transferred to St. Paul's, there was strong opposition from the Senior Chaplain to the Forces to the closing of the Garrison Church.

The Bishop reluctantly felt that the only alternative was to close St. Paul's. However, to avert this drastic step he was prepared to relinquish all civil rights in the building.

Canon Moreton was very upset at the Bishop's proposal. He suggested that his wife's cousin, the Reverend Noel Ambrose Marshall[4], then in India, would be an admirable man to undertake the joint chaplaincy, but if the military authorities' attitude made this impossible, he considered that the Reverend Marshall might be able to revive St. Paul's on his own. Surely it was better to give it a try rather than to consider closing St. Paul's.

Lord Plumer left Malta before the matter was resolved so it was passed on to the new Governor, General Congreve. He decided on the 1st October 1924 that all the services should be transferred to St. Paul's for an experimental period of six months, and that the Barracca Church should be closed whilst this took place. The new Senior Chaplain to the Forces, the Reverend Ernest Edmonds-Smith, though totally opposed to the scheme co-operated in the experiment, but wrote to Bishop Greig setting out the difficulties of the situation as he saw it. No matter how friendly and closely they could work together the Senior Chaplain to the Forces would be little more than an assistant curate to the Chancellor of St. Paul's and such a situation was impossible as a permanent arrangement.

He considered that the Barracca church was more conveniently situated for many worshippers, including the children of soldiers, who were not prepared to walk the longer distance to St. Paul's or into the rather unattractive neighbourhood where St. Paul's was located. He maintained that: *"the help to the Cathedral by no means corresponds to the greatness of our loss"*, and was convinced that the Barracca Church was so accessible that if St. Paul's was handed over to total Military control, he would advise that the Barracca church should continue to remain open for civilian use.

In the autumn General Congreve reviewed the experiment, and concluded that it had been justified, but he was not totally convinced by the result, and therefore proposed to reopen the Barracca and consider the matter further.

The Governor's decision was indignantly received by Canon Moreton who resigned from all church work in Malta, but he later reconsidered this action, and moved to Sliema where he remained as Chaplain of Holy Trinity until 1928.

His successor at St. Paul's was Canon Marshall who benefited from the initiatives that Moreton had introduced. It was Canon Moreton who had suggested building a Chancellor's residence along the north side of the Cathedral, even though the plan was shelved during the uncertain period 1923–25, it was later adopted.

Notes

[1] He left his pastoral staff to Holy Trinity Church, Sliema, where it was placed a few years later.
[2] Of the West Yorkshire Regiment.
[3] In fact Malta Government was to deal with local administration, and the Imperial Government would continue to handle certain other matters.
[4] After ordination in 1920 he spent three years in the Newcastle area, then in 1923 went to Calcutta.

Chapter 15

Canon Marshall's Improvements

Canon Marshall was installed as Chancellor of St. Paul's after some delay on May 24th 1926. He quickly tackled his difficulties and began to build for the future.

It was inevitable that a 'new broom' would meet some opposition and at the end of 1926 trouble arose when he asked Mr. Robinson, who had been organist since 1885, save for the years 1909–15, to resign since he left the church for a long period without appointing a temporary organist. Having been associated with St. Paul's for over forty years Mr. Robinson was offended and appealed to the Archdeacon but without success.

Apart from Mr. Robinson he tried diplomatically to replace some other church officials such as the aged Mr. Henry Twelves, and Michael the Verger, and did his best to win over 'difficult' personalities amongst the civilian members of St. Paul's. He also attempted to improve the relationship with the Service chaplains.

General Congreve whose health was never very good went into Imtarfa Hospital during January and died there on February 28th 1927[1]. His body was brought to St. Paul's at midnight on Ash Wednesday. After it had been watched through the night, a requiem was held at 8 a.m. and from 9.30 a.m. to 5 p.m. the body lay in state; a general dispensation had been given to the Roman Catholic Maltese, with whom the General had been very popular, to enter the building and over 15,000 people filed past.

The next day Canon Moreton and the Service chaplains received the coffin on board HMS *Chrysanthemum*, and it was buried at sea off the south coast of Malta in the Filfla Channel, with a memorial service being held at St. Paul's at 6 p.m. that evening.

When William Scamp built St. Paul's he had to carry out considerable structural alterations in the crypt so that the foundations of the walls and pillars in the church above were secure. Though nearly all the piers and arches were re-built, the basic layout as seen today probably still contains parts of the original Auberge d'Allemagne basement

For over eighty years it remained unused, but Canon Marshall supervised its preparation for use as a Church Hall for social events. At a cost of £200 the floor was tiled, the Verger's quarters improved, toilets and cloakrooms added, and the walls curtained. Bishop Greig opened it on Easter Monday 1927, in the presence of many members of the congregation, with the Band of HMS *Eagle* in attendance. In 1935 with the threat of war, and memories of the Great War, the crypt was converted into a gas-proof shelter.

Bishop Greig took up the post of the Bishop of Guildford in 1927, and so relinquished the See of Gibraltar, to Frederick Cyril Nugent Hicks[2]. Neither Bishops Knight nor Greig had considered Malta sufficiently 'alive' to justify an enthronement, but Bishop Hicks decided that the Statutes enacted by Bishop Collins in 1911 should be followed. He felt that a new era for St. Paul's had arrived and was anxious to do all he could to further improve its position and support Marshall.

He was enthroned in St. Paul's on 21st December 1927[3], by Canon Moreton. The ceremony was attended by one Service chaplain from each of the three Services who acted as his chaplains, plus the Archimandrite of the local Greek Orthodox community who took his place in the sanctuary and joined in the procession.

Hicks proposed to revive Bishop Collins' scheme of allotting Canonries to the Senior Naval and Military Chaplains and added the Chaplain from the newly formed Royal Air Force. By this move, the Chapter of St Paul's would become a reality, parade services at St. Paul's would be put on a better footing by the direct connection of the Service chaplains with the Cathedral, and he hoped a relationship somewhat similar to that of parishes to the Cathedral would develop. This farsighted plan however was deferred and remained unfulfilled.

At this time St. Paul's was beginning to take a more worthy position in Malta, partly due to a house for the Chancellor being built, and the conversion of the crypt into a Church Hall. These major improvements had been made possible by the raising of some £700 from amongst the congregation.

Whilst the foundations for the Chancellors residence were being excavated, a piece of stone was unearthed, with the inscription:

F·JOACHIM·SPAR·ORD
·S·JOH·HIER.MAGNS·BAI
ULS·ALEMANNIAE·1571

Clearly from the old Auberge d'Allemagne which was on the site previously, and therefore in April 1931 the People's warden Squadron Leader Forbes-Bentley suggested that the stone be placed in the Valletta Museum collection for safe keeping. Accordingly Professor Zammit was contacted and it was arranged that in return for the actual stone, a plaster cast would be made and kept at St. Paul's.

A Toc H group was formed in 1927 and in 1928 Bishop Hicks and Sir Thomas Vans Best, the Lieutenant Governor were initiated as members. An annual

Birthday Service was held on the Sunday following Armistice Day and the small chapel of the Holy Angels in St. Paul's was used by the Toc H members.

By refusing to press for closure of the Barracca church in 1926 and relinquishing the parade service in June 1928 Canon Marshall improved his relationship with the Service chaplains, and remained on good terms with the Reverend Edmonds-Smith and the Reverend A. Shell of the Dockyard Chapel.

Attendances at services were improving steadily and there was a rise in the number of communicants, which by 1931 were the highest since 1882 when records commenced. Most of this improvement was due to the efforts of Canon Marshall, whose innovations had also included the introduction of an annual Nativity Play.

Bishop Hicks wrote encouragingly about St. Paul's:

> *"There is every sign of the true spirit of prayer and worship within its walls, but the number of the civilian English population upon whom the Chancellor can rely are small. He is steadily building up a devoted band of helpers and to my mind the future is full of hope.*
>
> *The Cathedral stands, as no other of the English churches, Service or Civilian in Malta, can stand for the life and worship of our Church; it is a permanent memorial of the faith and vision and self-devotion of Queen Adelaide, but it is so large a building that except on special occasion it cannot easily be filled ... and its finance under present conditions is at best inadequate and may be precarious. We must see to it that by our prayers and by every kind of help that we can give, direct and indirect, the gallant fight which the present Chancellor is making is successfully carried through."*

Canon Marshall's success in bringing the English community back to St. Paul's however did not prevent the return of another financial crisis. In March 1931 an appeal was launched for funds to repair the fabric of St. Paul's and to supplement the stipend of the Chancellor. A band of top name signatories[4] sent a letter to the Editor of 'The Times' in London. After giving some details of the early history of the church the letter continues:

> *"After nearly a century of exposure parts of the building are now in immediate need of repair while at the same time it is essential to raise the incumbent's stipend to a living wage. A co-ordinated effort is now being made to enlist the aid of both the Service and civilian Anglican population of Malta, but it is impossible to expect that more than a fraction of the sum required for both these purposes can be found locally.*
>
> *We, therefore, urgently appeal to the general public for at least £10,500 to preserve the continued existence of Queen Adelaide's pious munificence...."*

By September the Cathedral Council with the aid of funds raised chiefly in Malta itself, had been able to restore all parts of the building which were in a dangerous condition, and to undertake some necessary repairs to roof, ceiling, cornices and pillars. Dilapidated portions of the floor had been renewed and minor repairs made to the organ, but there was no money left for future repairs.

Despite his successful work showing positive results, Canon Marshall decided that the time had come for him to hand over his post, since the climate was adversely affecting his health and nerves. He had recently become acquainted with the Reverend Nicholls, Chaplain of HMS *Eagle*, and persuaded Bishop Hicks to offer him the chaplaincy of St. Paul's.

Nicholls duly accepted and in May 1931 took over the Chaplaincy of St. Paul's. Of the retiring Chancellor the Bishop wrote:

> "He has spent himself without reserve; and he has left in every direction in Malta a memory and a legacy of faith, vision and activity which will, I hope, be a permanent possession of the Cathedral which he loved and of those who work for it and worship in it. It is, as he would wish it to be, above everything else, a house of prayer and a place of the presence of God."

A large congregation, including the Governor Sir John Du Cane[5], assembled in St. Paul's on Sunday evening the 10th May 1931. The Reverend Reginald Morton Nicholls, was installed as Chancellor, and during his thirteen years at the helm of St. Paul's he made detailed notes of many varied events in the life of the church, which are retained in the archives.

He maintained the tradition which Canon Marshall had established of presenting a Nativity Play at Christmas and wrote the following description of the Christmas 1931 version:

> "The Nativity Play has been given at St. Paul's for several years, and may now be said to be an established custom. It is given on Christmas Day at 5 o'clock and though this sounds a very unusual and inconvenient hour, and was strongly opposed at first, actually it is worth mention that it proves to be the reverse. It fills in just that part of Christmas Day which is apt to be rather empty; and the play was repeated on a weekday for those who could not come on Christmas Day. St. Paul's with its big sanctuary, its three vestries, and its Chancellor's house alongside connected at the east and west with the church is an ideal building for a stately production."

A difficult question, which soon arose, was that of the marriage of English servicemen to foreign women. Since in most cases the girls were 'artistes', often desiring marriage only to obtain British citizenship, Canon Nicholls made the rule that he would refuse all such unions, even when there was some case to be made out for the bona fides of those concerned.

On the other hand he may have seen an entry in St. Paul's marriage registers of an unfortunate occurrence three years earlier. Leading Seaman John Tatcher came to St. Paul's for his wedding to Mignon Blanche Jane Pearce, a 20 year old 'Music Hall Artiste', but she never arrived. She got into the wedding car to take her to the church but suddenly ordered the driver to drive anywhere but not to St. Paul's. She was later found at Birzebbugia in the car, still decorated with the wedding ribbons. The wedding was cancelled.

In November 1931, however, the Reverend John Clayton of Holy Trinity, Sliema, allowed his church to be used for the solemnisation of a 'borderline' case, which Canon Nicholls had already refused. Clayton's view was that each instance should be judged on its merits, and that as a working rule he would accept the opinion of the man's Commanding Officer or Chaplain.

The views of the Service chaplains on the matter varied. The Reverend C. Egerton Chadwick, the Army Chaplain General, was against all such marriages; the Reverend A. Watson R.A.F. *"we will not ourselves solemnize such marriages unless the circumstances are unique"*; but a meeting of Naval chaplains decided that each case should be judged on its merits. In the end an 'agreement to differ' between Canon Nicholls and the Reverend Clayton was reached and accepted by the Bishop.

Difficulties with the Roman Catholic Church continued from time to time. In November 1932 a law was published whereby offences against religions other than Roman Catholicism were liable to only half the penalty. In spite of protests by Canon Nicholls and the Reverend Clayton to the Governor, the law was later passed. Another example came in 1936, when pressure was brought on the local Rediffusion not to relay English religious services. However, these were made at a time of considerable political turmoil[6] on Malta and probably should be viewed against this background.

In the Archives are the 'Form of Service' Booklets for installation ceremonies, but we have an eye witness account of the 1933 installation of Harold Jocelyn Buxton, as the ninth Bishop of Gibraltar. He had been the Archdeacon of Cyprus so it was appropriate that a Greek Bishop, Germanos of Thyateira, was present at this consecration. After enthronement at Gibraltar on March 5th, the ceremony at Malta took place on 5th May.

The scene in St. Paul's is well narrated:

"Four o'clock on a hot Friday afternoon does not sound a propitious time, but before that hour a congregation of near six hundred had assembled. The

procession to the choir stalls was led by a seaman cross-bearer; then the two senior churchwardens of St. Paul's and those of Holy Trinity, Sliema, with their staves of office, followed by the choir-boys of St. Paul's and representative boys from Holy Trinity, and from the Dockyard Church and the Barracca Military Church.

Following these came St. Paul's choirmen and some fifteen Chaplains from the Services. The Archmandrite of our local Greek Orthodox community in his bright green vestment brought up the rear. The hymn was 'Light's abode, celestial Salem' and above the descants in the later verses, soaring clear and high above the solid melody sung by the men's voices and the congregation, was a solemn and inspiring overture.

The ceremony of enthronement followed the usual course. The Bishop attended by the Rev.John Clayton, Incumbent of Holy Trinity, Sliema, who acted as his Chaplain, knocked thrice on the main door (every window of the surrounding houses filled with Maltese onlookers); the Hon. R. Strother Stewart, in wig and gown, acting as Bishop's Registrar, presented the necessary papers to the Chancellor of the Cathedral; and the Bishop vested in cope and mitre was conducted up the church as the choir chanted, very sweetly, the appropriate psalms.

Then followed the reading of the documents by the Registrar, the taking of the Oaths and the signing of the Cathedral Roll and the Bishop was escorted to his throne by the Chancellor. The latter and Mr. Clayton made their obedience, and the Service Chaplains (who owe allegiance not to Gibraltar but to Canterbury) came out of their seats in stalls and sanctuary and bowed to his Lordship. The Bishop then left his throne and standing at the foot of the chancel steps was greeted by the chief representatives of the Anglican community – His Excellency the Governor, the Naval Commander-in-Chief of the Mediterranean, His Honour the Lieut-Governor, the Vice-Admiral Malta, the Brigadier commanding the troops, the Commodore Royal Air Force, and the Churchwardens.

Then followed the Installation of the Bishop as Dean of the Cathedral; an oath to keep the constitutions and another signature; a merry anthem – Martin's setting of Psalm cl, with the Easter Alleluias tumbling over one another like a peal of bells; a short sermon; a solemn procession of over fifty choir and clergy round the Cathedral. The Blessing, given by our new Bishop, ended a truly memorable service."

Referring back to the Nativity Play which was performed every year until 1938, heading the cast list for the 1933 production were Miss.Clayton as 'Our Lady' and Midshipman P. Wyatt as 'Joseph', in pencil alongside their names it says "Married in 1937".

Notes

[1] He took special interest in the Boy Scout Movement, and a memorial archway to him stands at the entrance to the Boy Scout Headquarters in Floriana.

[2] Bishop Hicks became Bishop of Lincoln in 1933.

[3] His Pastoral Staff is in St. Paul's, inscribed "This crozier belonged to Nugent, Bishop of Gibraltar 1927–1933, afterwards Bishop of Lincoln. b.1872 d. 1942. Given to Malta Cathedral in perpetual memory of him by his wife Kathleen Hicks. He was the first Anglican Bishop to be enthroned in Malta."

[4] The signatories of this letter were the current Governor of Malta, General Sir John Du Cane, three former Governors, General Sir Charles Mansfield Clarke (1903–1907), Field Marshall Lord Methuen (1915–1919), Field Marshall Viscount Plumer (1919–1924), Celia Congreve the widow of General Congreve, H. C. Luke Lieutenant-Governor of Malta, The Bishop of Gibraltar, Admiral Ernle Chatfield, Commander-in-Chief, Mediterranean Station, J. L. Forbes, Air Officer Commanding RAF Mediterranean, Admiral F. L. Field, Former Commander-in-Chief, Mediterranean Station, 1928–30.

[5] He resigned the following month.

[6] The Constitution was suspended in 1930; Self-Government restored in 1932, but suspended again at the end of 1933.

Chapter 16

Canon Nicholl's Influence

The Abyssinian crisis of 1935–6 caused some alarm in Malta, as it was likely to be the first victim in any outbreak of a war with Italy. Due to hurried troop movements St. Paul's lost four successive organists, four servers and twelve choirmen all within a few months. Important naval conferences were held in Malta, and at one evening service there were no less than three Admirals in the Commander-in-Chief's pew – Admiral Fisher, C-in-C Mediterranean, Admiral Pound, Chief of Staff, and Admiral Backhouse, C-in-C Home Fleet.

Early in 1936 Malta joined in the mourning for King George V, who had died during the night of Monday 20th January. The memorial service, held at 11.30 a.m. on Tuesday 28th January at St. Paul's, was conducted by Canon Nicholls, assisted by the Assistant Chaplain General to the Forces and the Senior Naval Chaplain. Men of The Lincolnshire Regiment formed the guard of honour and the band of the Rifle Brigade played appropriate music. The Lieut-Governor, Sir Harry Luke[1], represented the Governor who was too ill to attend, and staff and other officers of the Army, Navy and Royal Air Force were present.

> *"The service was most lively, solemn, dignified, spectacular, the choir chanting unaccompanied"* wrote Canon Nicholls, *"After the band had played the Funeral March the congregation waited for the signal gun to announce the beginning of the two minutes silence. Not a sound was heard within or without the Cathedral till the second gun brought the silence to an end. The service then closed with the singing of the National Anthem".*

He also noted the following conversation, *"A bandsman of the Rifle Brigade said; I enjoyed it very much. To play Sunday by Sunday in our Gym for Mattins is one thing; to play in St. Paul's for a service like that was almost like playing in Winchester Cathedral."* (N.B. the Rifle Brigade Depot is Winchester).

A second service was held at St. Paul's the following day for men of the Destroyer Fleet who had not been present on the 28th. The Memorandum issued from HMS *Keppel* gave the details. Lieutenant Nicholls of HMS *Verity* was appointed to carry out the duties of Pier Master at the Marsamuscetto

Ferry Landing Stage. The attendance ordered was a total of 700 men from the seventeen ships[2], accompanied by 80 Naval Officers.

A couple of months later, on Tuesday the 17th March, another memorial service was held in St. Paul's, this time upon the death of the Governor, General Sir David Graham Campbell, at which Non-Conformist as well as Anglican chaplains were present.

The new Governor, Sir Charles Bonham-Carter, arrived in March on board the P. & O. liner *Strathmore*, escorted by the destroyers *Wren* and *Wishart*, and was immediately embroiled in the political troubles on Malta. Within his first year he introduced an interim Constitution, and just prior to the outbreak of World War Two, the 1939 Constitution[3].

At St. Paul's meanwhile Canon Nicholls was making steady progress, though one small activity was facing a predicament, and called for some modification. During 1937 there was a dearth of bellringers. It was decided that the bell pulls should be so arranged that all six could be operated by just one person. To make this possible a board with six levers was constructed. A young pre-war resident recalls this event:

> "*I was living with my parents as guests of Mr. Clements and his wife, he was verger of St. Paul's at that time, 1937. He had a flat in what I gather is now the Chancellors Lodge. The 'Keyboard' of ropes was made by a member of TOC H, a Staff Sergeant Leonard 'Bugs' Waldron, Royal Artillery, serving at Tigne Barracks. Mr. Clements and myself were 'recruits' to hang onto each rope as it was brought onto the board and secured. The long wooden handles made the bell ringing a task for one person only.*
>
> *The bells were then played for all services by a Sergeant in the Pay Corps, and he was followed as ringer by my husband Sapper J. Collyer, who was serving as a Sapper with the Royal Engineers at Lintorn Barracks[4], Floriana, (now the Inland Revenue Offices). He was also a server, this was during the time that Canon Nicholls was in residence.... My father, brother and myself were all in the choir during the time my father was serving in HMS Hood, on station in Malta at this time.*
>
> *PS. For special occasions a broom handle placed over the bell handles enabled all the bells to be played at once! not terribly good for the structure!*"[5]

In 1938, Admiral Sir Dudley Pound, the C-in-C Mediterranean Fleet was given authority by the Admiralty to dispose of the Colour of the Mediterranean Fleet bearing the cypher of the late King George V[6]. He offered it to the Cathedral and accordingly a 'laying up' Service was prepared. On the 27th February the impressive ceremony took place. A Royal Navy guard of honour, headed by the band of the Royal Marines, escorted the Colour from the Flagship in Grand Harbour to entrance of St. Paul's. The Colour Party comprising a Royal Naval Lieutenant carrying the Colour, flanked by two sailors bearing rifles with fixed bayonets, and a Petty Officer with drawn cutlass, entered the building to a fanfare of trumpets.

Following a hymn and prayers, the Admiral read the Lesson. A psalm and another hymn were sung before the Colour Party marched slowly down the Nave towards the altar, in front of which they halted. Captain V. A. C. Crutchley V.C., D.S.C., R.N. in full dress uniform stepped forward, took the Colour and offered it to the Chancellor, saying *"This Colour carried in the service of King and Empire."* The sermon on this occasion was preached by the Chaplain of HMS *Warspite*, the Reverend R. T. Venn. The Colour was later hung by a wooden staff on one of the pilasters on the south wall[7]. During May Surgeon Capt. Sheridan undertook to arrange for a suitable plaque to be produced.

The Service chaplains varied in their attitude to St. Paul's. Having been a Service chaplain himself Canon Nicholls wished for closer co-operation with his fellow clergymen and instituted celebrations for the Royal Air Force on a Wednesday, Royal Navy on Thursday, and the Army on Friday, but while the first two were regularly conducted by their respective Service chaplains the Army took no part. The early hopes that the Reverend C. Egerton Chadwick, A.C.G., would prove co-operative were not realised. At Bishop Buxton's enthronement he insisted on walking alone, being an Archdeacon, and subsequently made a practice of being absent during the Bishop's visits. Perhaps due to the many years of discord between the Military and successive Governors on one side, and the Bishops of Gibraltar on the other, was the reason why the Reverend Chadwick in March 1936 had dedicated the Barracca Garrison Church, with the name of St. George's Church.

An attempt was made by the Army Chaplains in 1938/1939, though in an amicable way, to secure the right to hold Military weddings in their own churches, but after considerable discussion between Bishop Buxton and the Chaplain-General no progress was made and they agreed to leave the situation unchanged.

At the Vestry meeting held on 24th April 1938, the council members elected were Mr. Barrett Chaplain's warden, Sir Harry Luke People's warden, Capt. Coldwell and Capt. Ohlson Lay wardens, Surgeon Capt. Sheridan R.N. Naval warden, Hon. Sec. W. A. Griffiths, and Hon. Treasurer Pay Captain Trevor Hayles. They also confirmed the appointment of Mr. Nicolle as organist. Three months later Sir Harry Luke announced his resignation since he was leaving Malta to become the Governor of the Fiji Islands.

Around this time the relationship with the Non-Conformists took an unfortunate turn, through an action by Toc H. The headquarters of this organisation told the Malta branch that it inclined too much towards the Church of England, and as a result the local officials invited a Non-Conformist to preach to them in St. Paul's. Even though the invitation was not performed, it caused some disharmony.

Notwithstanding that the threat of war was ever present, there was certainly a greater stability in the life and work of St. Paul's than for many years, for which Canon Nicholls must take the credit. In 1939 he made this summary:

"Malta has a very definite 'season', from July to October it is blistering hot, September being the worst month of all owing to the very high humidity – and also to the fact that those who have been here all the summer are less fit to stand its utterly enervating character. During the 'sirocco' weather everything is wet when the dawn breaks and indeed often all day where the sun does not reach. How one sniffs the air for the smell of rain – unknown for four or five months and perhaps overdue!

And when it does arrive, get out your sponges and buckets, for it comes down in torrents and pours through the wooden window frames shrunk by the heat and is a rising tide under the doors.

But there is also a season within a season. Resident civilians diminish year by year and the congregation at St. Paul's is largely drawn from the Navy, whose movements thus cast an influence over us. The Fleet is usually away for a short time in January and during Lent (I complained to the Commander-in-Chief about it!) and also for four months in the summer.

Towards the end of October the berths on the liners are all booked up, and thousands of people come to this little Island to await the return of the ships with their crews numbering something like 20,000 men. Thus our Church 'season' begins with Harvest Thanksgiving, generally on the second or third Sunday in November. The Armistice Service comes just about that time. Since a formal parade and March Past were given up, it has been shorn of much of its magnificence: but it is a great moment nevertheless, with a large Union Flag in the Sanctuary and the Red, White, Blue and R.A.F. Ensigns round it. The firing of guns announces the silence, and afterwards buglers on the Cathedral steps sound the 'Last Post' and 'Reveille' over Marsamuscetto Harbour.

Advent approaches with its splendid solemn hymns and its call to the deepest spiritual thoughts. Meanwhile, the Nativity Play is under way and rehearsals take place every Monday evening for eight weeks. On the Sunday before Christmas, instead of Evensong we have the Carol Service of the Nine Lessons, in which the story of the birth of Christ and the preparation for it is read by different layman including the verger, and a choirboy who has a lovely speaking voice.

Christmas is ushered in by the Midnight Eucharist which is held in several of our Anglican churches here. Afterwards we ring a merry chime on our six beautiful bells. Nobody complains, for all the deep toned bells of Malta are also sounding, but our 'bobs' and 'grandsires' are easily distinguished against theirs because the bells in Malta, splendid though they be in tone, are just clanged.

Christmas Day is very strenuous indeed. No sooner is the last service over – about 11.30 – than feverish preparations begin for the Nativity Play in the Cathedral. 'Surely not on Christmas Day?' said someone to Canon Marshall when he started it. He replied 'What better day ?' Indeed for men of the Services in ships or barracks or camps – even at home, but much more so abroad, – Christmas Day can be a very lonely time.

Our curtain goes up at 5.30: and at least seventy performers, singers and staff, every one of whom is indispensable – are in their places for what is a beautiful representation of Christian devotion and artistic loveliness. All ranks and ratings, soldiers, sailors, airmen, civilians; men, women and children; every one a believer who almost without exception, has knelt earlier-in the day at the altar of one of our churches. Our twelve years experience has collected a tradition of good acting, the best music, mostly unaccompanied from the west gallery, exquisite lighting and sumptuous dresses. After Christmas there is s a welcome lull.

The 'Festival of St. Paul Shipwrecked' falls on February 10th. It is a local Feast of the highest honour, and by the Constitution of the Cathedral it is also our Patronal Festival. We try to make it a kind of dedication of the Church of England in Malta. Holy Eucharist is sung, and the Epistle and Gospel usually read by the Chaplain of the Dockyard and the Assistant Chaplain General to the Forces, vested in copes.

Evensong on the adjacent Sunday takes the form of a Service for Seafarers. Hymns, psalms, lessons, and sermon are all about the sea; they that go down to the sea in ships and occupy their business in great waters; the Navy of Hiram King of Tyre; the story of the wreck at St. Paul's Bay, nine miles to the north west of the Cathedral. The lessons are read by Captain G. J. Coldwell, a former Commodore of the P. & O. Fleet, who is a churchwarden, and by the Naval Commander-in-Chief.

And so we pass to Lent and Easter. The Three Hours Service consists of Litany, Ante-Communion, the Reproaches, and ends with Evensong; and three Sermons are interspersed. Twice within the last few years we have been fortunate in having the Bishop with us, to lead our meditations. The 'Passion according to St. John' being the whole of chapter xviii and xix, is sung to the setting of William Byrd. It is marvellously dramatic and moving. The

Narrator chants the story and the words of the Christus, of Pilate, of Peter and of the crowd are sung by members of the choir.

With Easter the great Fast is over, and the Christian joy is full. About this time the Bishop usually visits us. Sometimes he stays for two Sundays, sometimes for three.

I have said nothing of the vital pastoral work which in its limited circle does not differ very much from that of an English town-parish. Nor have I mentioned Holy Trinity Church, which by all accounts is going great guns. I have simply picked out a few highlights, within the Cathedral itself."

The life of St. Paul's was strengthened by its connection with various organisations. Toc H has already been mentioned. A branch of the Girls' Friendly Society[8] had been established in Bishop Sandford's time, and his wife had taken a keen interest in its activities until her death in 1901. It then appears to have been inactive for several years before it was reorganised at Easter 1913 by Mrs.Barnes, wife of the locum tenens of St. Paul's. After the Great War of 1914–1918 very valuable work was done by Mrs.Coldwell, the Hon. Secretary whose house was used for meetings from July 1928 to October 1931.

On the 28th of the latter month the Coldwell Hostel for Girls in Strada St. Ursula was opened by Lady Campbell[9], wife of the Governor, fulfilling her first public engagement in Malta. The house had on the ground floor, entrance hall, restaurant and kitchen; on the first floor were sitting, reading, and writing rooms: and above were three bedrooms. Representatives of the Y.W.C.A., Girl Guides, Friendly Wives (an organisation for Naval families) were on the Hostel Committee. Mrs. Coldwell died on June 16th 1936, and her work was carried on by Mrs.Nicholls, the wife of the Chancellor.

A Mothers' and Churchman's Union was in existence before the 1914–1918 War, and continued during the peaceful years which followed. When a Diocesan 'Mothers Union' Council was formed in 1928, Lady Du Cane, wife of the Governor became a Vice-President. Branches were formed at Sliema and in the Dockyard area, as well as in Valletta where Mrs.Trevor Hayles, the Hon. Secretary organised monthly meetings. A united service was held annually at St. Paul's on Lady Day.

Notes

[1] He was a Churchwarden of St. Paul's for seven years.

[2] 50 each from HMS Keppel and Douglas, 40 each from Witch, Whitshed, Wren, Valorous, Wessex, Wild Swan, Whitehall, Veteran, Verity, Viceroy, Vega, Venetia, Wolsey, Mackay and Encounter.

[3] Sometimes called the 'MacDonald' Constitution.

THE ACTS

Chapter 27

40. And when they had taken up the anchors, they committed themselves unto the sea, and loosed the rudder bands and hoisted up the mainsail to the wind and made towards the shore.
41. And falling into a place where two seas met they ran the ship aground; and the forepart stuck fast, and remained unmoveable, but the hinder part was broken with the violence of the waves.
42. And the soldiers' counsel was to kill the prisoners, lest any of them should swim out, and escape.
43. But the centurion, willing to save Paul, kept them from their purpose; and commanded that they which could swim should cast themselves first into the sea, and get to land:
44. And the rest, some on boards, and some on broken pieces of the ship. And so it came to pass, that they escaped all safe to land.

Chapter 28

1. And when they were escaped, then they knew that the island was called Melita.
2. And the barbarous people shewed us no little kindness; for they kindled a fire and received us every one, because of the present rain, and because of the cold.
3. And when Paul had gathered a bundle of sticks and laid them on the fire, there came a viper out of the heat, and fastened on his hand.
4. And when the barbarians saw the venomous beast hang on his hand they said among themselves, No doubt this man is a murderer, whom though he hath escaped the sea, yet vengeance suffereth not to live.
5. And he shook off the beast into the fire, and felt no harm.
6. How beit they looked when he should have swollen, or fallen down dead suddenly: but after they had looked a great while and saw no harm come to him, they changed their minds, and said that he was a god.
7. In the same quarters were possessions of the chief man of the island, whose name was Publius: who received us, and lodged us three days courteously.
8. And it came to pass that the father of Publius lay sick of a fever and of a bloody flux: to whom Paul entered in and prayed, and laid his hands on him and healed him.
9. So when this was done others also which had diseases in the island, came, and were healed.
10. Who also honoured us with many honours: and when we departed they laded us with such things as were necessary.
11. And after three months we departed in a ship of Alexandria, which had wintered in the isle, whose sign was Castor and Pollux.

[4] Named after the Governor of Malta from 1884–1888, General Sir John Lintorn Simmons.
[5] Letter 14th February 1989 from Mrs. Kathleen Collyer, nee Moore, of Thatcham, Berks, RG13 3EU.
[6] The White Ensign on rich silk with the Royal Cypher and cross of gold.
[7] By 1955 it was so badly disintegrating that it was taken down.
[8] Established in 1875 by Mrs. Mary Townsend to help country girls who found themselves in moral danger when they moved to towns seeking work. The first GFS Hostel was opened in London in 1877. The present headquarters is located at Townsend House, 126 Queen's Gate, London, SW7 5LQ.
[9] Janet Aikman, daughter of Sir Robert Aikman, married Sir David Campbell in 1899.

Chapter 17

St. Paul's Interior Appearance Pre-War

For more than thirty years after the consecration the appearance of St. Paul's interior remained unchanged, the only ornamentation being the carved capitals of the Corinthian columns and pilasters, and consequently the church looked somewhat austere.

Behind the altar were five large zinc panels, of which three were painted. The central one with the Ten Commandments and the flanking ones with the Lord's Prayer, and the Creed. These panels were the work of Mr. Friars, of Hannover Street, London.

At the west end of the building was the font, of unusual design. Mr. Sconce wrote early in 1844: *"The font was given by Mr. Bowden, the writer of the 'Life of Pope Gregory', so of course you will think it an orthodox font, only it is too small. It is a marble copy of a good Grecian Vase."*

The first memorial panels to be affixed to the walls were large ones in the bays between the pilasters, to Archdeacon Le Mesurier and Bishop Tomlinson. One was later added for the Reverend John Cleugh. The Bishops had only been in favour of ecclesiastics being remembered in this manner, but an exception was made in the Spring of 1898, when a large memorial panel for Lady Houlton was placed in the bay next to that of Bishop Tomlinson.

Two further large memorials were subsequently installed, for Mr. Henry Lumsden Gale in 1905 and Mr. William Hardman in 1909, both long serving members of St. Paul's and deserving of such recognition.

When Lady Fremantle died in 1898 a brass plate was mounted in her memory and her husband the Governor, also had two white marble steps laid in the sanctuary so raising the altar about a foot. They were inscribed:

IN MEMORY OF LADY LYON FREMANTLE 1898

Over the next few years several other metal and marble memorial tablets were approved. In 1902, Colonel Stringer Commanding the 3rd Battalion Royal Garrison Regiment received permission to erect a brass tablet in memory of the men who had died during the regiment's service on the island. The following year General O'Callaghan submitted a request for a marble plaque, identifying the site as the former location of the Auberge d'Allemagne, to be fixed on the outside of the church under the portico.

Apart from these minor additions, and the installation of new lighting, the only significant change was in 1885 when the organ was moved. The organ was first set up in St. Paul's during 1854. Originally built by Father Smith (c1630–1708) for Chester Cathedral it was taken in part exchange by the organ builder[1] when Chester required a new one in 1844. Thus it became available for St. Paul's, and was installed by Robson & Company[2].

In 1885 it was rebuilt and moved from its original location at the west end of the church, to a gallery above the choir at the east end. The instrument was rebuilt again in 1905, by the Swiss firm of Goll & Company who were based in Lucerne[3].

The first effort to make the interior more appealing was in 1925 when the organist, Mr. Robinson offered the church a beautiful painting by a Maltese[4] artist depicting 'Our Lord as the Good Shepherd', in memory of his friend and late churchwarden Mr. John W. Starkey. The offer was taken up, and it was hung as the centre panel behind the altar. Mr. Harrison, the secretary to the church council wrote a letter of appreciation to Mr. Robinson and added:

> "H.E. the Governor has expressed his admiration of the picture and it is universally considered a great addition to the church."

Canon Marshall initiated a Restoration Fund in 1931, but had left Malta before any practical work could be done. Canon Nicholls made a start by preparing a memorial chapel to Bishop Collins at the end of the south aisle, and this project commenced in 1933. Timber for the altar was provided as a gift by the Anglican and Eastern Churches Association, and was built as a labour of love by three joiners of the Royal Navy who were members of the congregation.[5]

By 1936, the painted inscriptions on the zinc panels flanking the altar were looking badly worn, so green silk curtains were hung in front of them, and when Elizabeth Coldwell died that year, her husband presented a Kirman carpet in her memory which was laid over the altar steps.

These were still relatively minor changes, but in April 1937 Bishop Buxton informed the church Council that an anonymous donor had made a gift of £500, which could be used, for beautifying the sanctuary, or added to the endowment fund.

Canon Nicholls was in favour of improving the appearance of the sanctuary, and Mr. W. D. Caröe the celebrated ecclesiastical architect prepared a comprehensive plan, but he died before the work commenced. In 1938 under the supervision of his firm, Caröe and Passmore of Westminster, the alterations began.

Since this plan involved a complete change, the painting donated by Mr. Robinson in 1925 was taken down, and he was informed that it was going to be moved, but its whereabouts today is unknown. In 1994 Canon Cousins attempted to trace it both in Malta and in the 'Art World' but without success.

The six plain pilasters in the sanctuary were carved with tulip motifs for the lower ten feet, then fluted from there up to the capitals. The tulips, the fluting, and the leaf design of the capitals were all gilded. This work was completed by Passion Week 1939, save for the western faces of the end pillars, which were not gilded, as the carving of the northern one would have involved risk to the organ. The gilding work on the pilasters was carried out by John Sammut[6], and Mr. E. Paris.

Lady Bonham Carter, the wife of the Governor, made enquiries about a suitable damask to cover the old zinc panels. By Holy Week the five $9' \times 5'$ panels, which had formerly been covered by green silk curtains, were filled with this very beautiful blue and gold cloth, 'Crown Brocatelle' pattern, mounted on wood. This fabric was made by Warner and Co., and was of the same weave as that used to cover the galleries of Westminster Abbey for the Coronation of King George VI in 1937. A new pulpit fall was also made from a piece of this cloth.

> *"The effect is, I think, most beautiful"* wrote Canon Nicholls. *"I contemplate it mostly from the north corner of the communion rails, and the light shines from a different angle on every pilaster and panel. One will glint like dew upon golden daffodils, and the pattern of the panel next to it will stand out in a glowing blue. The other four panels will all be different till the eye reaches the one above me; that one is almost sombre grey."*

There remained a balance of about £150 from the original amount but Mr. Caröe's other plans, which included a better sounding board for the pulpit, cresting over the throne and a ten-foot altar and frontal were postponed with the outbreak of war.

Of a much minor nature, but a very practical suggestion was made in March 1938. Pay-Captain Trevor Hayles, R.N. drew the Canon's attention to the uncomfortable pews, caused partly by them having straight backs and suggested they be altered by sloping the backs. This was agreed and the matter put in hand immediately.

Below the organ before the war there was an area called 'Museum Corner'. On show was a small portrait of Queen Adelaide and her husband King William IV on a pear, entitled 'A pretty pear'; Queen Adelaide's letter to the Protestants in 1839 set in a wood and red plush frame ornamented with silver filigree work; a plaster cast of an inscription from the German Auberge dated 1571. A glass case contained the leaf-shaped silver trowel used by Queen Adelaide in laying the Foundation Stone, and the boxwood rammer used on the same occasion was kept in the sacristy and displayed on Sundays and special occasions. Other exhibits were a small reproduction of a picture in Greenwich showing Queen Adelaide on HMS *Hastings*, en route to Malta; an old Prayer Book and Bible (dated 1628) presented by Messrs. Foyles, the famous London booksellers.

By way of a flight of stairs at the west end it was possible to reach the small Chapel of the Ascension. Whilst in England during 1932 Canon Nicholls was contacted by Mrs. Lay whose son Hugh was killed when his Aero Bison aircraft crashed into the sea about five miles east of Valletta on 22nd October 1926. She wished to have a memorial to him placed in the Church, and after some discussion it was felt appropriate that a window would be installed in the Chapel of the Ascension, in memory of the four-man crew[7]. A design was submitted by Powell & Sons, which was approved, and by September 1934 the window was complete. It was and still is the only stained glass window in St. Paul's.

Such was the interior of St. Paul's prior to the Second World War.

Notes

[1] Gray & Davison
[2] A full description, specification and playing qualities of the organ appeared in "The Organ" magazine in April 1940.
[3] Goll & Co. was responsible for the famous organ in Lucerne Cathedral.
[4] Giuseppe Cali, now considered the outstanding Maltese artist of the 20th century.
[5] Of which Bishop Collins was President from 1906 to 1911
[6] Of 113 Cross Roads, Marsa.
[7] A memorial service had been held on board HMS *Eagle* on 30th October 1926. The four men who lost their lives were, Lieutenants Lay, Carslake and Anderson, and Leading Telegraphist Gibbs.

Chapter 18

Outbreak of World War II

When World War Two broke out in September 1939 Canon and Mrs. Nicholls were away on holiday but hurried back across Italy and looked after both churches until the Reverend Hugh Farrie, the Chaplain of Holy Trinity Sliema, returned from England. As a result of military deployments and difficulties encountered in wartime the congregations were continually changing.

Due to the war no Armistice Day service was held, also the Nativity Play, which had been presented at St. Paul's every year since 1931 was cancelled.

Canon Nicholls noted: *"We must be grateful that we are not in a war zone."* But even in the un-natural calm of the first winter of the war, the Royal Navy was on active service, and his son Lieutenant A. H. Nicholls, was lost in HMS *Sphinx* during February 1940.

Canon Nicholls expressed his feelings at this family tragedy:

> *"The price to be paid to cast out the evil spirit which Germany fostered and has now let loose upon the world is a heavy one. We had set aside money for the additional income tax, had lent as much as possible to the Government, had rationed ourselves voluntarily in food and in coal (living in the study to save using coal in the drawing room: it had been a cold winter here): now the biggest payment of all (and the only one that matters) has been demanded and paid.... So there it is, and we must treasure the gracious memories which we have of his beauty and talents and quiet reserve: and look forward to seeing him again in a life where war is not."*

At that time Canon Nicholls was able to record that the financial situation of St. Paul's was better than he expected. The Annual Appeal during April/May brought in £110 from the congregation on Malta. Due to the prohibition on the use of private cars many English residents were unable or unwilling to reach Valletta, but in spite of reduced numbers attending Sunday services, the amount of money put in the plate at collections remained steady.

But life on Malta dramatically changed on the 10th June 1940 with the entry of Italy into the war as a partner of Germany. This placed Malta, not only in a war zone but also within striking distance of enemy airfields, for Mussolini's Regia Aeronautica airfields in Sicily were only fifty miles away.

Many books have been written about the 'Siege of Malta' during the Second World War. Canon Nicholls at St. Paul's kept notes of his experiences, which graphically illustrate various aspects of life during those nerve-racking days. The manuscript is fifty A4 size pages long, and the next chapter is composed of extracts mainly concerning St. Paul's, and has been left exactly as written, in the Canon's own words.

Chapter 19

Siege of Malta 1940–1942

1940. It was on the night of June 10th that Rose Foss rang up to say that Italy was declaring war as from midnight.[1] It was only at six o'clock that very evening that H.E.[2] had made a short broadcast which was not more ominous than expected. But there had been one particular sinister thing which made the immediate outbreak of war seem definitely certain within a few hours, viz. the departure of the Italian Consul-General from the Island.

On Tuesday June 11th, we woke at 06.45 to the scream of the air raid siren. It is not a scream really, but quite a melodious pair of notes – a major third, I think. But, since it rises from a low note to a high one, and then warbles up and down continuously in a chromatic scale, it gives the impression of a shriek. Probably this is emphasised psychologically, by the fact that its warbling note means danger. Indeed when with its steady note it announces "Raiders passed" it has quite a pleasant sound.

On the first morning of the local war, the siren practically synchronised with a furious outburst of anti-aircraft fire all around us. We hurried into dressing gowns, and ran to the Crypt collecting the two frightened maids as we went. The fire was severe; windows and doors rattling, and the crump of bombs falling. There are three A.A. guns 600 yards away, clearly visible from our drawing-room windows, and indeed guns on all sides of us at about the same distance. I do not know how long the action lasted – perhaps 15 minutes. Ten planes, we were told, in two formations. We had 8 raids during that day, by far the worst being the last, when firing went on for about 30 minutes at about 7.30 p.m. It was a terrifying experience. I could hear bombs dropping. The sound is quite different from gunfire. It is a thick sound, and the word "crump" just describes it.

Since then we have had raids practically every day. The total to date is 53 in 22 days, and perhaps 5 days on which we have been exempt. In the first eight days we had 37 civilians killed and 112 wounded, as well as a few soldier casualties.

On July 10th we had a particularly unpleasant affair. At 8 o'clock, just as we were about to start Mass, it began. The guns near us were firing furiously, and we could hear bombs exploding. Suddenly there were bombs all round us, and then two almost simultaneous frightful blasts. The maids cried out (perhaps we also) and we all four closed towards one another to touch one another. The bangs were followed by the crash of falling stones and breaking glass; I felt sure that some part of the house was hit.

The plaster round all the doors had fallen; the soft iron bolts of doors were nearly all forced off; and both inside and outside the house there was dust, plaster, and glass. The stained glass window in the Chapel of the Ascension had got it worst. That faced the bombs. It is a window 9 ft. by 6 ft. built on a criss-cross of stout wrought iron bars some one-inch and some half-inch thick. These bars had bulged inwards about an inch; and where the bars had been let into the stonework pieces of the stone had been broken clean away, and the end of the bars left exposed. None of that glass was broken, thanks be to God; but there were about 40 panes broken elsewhere, facing the explosion, at right angles to it, opposite to it, and (strangely) also in the Verger's yard below. But considering the violent noise not much damage was done.

24th July 1940. Up to the present, we have had about ninety raids; it would have been more; but last week there was a lull, and for three days we had a welcome rest. Previously there had been about two raids daily.

St. Angelo has been hit more than once, and the Navy there has had to resort to underground quarters; Bighi Hospital got hit by a lone glider; not a sound was heard until the two bombs dropped. We heard them clearly, and ran for it; and since then we have never felt quite happy during that hour after sunset. An innocent Sick Berth Assistant was killed and a doctor slightly wounded, the Operating Theatre and X-ray room were demolished. About 100 unfortunately have been killed – nearly all civilians – and about double that number wounded.

Domestic life has suffered. The house is dark. We keep all rooms, not at the moment in use, shuttered. There is no time, in many of the raids, to shut windows and fasten shutters; with guns banging in the distance and others nearer to us opening fire, one has an irresistible urge to get under cover as quickly as possible!

At the Manoel Island raid, there were half a dozen lumps of bomb in the garden and on the roof. There was also an enormous piece of bright steel, or polished iron, half the size of your hand and weighing at least a pound lying outside the French window of the dining room. It was very hot.

Then, again, the raids are roughly twice a day – sometime in the morning, and some time in the evening. One never knows when. But always on Saturday night and Sundays. I often ponder the psychology of this. Is it a gesture of contempt against the Christian Religion?? Mussolini launches his barbarous attack against the harmless Albanian people on Good Friday 1938, and I can conceive of no reason why he should have chosen that day except a gesture of defiance against the Pope and the Christian democracies.

Our domestic upset is however infinitesimal compared with those who have left their homes. With the early raids in the neighbourhood of the Dockyard and Pieta, the inhabitants of the Three Cities and Valletta and Sliema, fled pell mell to the country and quartered themselves higgledy piggledy upon their relations. The noise of gunfire is of course much less. But nowhere is safe. Nevertheless, the people are wise to leave the centre of the target. Many of the poorest classes transferred themselves, their beds, their pots and pans into one or other of the tunnels under Valletta.

An air raid a day keeps concentration away. We sleep in the Crypt[3]; eerie, but one need not get up to go below in case of an alarm. It is also very cool in the Crypt; and it has been a cool year – another thing to be thankful for. For a fortnight I slept in my clothes – a form of funk, I think. Perhaps I had an idea that I might be called out for casualties.

The worst thing of all is to wake up happy having forgotten that there is a war on. This has not happened to me for some time. But for years I have slept blissfully unconscious, then wakened fresh and ready for the day's work. Then in 1935 when the first prospects of war with Italy approached, one woke miserably daily, for about six weeks. (I recall the same feelings in 1914) On the outbreak of the 'Second German War' it was the same, but then came that strange eight months when nothing seemed to happen.

I used to wake happy, and then would suddenly recall Anthony sweeping up mines in bitter weather and foul gales in the North Sea. That is over now, and he lies with about 5,000 other seamen in the deep. And so one wakes miserably; glad, of course, of the night's rest, glad not to have been molested; but dreading what the day has to bring forth. Dreading raids on a more serious scale; fearful of casualties among loved ones at home at Portsmouth and in the Midlands; anxious for what one may read of further devilment's, in the wisp of a newspaper, which is hardly worth the name. Anxious for London, for other countries attacked by Germany, or dragged into the Totalitarian circle, anxious about invasion.

On September 2nd, a Convoy arrived – two I think; one from the West and another from the East. One does not ask many questions about such movements because some people talk too much. We know that many guns arrived, for they were seen; and timber on deck. Some Australian mutton, we are told; at least one hundred tons of butter. I hope also a lot of oil. One of the ships was bombed, and hit on the after end. The Master was praised for getting the ship to harbour.

On September 8th being the Day of National Prayer, we reverted to holding our services in the Cathedral instead of in the Crypt. It has proved very successful and evidently meets a need in spite of the difficulties of getting to church. Hedley Nicolle, the Choirmaster, went over to St. George's Barracks, where there are a large number of families housed, and sought out our choirboys. Not only did they rally round, but other boys from Dockyard and Barracca, and Holy Trinity – in none of which are there any sung services so that with such of our men as can attend, together with a few from elsewhere, we now have a temporary choir of about 25.

(On September 22nd Canon and Mrs. Nicholls were guests of the Governor, General Dobbie at San Anton Palace, for five days. Here they were able to relax and even play a few games of tennis. The Governor and his wife were Plymouth Brethren, so tee-total and non-smokers, and though they drank the toast to 'The King's Health' in water, their guests were provided with something stronger.)

14th November 1940. I am told that the BBC in a broadcast made some allusion to the base from which Naples was bombed – and hazarded that it might be Malta; which seems a mighty stupid thing to say. I have no doubt that Malta it was; but we ourselves were very careful not to publish our own conviction. The BBC kindly did it for us.

(The organist of St. Paul's, Mr. Hedley Nicolle, employed by Gieves & Co., was evacuated to Alexandria, and sent his letter to Canon Nicholls from:

"Modern Imperial Hotel, Sliema, 28th December 1940, Sirs, It is with very deep regret that I ask you to accept my resignation with regard to the organistship and choirmastership of St. Paul's, a position which I have held since February 1938... I have learned to love St. Paul's, Malta during my stay and in spite of difficulties due to changes of personnel at various times I have always tried to do my utmost to make the musical portions of the services as a worthy contribution to the Glory of God. I wish to thank Canon and Mrs. Nicholls, the Churchwardens, ... and all members of the choir past and present for all kindnesses shewn to me. May I wish you all God speed and I can assure you that I will never forget St. Paul's and sincerely hope to revisit you at some future time.")

1941.

13th January 1941. I have neglected this record for many weeks; and during that time a number of exciting things have happened. London had its frightful fire-raising raid on December, when the Guildhall was burned down, and among other cherished buildings the church of St. Lawrence Jewry, my brother-in-law's church. Coventry also had a frightful time on November 14th. Poor dears.

Germany has at last decided to come to the help of Italy, which is said to be full of German troops and aeroplanes. The Aircraft carrier *Illustrious* was hit 6 times, and her after deck was a mass of flame. But the fire was put out and the ship reached Malta under her own steam, after steaming about 180 miles. The *Southampton* was also hit and set on fire. Blazing from stem to stern she had to be sunk by one of our own ships. *Gallant* hit a mine and the whole of her bows were neatly cut off at the bridge. She was towed to Malta stern-foremost, she had about 70 killed; *Illustrious* about 50 and 80 wounded. The *Ark Royal* was also engaged, but we think arrived unhurt at Gib.

On Thursday January 16th the German raids began, and continued on Saturday and Sunday. The attack was very fierce indeed.[4] The barrage was frightful, but many bombers got through, attacking continuously in small formations from every direction.

Many people watched the raids from a distance, or from reasonably safe places; They saw Valletta as one great cloud of smoke; the enemy planes skimmed the roof tops as they rose out of the dives. The *Illustrious* was hit once and the Captain's cabin demolished. The *Essex*, a fine new P. & O. 4 years old, was also hit and had about 16 killed and some injured. The Dockyard is badly messed up and probably pretty well finished as a repair shop on any large scale. Senglea (I am told) is badly cut up and of course the inhabitants have wisely fled to the villages as they did in June.

The noise in our Crypt was just terrible. There were about 250 people there huddled together, many of them crying, but many were very brave. The roar was like the loudest thunder one has ever heard, but absolutely continuous, and it was not possible really to distinguish the guns from the bombs, except when one fell close to us – about 70 yards. That brought down a block of flats and 5 people were killed. We sat, holding hands and praying aloud.

Today has been an anxious one for the authorities. *Illustrious* is, I think, going out tonight. I only heard at 3.30 p.m. and then I was not told; somebody whispered that it was to be hoped that there would be no raid today ... I passed the Dockyard shortly after, and *Illustrious* was obviously raising steam. On and off after that I was praying for darkness to fall before any reconnaissance plane came over. Later, I noticed that the two destroyers in Sliema Harbour had cast off their cables from the buoy, and were held only by a wire. It has been dark now for two hours and I pray that the ships have got out. With luck *Illustrious* may yet reach Singapore, and be repaired.

(4th February) The first anniversary of Anthony's death, and Padre Marson had kindly said a Requiem for us that morning. The previous few days had been rather racking. I thought of Tony writing what turned out to be his last letter ... the setting out for the minefield ... the approaching plane ... the explosion ... dealing with the dead and wounded ... towing the ship ... the cable parting ... the rising seas ending in a furious gale ... the sudden capsizing. Oh, the sorrow of it all.

7th February 1941. *Illustrious* did get away on January 23rd and is now safely in Alexandria if not farther afield. In spite of her severe superficial damage, and the loss of a number of her planes, she was able to steam 23 knots.

On February 8th/9th we had no less than ten hours of raiding, from 3 p.m. to 3 a.m. There were about 140 people sleeping in the Crypt. I got them to bring cards, draughts, etc., as they just do nothing but sit about – or lie about. I have produced about 20 old hassocks from the church, which they use as head pillows and some bring deck chairs, etc. I feel sorry for the women with babies.

That night there were long intervals of silence punctuated with sudden burst of furious gunfire. On the 9th itself we were alert for 4 hours; on the 12th we had constant alarms from 9 p.m. till 2 a.m. On Sunday 16th we heard the alarm siren no less than eleven times between 7 in the morning and midnight, but we held our services all the same.

And yet human nature can stand it! A few babies are born at K.G.V. Hospital; we held our Sung Eucharist on St. Paul Shipwrecked, February 10th. All Chaplains attended bar one.

21st February 1941. This morning I had a very moving incident at 8 o'clock. We, Clement (the Verger) and I, were saying Mattins preparatory to the Mass, when I heard the click of the Cathedral door opening. I got up and went to meet the newcomer. I saw an old, old soldier coming up the aisle, his heavy hobnailed boots scratching upon the tiled floor. He wore the ribbons of the 1914/18 and the other two medals of the veteran; his hair was greying and towzled; his face lined with toil, his hands gnarled and stained. *"I've just come in to say a prayer; I only get leave once in 8 days"* he said.

I explained that we were about to have Holy Communion, and that if it was any use to him and if he had time, would he wish to receive the Holy Sacrament? *"I've been confirmed"* he said in his rich voice with a strong burr *"in 1916"*. So we started the service. He seemed to follow it, as I heard a soft voice joining in. When we reached the Communion, he rose from his place without hesitation and knelt at the rail, holding up his two huge coarse hands high for the Bread of Life. I was much moved and with difficulty finished the service.

Most soldiers are young; here was one relatively old, dragged from his home to serve 2,000 miles away. Not a conscript, he said, but a pensioner, and the London Fire Brigade. *"A soldier's got to be practical"* he said, *"but I always go to church at home. This is a lovely building"*. And so we parted.

On Thursday 28th at 5.15 a.m. we had our worst experience hitherto. At 5.15 when the siren blew, I dressed as usual, but Phyllis stayed in bed[5]. There were rather less than the usual 100 persons taking refuge. I went upstairs for a few moments, and returned below. Five minutes later there was a loud explosion very near indeed. A cry of fear rose from the people and they surged towards our corner. Two minutes later there was a most frightful roar of stupendous power, or perhaps two in quick succession. I scarcely retained consciousness, as it seems now.

Phyllis was sitting up on her bed, I on the edge with my arms around her, her head buried on my shoulder. Mrs. Gale at the other end, her face in her hands, shivering with fear, screams from many people; myself saying *Keep calm* in an automatic voice! Banging, tearing, splitting, rending, and through it all a great wind rushing through the funk hole. I truly thought that we were directly hit and the building coming down. Then no more.

When the raiders had passed, I inspected the damage. A large part of the outer side of the dining room and the housekeeper's rooms are framed glass and the French window. Glass and frames were all over the floor. Upstairs, about a quarter of a ton of stone from the roof was lying upon Phyllis's bed and the floor.

In the drawing room, some of the ceiling stones, of which the roof is made, had fallen; the window frames were torn from their seating and were lying about having broken tables in their fall. There was a twenty-pound stone on the lid of the piano. The skylight glass of Mrs. Micallef's bedroom, 12 sq.ft. of it, one inch thick had crashed to smithereens two feet from the old lady's corpus.

The Cathedral itself was fortunate. Nearly all the windows and frames have gone, and the huge doors were snapped from their hinges and flung about. Some had the hinge pin neatly sheared off. There are a few holes in the plaster ceiling and most of the plaster of the portico has come down. What is left must be demolished. The stout wooden boards which we put up in the Chapel of the Ascension some months ago were shattered to pieces.[6] Yet blast is a strange wanton, wayward thing. Clocks were ticking, wireless and telephone working, and many delicate ornaments standing quietly in their places.

We have swept up the worst of the muck, but yesterday there was a high wind, and more dangling glass fell as well as gallons of dust and rubble. Next week the Demolition Officer is sending a gang to demolish the loose ceiling stones. He says that the house is not structurally unsafe as yet; but the whole roof needs to be properly vetted.

(The Governor and his wife came to see the damage at St. Paul's for themselves, then invited Canon and Mrs. Nicholls to come out and stay at St. Anton Palace for a few days).

Labour is frightfully difficult to obtain; but the P. & O. night watchman is a carpenter in his spare time, and he came along and put some of our doors and window frames back, and did it very well. Also the Gas Company lent us their carpenter, and we were allowed to buy £3 worth of planks, with which we boarded up the dining room and the housekeeper's rooms, and put padlocks there.

(On 12th March 1941 having secured the damaged Chancellors House, Canon and Mrs. Nicholls left Valletta for St. Anton Palace. This time for eight days rest and relaxation, though the Canon travelled into Valletta every day to take a service in St. Paul's. Both enjoyed walking in the spacious and flower stocked Palace gardens, which also held around 500 orange trees, yielding large quantities of fruit which was distributed to the local population.

The Governor persuaded them to stay a little longer, and during this time they had the chance meeting with the British Foreign Secretary Anthony Eden, and the C.I.G.S. Sir John Dill, who had arrived by Sunderland flying boat from Athens but were forced to wait at Malta for twenty four hours, since the sea was too rough for the plane to take off.)

The Day of National Prayer. Mass was said in the Crypt, but the 10 o'clock was not, I am thankful to say, disturbed. I had devised a Service in three parts – Repentance, Thanksgiving and Self-dedication – with a Short Address, Psalm, Lesson, Hymn and Prayers for each section. At noon and in the afternoon, the attacks came. They were very severe indeed. There were four people with us in our funk-hole. One dockyard man held his fingers in his ears, with his head between his knees; another a N.O. (temporary) who has a most dangerous job of detonating unexploded mines was white as a sheet. I stood among them reciting psalms, and as the barrage and the bombing increased in intensity I had to raise my voice louder and louder, until I was actually shouting the words.

In the afternoon it was, if anything, rather worse – a continuous roar like the loudest thunder, and the expectation of hearing one drop very close or actually on top of us. I was smoking and reciting the Creed, etc., and at the same time watching my hand as it held the cigarette. I was amazed at its steadiness: *"I believe in the Resurrection of the dead, and the life of the world to come, and my hand is perfectly steady and I can't think why, for I'm terrified and any moment may be my last, but I believe in the life of the World to come, Amen."* Comic!

18th April 1941. Easter has come and gone, and it has seemed very strange in some ways. We had quite good congregations on Good Friday (11th). We decided to try to carry through the usual Liturgical Three Hours, and by the grace of God we were not disturbed, except that a mine went off with a frightful roar when I was saying the Church Militant prayer. Of course I stopped; then I turned to the congregation and said, *"I think that was a mine"*. A man in the front row said 'mine' with his lips, so we continued the service.

On Easter Day we had over 100 communicants, which was good considering; and one or two at odd times from the Reserved Sacrament. We could not sing my descant to Hymn 134, which was a disappointment to me, as we have it only twice in the year, at Mattins and Evensong on Easter Day itself. I dislike having that hymn on any other day. Just as we were singing the "Easter Anthem", we were given our 500th 'Alert' and we had some difficulty in accommodating the large congregation in the Crypt. On that night and on the eve, we had several hours of night bombing raids.

The Huns have been very active here lately, and the strain is somewhat severe. At night when the siren wakes us, I find myself shivering as though I had the ague. That is only at night. It is horrible to hear the drone of the enemy getting louder, and then the crumps. But what about poor London, which has just had it's worst raid of the war.

We have had night Blitzes on April 18th, 19th, 22nd, 24th, 28th, 29th, 30th, and May 3rd, 6th and 7th. On the 22nd three big destroyers had brought us a magnificent mail – we had at least 60 letters and packets[7]. Our water has been cut off several times for long hours at a time, we have had no gas for a week, and we were minus Rediffusion for some days. But the telephone has come through unharmed.

(The raids on Valletta continued so on the 29th April they decided to spend the nights at Mr and Mrs. Burrell's house in Birchicara.)

21st May 1941. It is now three weeks that we have been sleeping out at Birchicara. It is very pleasant relief as we leave Valletta and arrive in that pretty country wied or valley, with pleasant trees dotting the road. It is also much better at night, as the guns are far less loud.

Ten days ago (27th June) we returned to Valletta to sleep. Our dear Pussy has disappeared. Whether he was killed by a splinter, or blast, or when wandering about at night, for the outside door will no longer shut, got entombed, I cannot guess. There are many buildings in ruins near our house. Or possibly he was run over by some military car, which are sometimes heard rushing about at night at great speed. Anyhow he must be dead.

He was a great friend, and we both miss him tremendously. Every morning he greeted me affectionately. A whistle from the loggia, and he would come lolloping up from the garden over the precipitous stones and up the steps, making queer welcoming noises in his throat. For hours he would sit or lie in his special place on the top of my writing table. He had a good knowledge of English! and no little sense of humour. exemplified sometimes in a gentle nip of my hand with his powerful jaws – for he was a huge beast – or a frigid and calculated refusal to obey orders, such as *"Go into the study at once when I tell you"*. Another war-casualty. Rest his soul, if he has a soul.

(Whilst out shopping in Kingsway[8] on 25th July Mrs. Nicholls had a narrow escape when an Italian fighter plane, pilot-less, swooped screaming over the roof of the Palace, then over the Casino Maltese missing the top by a few feet, roared up Kingsway and crashed into an already blitzed building. She had seen the planes overhead and took shelter in the chemist shop of Collis & Williams, at No.300 Kingsway, when this plane came down just five shops away.)

20th August 1941. I have neglected this diary. Today the Master of the S.S. *Port Chalmers* – one of the Convoy – came to lunch with me, and told me something of their voyage. It was his first time in action. He left Avonmouth, and rendezvous-ed with ships from Liverpool off the Isle of Man. Thence to N. Ireland where other ships joined them all exactly timed. Then down to Gib. with some other ships for the Cape. Suddenly they found *Nelson* on their quarter! When they entered the Med. a destroyer fired a rocket with a line attached and they drew on board their sealed orders.

On opening these the Master (Captain Higgs, a splendid specimen of the Merchant Seaman), found a thrilling document. It spoke of Malta's defence, of her need for stores, coal and ammunition and said the Convoy must go through. The Navy would give all possible help but the convoy could assist by making as little smoke as possible, by not signalling at night, by keeping station. It ended with the same slogan, in capital letters this time "THE CONVOY MUST GO THROUGH".

It gave them all a buoyant feeling of determination, and was finely phrased, said the Master. Next morning it began with air attacks. *Fearless* was sunk and *Manchester* compelled to turn back. That night the E-boats got among them, and between the two lines of ships, for *Sydney Star* was holed (40ft long) on the port side but was on the starboard side of *Port Chalmers*. There was a tremendous firing from the ten T.B.D.'s and *Edinburgh*, *Renown* and *Ark Royal* went with them about as far as Sardinia, and then disappeared. When they reached Malta on the next afternoon, Captain Higgs said they were very thrilled by the cheering crowds on the bastions to greet them.

11th September 1941. I heard of the worst case of pilfering from the convoys today. Somebody got away with 470 cases of whisky, not bottles. The size of the haul makes one give a grudging admiration, when I have lads in prison for stealing a few packets of cigarettes! With whisky at, say 15/- per bottle, this is a value of over £4000. It must have been a whole lighter full, and there must have been a number of people in the syndicate. We are told that somebody is suspect.

After Mattins we had our first Carol practice, and in the middle Clement called out from his seat in the loggia *"Convoy"*. We rushed out of the drawing room and there on the horizon, a marvellous sight. The biggest Convoy since the war. We counted about 15 ships. Actually 9 merchantmen, 5 cruisers, and ten destroyers. The merchantmen about 12,000 tons each. They had been escorted into the Med. by *Nelson, Prince of Wales*, and *Ark Royal*. *Nelson* must now be detached from the Atlantic.

19th November 1941. Once again I find that a long period of time has passed since I wrote in this 'diary' of the siege. We have a new horror. For two months past depth charges are let go in Sliema Harbour immediately below our drawing room window. At first it was very secret, but now we know in part. They are only small charges, 6 lbs. I am told; but they shake the Cathedral to its foundations, the glasses rattle, and pieces of plaster fall down from the walls and ceilings. These big detonations go on from nightfall almost every night, and continue at intervals of perhaps 15 or 20 minutes till dawn.

The stolen whisky has been found – 300 cases (not 470). They were stowed in Zaccaria St., and 4 NAAFI, men are under arrest. The officials are now trying to find the bosses who are responsible. In the same cellar were found 250 cases of 'undeclared' whisky.

17th December 1941. It seems as though once per month is to be the average attention which this story of the Siege of Malta can receive. For days past I have wished to continue it, and have failed. Rear-Admiral Rawlings who has safely arrived here for a few days in "*Ajax*" came to tea yesterday and said he hoped someone was keeping a diary of this 'fantastic' siege. So I am encouraged to go on.

I have had one personal trial hanging over me for three months which to my great relief did not materialize as I feared it would. An English soldier from the West Kent Regt., quarrelled with another soldier over a slut of a girl. He knocked the other man out with a rifle-butt, then cut his throat, and with the assistance of another man put the body in a sack and threw it into a dry watercourse. Justice here is terribly slow, and the prisoner was about 4 months on remand. I saw him every week, and he used to say *"Well, if they hang me . . ."* and I felt certain that he would be condemned, as two Maltese had been put to death either this year or last – the first for about 20 years. But he was lucky.

The jury voted 7 to 2; and as the vote for execution must be unanimous, he got a life sentence. The English barrister-soldier who defended him said that in all his experience – which was not small – he had never known a more sordid murder. Anyhow, thanks be to God, I was saved the horrid business of seeing him put through his last earthly punishment. Now I see him weekly.

St. Stephens Day. Boxing Day. We are having our third noisy raid today, so I will add a little to this. Yesterday, God be praised we did not do so badly. The first alert was just as I was communicating the last five people at the Sung Eucharist; so we came down to the Crypt and finished the service there – a thing we have not had to do for several months. It was a very spiritual Christmas. There were 99 communicants at the three celebrations, which is a good number considering the transport difficulties. The shortened 'Service of the Six Lessons' was very beautiful. The lessons were read by the Verger, a Choirboy, a Sidesman,

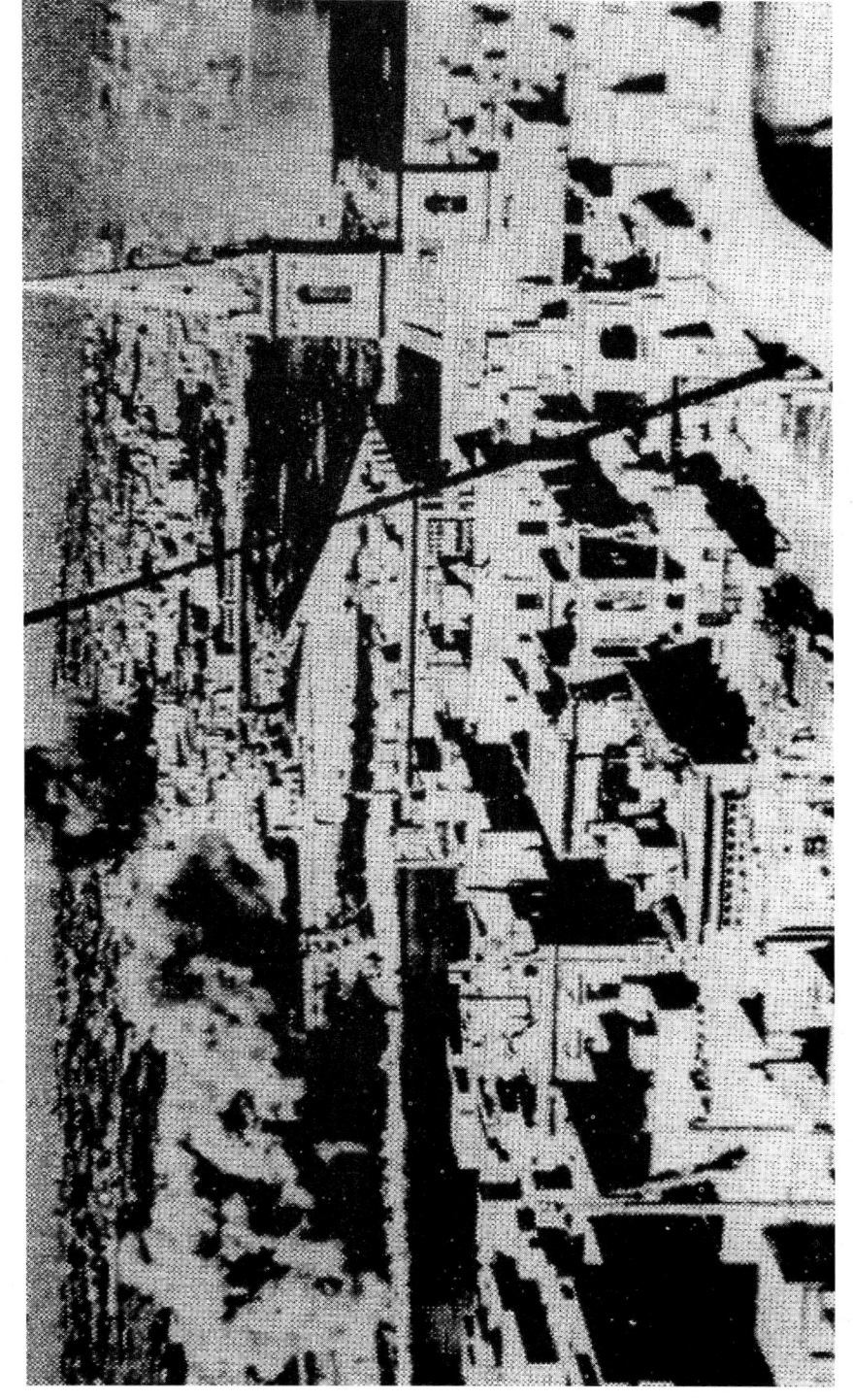

1941 – Bombs exploding at Fort Manoel and in Lazaretto Creek behind St. Paul's Spire

a Churchwarden, the Governor, and the Parish Priest (me). It was very nice to have the Sung Eucharist again, with a choir and congregation of about 60 people, who sang Pange Lingua very well.

1942. 15th January 1942. Boschetto House, near Rabat. We came here on Tuesday in an interval between the 17 Alerts which we had on that day, many of them serious raids over the harbour and therefore over our heads. There were a number of bomb-holes in Floriana as our bus passed through, but we got to Mdina safely; a fresh Alert was sounded as our carrozi started on the two-mile drive to Boschetto.

Later. It was very cold; but being a hospital-type there was a small ration of coke, and the fire was lit after lunch, or even occasionally before. Mrs. Geoghegan is a wonderful manager. She contrived to feed us splendidly in spite of being so far from any shops. I had lately had certain disturbing symptoms about my heart and I had been examined by Dr Stones of KGV Hospital, and by Lieut-Colonel Hamilton of Mtarfa Military Hospital.

It was on their recommendation that we went for this rest, rather than for treatment in the hospital itself. While we were there three Merchant Captains arrived,[9] and we were glad of their company. One arrived late one night having had great difficulty in getting there. As he left his ship a stick of bombs dropped alongside in the harbour. Mrs. G. put him to bed and kept him there for two days. They had come from Alex. and had been thoroughly bombed on the journey. He was very shaken.

On the recurrence of the date of the *Illustrious* blitz, the newspaper reminds us that in these hectic days we destroyed 39 Hun planes for certain, 5 probables and 9 damaged. Between June 11th/40 and Jan 15th/42 we have had 1285 Alerts. The sirens must be wearing out!

The 5th (February), I was walking back from visiting KGV[10], believing that there was no immediate danger; just as I got to the Casino Maltese a roaring barrage broke out overhead. I ran for the shelter of the Arcades. As soon as it was over – perhaps three minutes – I continued down Teatro for home and saw two huge black columns of smoke of exploded bombs appearing over the roof of St. Paul's. They had fallen on Manoel, as usual these days. That was a bad day for Sliema. The Gaiety Theatre, a very fine theatre was gutted (luckily it was empty), the Union Club hit, Barclays Bank destroyed, and the cashier, who was just wishing to finish a job at his desk, killed.

February 12th. A corner of the Palace was knocked off, a bomb dropped in Palace Square; it was one of those which goes off on the slightest impact and does not bury itself in the earth. It made only a very small saucer like hole, but walls within 100 yards have large chunks chipped out. But it killed at least two people. A man who heard it coming flung himself down and got away with it. But a lady continued her walk and was hit in the face, and a well-known man Mr. Reggie Smith[11] who was going to the library had his leg blown off. He died a fortnight later. At his funeral which I took in the Chapel at Ta Braxia itself a large number of Maltese actually came into the building, encouraged by Mr. Charles Edwards.

10th March 1942. Things are bad in the Far East, Singapore has fallen, and there were 70,000 prisoners. Burma is also under attack, and Rangoon in great danger; the Dutch East Indies, Java and the Naval base of Surabaya lost also. Australia has been attacked for the first time in her history Port Darwin bombed.

On the 14th there was less activity; but Sunday was a tragic day; three alerts without ceasing, and at 6 p.m. another blitz over Manoel. Later we knew that the Casino Maltese had been hit, and the Regent Theatre next door. Mr. Caruana Galitzia, a popular and prominent Maltese was killed, and Phyllis's Maltese doctor[12] of whom we were very fond. Mr. Parnis,[13] a Maltese who had lived in England and won the M.C. in the last war was wounded and died about a week later. About twenty-five civilians were killed in the Regent Theatre.

On Sunday 22nd my old heart conked out after early Mass, and Captain Coldwell and Captain Ohlson took Mattins between them, most reverently as I was told and should expect. Dr. Stones happened to be in the congregation and he came to see me. After resting I was able to take the Office of Evensong, but did not preach.

I have no notes of what took place on the next few days, until Friday when poor Manoel suffered yet again. It lies exactly opposite our home, at a distance of 500 yards. It is the Submarine Base and is called **HMS** *Talbot*. There are usually at least 4 submarines lying there, resting and replenishing between their 'patrols' which occupy about a fortnight at sea. The men live ashore in an old building which used to be the 'Lazaretto' or infectious hospital. It is heavily defended with 4 big A-A 3.5 guns as well as smaller stuff. The barracks have been hit several times, the Chapel which has a very attractive facade which faces us has been gutted, but the facade still stands.

On this Friday the 27th, some English ratings and two Greek officers who are part of the Ship's Company of a Greek submarine which has been working with us were killed. In the afternoon I buried these two Greek officers. The Orthodox Community no doubt wished that they should be laid among their own people – for we have a section for the Orthodox in our Cemetery. [14]It was a most moving service.

At the burial, as the bearers began to lower the first coffin, one of them gave a loud blubber. That was enough. The other sailors, about 30 of them followed suit. After the service a young officer read a panegyric. There were a large number of the Greek civilian community present, both men and women, and during the speech the whole gathering wept openly and unashamed. It sounds pretty awful to the English sense of self-control. But it was not in the least shameful nor unpleasant – except for the difficulty which I had, and perhaps Captain Phillips, in keeping my own tears under control.

I got back feeling pretty dicky, as I was caught in my carrozi under a barrage in Kingsway, with bombs falling, and just managed to dash into a shelter. I had not been back more than a few minutes when I was rung up to say that there was a bad casualty at the Central Civil Hospital[15]. I tried to get the RAF Chaplain on the telephone, but failed, and so set off feeling scarcely able to walk. Luckily I found a carrozi fairly near which raced off to the hospital, with the 'Danger Imminent' flag flying. The cabby agreed to wait. The RAF man was unconscious, so I said the Office for the dying, and the Commendation.

At 6 o'clock Manoel was again the target, and the worshippers took refuge in our funk-hole. Then we went to seek for Manoel, which was again completely blotted out by smoke and dust. The popular Sliema church of Stella Maris was also hit.

This brings the account of our siege more or less up to date. I struck a bad cold that Friday, and have taken things as easily as possible, resting in bed for part of the day, reading the History of the Papacy, and writing. I will end this section of this scribble – by a piece of what we hope is going to prove very good news.

During these bad weeks we have felt rather helpless; as though the Germans really had got the upper hand. But there have been rumours of the coming of Spitfires. Oh, for a few Spitfires, we have thought again and again. But we do know that the runways of the dromes have been lengthened, and somebody whispered that this was the real secret. Spitfires need a longer runway than we could hitherto supply. Last week there was a rumour that they were really coming – that some pilots had actually arrived.

Last Saturday some positively did, and Spitfires were flown over the island for recognition purposes. On Sunday and Monday they were in action.

Notes

[1] Mussolini made the Declaration of War at 6 p.m. at the Palazzo Venezia in Rome.
[2] The Governor at that time was Lieut-General William George Sheddon Dobbie.
[3] Nowadays generally called 'The Undercroft'.
[4] German Luftwaffe Junkers JU88's and JU87's which became better known as the Stuka dive-bomber.
[5] Canon and Mrs. Nicholls had their beds in a corner of the Crypt (Undercroft).
[6] The stained glass window was repaired and re-installed after the war.
[7] During April the Malta Post Office issued stamp labels bearing the White Ensign and RAF Ensign, with the words 'Malta is grateful to the Royal Navy and the Royal Airforce for the safe arrival of this letter'.

[8] Now named 'Republic Street'.
[9] Convoy MF3. Four merchant ships sailed from Alexandria, the *Ajax*, *Thermopylae*, *Clan Ferguson* and *City of Calcutta*. The *Thermopylae* was sunk en route to Malta on January 19th.
[10] King George V Hospital was totally destroyed shortly after on 26th April 1942.
[11] Son of Thomas Corlett Smith, and great grandson of Thomas Corlett.
[12] Dr. Robert Bonello MD.
[13] Capt. William C. Parnis OBE, MC.
[14] Ta Braxia cemetery.
[15] Now the Police Headquarters in Floriana.

Chapter 20

Centenary of Consecration

Both Chaplains were suffering from ill health as a result of the conditions, that they had endured for the last twenty months. Canon Nicholls was ordered back to England, and left Malta towards the end of April, leaving the Reverend Farrie to look after St. Paul's as well as Holy Trinity.

The day to day business at St. Paul's carried on despite wartime conditions. At the 1942 Annual General Meeting, the churchwardens who had served throughout 1941, were re-elected, namely, Mr. A. L. Barrett as Chancellor's Warden, Capt. C. J. Coldwell People's Warden, Commander B. J. Ohlson, Mr. Gordon Firman, Mr. Charles Edwards, with Pay Captain Trevor Hayles R.N. (retired) as Treasurer and Mr. T. D. Trudgeon as Secretary.

In July Bishop Buxton arrived by air to help out by taking over at St. Paul's, but he was very soon on his own looking after both churches since Farrie was suffering from an attack of jaundice, and was sent to an inland village to rest.

During this visit discussions took place with Chaplain Farrie and the Churchwardens about the immediate repair work needed for the Cathedral and the Chancellor's House. Professional advice was also sought from a qualified surveyor and from the Royal Engineers.

The Bishop also met the Lieut-Governor, Mr. David Callender Campbell[1], to talk about the financial position of the church. The Anglican Church Commission which held the properties had never accepted responsibility for their maintenance, and while the churchwardens of St. Paul's had assumed the care of the fabric and finances of the building, without prejudice to the legal position, the large scale repair work due to war damage raised a fresh financial issue. Mr. Campbell thought that the Government would be willing to contribute to the cost of temporary repairs, though the War Damages Bill was not yet in force.

In April 1941 nearby bombing jarred the organ so severely that it was unplayable. *"At first it did not appear possible to have the organ repaired locally"* wrote the Reverend Stevens in 1942. *"It seemed that it would have to wait until the end of the war when it could be shipped to England."* However, as a result of a chance conversation between Major-General C. T. Beckett C.R.A., and Lieutenant F. W. Rimmer[2] who was in charge of the music at the Cathedral, Lance-Bombardier

Interior of St. Paul's 1844

Silver Gilt Chalice inscribed
'Malta Government Chapel, A.D.1809'
mounted with the
Pectoral Cross of Bishop Knight in 1912

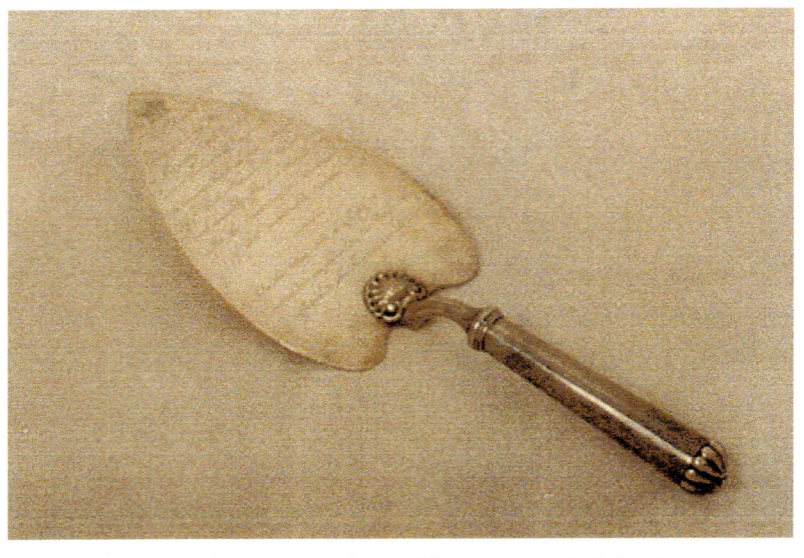

The Silver Trowel used by Queen Adelaide
to lay the Foundation Stone
of St. Paul's Church, 20th March 1839

View of the High Altar 1999

Chapel of the Ascension

Royal Marines Memorial Gates

View of the Baptistry 1999

J. Poole of the Royal Artillery was discovered and given permission to devote the necessary time to restoring the organ. Poole had considerable experience having worked with one of England's leading firms of organ-builders, and later he was assisted by another Royal Artilleryman, Gunner J. G. Lodwick.

> *"This restoration was a long task. There was little material and none of the tools normally required for such a job. Major General Beckett took great interest in the work, and actually brought back some of the requirements from a visit to the Middle East. He also caused appeals to be made for old kid gloves, split skin, and bedding leather. This was urgently needed for the envelope valves, many of which were in bad need of repair. The appeals met with a ready response and soon sufficient skin was available to make a start. Later a complete set of tuning cones, bells and knives was made in the R.E.M.E. workshops by kind permission of Lieut-Colonel L. N. Tyler, work went on through the long 'blitz' months of early 1942, and fortunately although many bombs fell near the Cathedral no further damage was caused to the organ."*

As a result of the efforts by Poole and Lodwick, the greater portion of the instrument had been restored by the end of the year. Only a few stops were so badly damaged that they had to await the full-scale reconstruction after the war. Funds for the organ repairs had been raised by Mrs. Ohlson[3], wife of the churchwarden. On December 27th Lieutenant Rimmer was able to give a special recital on the newly repaired organ.

The fortitude of the Maltese people had been honoured in April, and on Sunday 13th September 1942, the George Cross Medal, which had been awarded to Malta by King George VI on April 15th, was publicly presented to the people of Malta, by Lord Gort the Governor, in front of a vast crowd in Palace Square. It was accepted on their behalf by the Chief Justice Sir George Borg.[4]

An hour later Lord Gort accompanied by his Staff Captain, Guy Russell R.N., and Major the Earl of Munster, arrived at St. Paul's to attend the ceremony for installing the Reverend Hugh Farrie as a Canon of St. Paul's. An honour he richly deserved. Bishop Buxton, the Reverend Farrie and the Reverend J. G. Gethin-Jones received them at the door of the church, and the Churchwardens, Mr. A. Barrett, Mr. Charles Edwards, Mr. R. Firman and Cmdr. H. Ohlson conducted H.E. and his party to their seats. Other dignitaries present included Admiral Sir Ralph Leatham, the Vice-Admiral Malta, and General Mack Scobie, the General Officer Commanding Troops Malta. The congregation was composed of civilians and forces personnel including a large detachment from the Royal Navy. After the sermon by the D.A.C.G., the Reverend J. G. Gethin-Jones, Hugh Farrie was installed as a Canon by the Bishop, who then celebrated the Eucharist.

Canon Nicholls' post was kept open pending his return and a locum tenens was found, the Reverend H. E. Stevens, who had spent ten years as a Naval chaplain and knew Malta. He arrived in October, "*I am now settled in with the dear old Verger and his wife for butler and cook, and quite happy with their help*" he wrote: but it was no easy task he had undertaken. Fortunately the roof over the study and bedroom of the Chancellor's House had been repaired and he lived in these, there being insufficient fuel for the drawing room. Food was still very short, but the air raid alerts had been diminishing in recent weeks, so Christmas was fairly peaceful. For the Verger, Mr. Murray Clement[5] the festival was overshadowed by the news that his son had recently been killed on active service with the Royal Air Force.

1942 was without doubt the most eventful year for the people living on Malta. There had been over 2,000 air raid alerts; some Spitfires arrived in March to strengthen the air defences; on 9th April the Mosta Dome bomb incident; 7th May the clandestine change over from Governor Dobbie to the new Governor Lord Gort at Kalafrana; in August the thought of surrender due to shortage of food and materials narrowly averted by the arrival of the Santa Marija convoy; and in September the George Cross ceremony.

In his New Year's Eve message Lord Gort rightly said:

"*... the last night of a year which has brought not only great trials, but also great glory to Malta, to wish you all, fighting Services and citizens alike, good fortune in 1943 ... May the year which begins tomorrow carry us far along the road which leads to the portals of victory! ... Let us go forward with confidence into 1943.*"

So the New Year opened with some optimism that the course of the war had at last turned in the Allies favour.

At the personal level however, there were still many problems. A ten day musical festival arranged by Lieutenant Rimmer with organ recitals at St. Paul's had to be cancelled, since all theatres, cinemas and places of public entertainment were ordered to close due to an outbreak of infantile paralysis (poliomyelitis).

Some temporary repairs to the building had been undertaken, as noted by the Reverend Stevens:

"*All the Cathedral windows have now been filled in with wood, which produces a dim religious atmosphere not unpleasing when you become accustomed to it. The Chancellor's damp and much blasted house has been further repaired and it is no longer necessary to put up an umbrella when passing through the lounge even in the heaviest downpours*".

During the summer of 1943, there was great activity in Malta. Troops came to the island in large numbers, whilst the Royal Navy assembled about 175 ships, plus 23 submarines and around 1,300 landing craft of all types. They were joined by an American Fleet of about 65 ships, with another 700 landing craft. This vast accumulation of soldiers and sailors kept the Reverend Stevens extremely busy, but he managed to cope in spite of being slightly handicapped by a leg disability.

Large congregations attended the services at St. Paul's, and activities such as a Servers' Guild, a revived Toc H group, and a Servicemen's Rover Scout Crew were running. The personnel of these groups changed constantly as the war continued. The Reverend Stevens recorded:

> *"Many of our most faithful worshippers are leaving the Island as the battles move further and further away from us, and the sadness of farewell is relieved by their appreciation of what St. Paul's and Holy Trinity have meant to them, especially during the severest blitzs."*

The top Military leaders conferred on Malta and both General Alexander and General Montgomery attended services at St. Paul's. Sir Andrew Cunningham, C-in-C, Mediterranean[6] moved his Headquarters from Algiers to Malta on July 3rd, in preparation for Operation Husky, the invasion of Sicily, which took place on 10th July.

Thereafter events moved rapidly. By 19th August all restrictions were lifted on the ringing of church bells which had been banned since they were only to be used a signal of an enemy invasion. Italy signed an armistice on 3rd September 1943, which was announced on the 8th. One of the terms included the surrender of the Italian Fleet, and Italian Naval and Merchant ships of all classes were ordered to sail to Malta. Morale was further boosted during the year by visits from His Majesty King George VI in June, Winston Churchill in November and President Roosevelt in December.

At St. Paul's by February 1944, the Reverend Stevens resigned owing to continued ill health[7], but without doubt had worked hard on behalf of the Anglican community on Malta. Canon Nicholls writing from England said that he would not be able to return and resume his duties, on medical advice. Bishop Buxton therefore had to find a new man for the post. He invited Canon Nicholls to retain his Canonry, and wrote of the Reverend Stevens tenure; *"He has endeared himself to all the padres here, as well as to countless officers and men. And he has made his house a house of call for an endless company of friend of St. Paul's."*

Canon Nicholls[8] sent a letter to Mr. Trudgeon, one of the churchwardens thanking them for their good wishes and continued:

"I loved Malta and the work there. It was not easy; but difficulties are made to be overcome. I wish I were still there; but in any case it was time that a new man with new methods took over the work. Give the joint greetings of Mrs. Nicholls and myself to all members."

As early as the autumn of 1943 some rebuilding had taken place in Valletta, and though conditions were very far from normal, development schemes for the future were being prepared. By October 1944, a detailed programme for the reconstruction of Floriana and Valletta was on show at Office of Public Works in Valletta.

Work on repairing the spire of St. Paul's commenced on March 1st 1944, under the supervision of the architect, Silvio Mercieca. It was financed by a loan of £2,000 from Diocesan funds. The contract was entrusted to Mr. Joseph Sammut of Gzira, and with the employment of thirteen workmen the task of restoration began. Scaffolding was erected to the height of 130 feet above ground level, but the work had to proceed with some caution since it involved handling large blocks of stone weighing up to three-quarters of a ton each, in a confined space. However, the job was completed in just five months, three months ahead of schedule.

By that time the new Chaplain the Reverend Francis William Hicks[9] had arrived and enabled Canon Farrie to take a well-earned holiday. He was installed as Chancellor and Senior Canon later in the year. There was no gas supply available, but otherwise the daily living conditions were steadily improving. The Chancellor's House needed very extensive rebuilding, and it was estimated that the repair and reconditioning of the organ alone would cost £2,500. With these and other improvements in mind it was decided that the time was ripe to launch a special appeal to the public to raise the necessary money.

Accordingly, the "Saying 'Thank You' to Malta and Gibraltar" Fund was opened in October 1944:

"There can be few among us who are not aware of the vital part played in the war by Malta and Gibraltar. Malta, unconquered after two years of siege, and backed by the Fortress of Gibraltar, made possible the successful North African campaign, and the re-opening of our Mediterranean life-line.

It is felt that there are many, not only at home and throughout the Empire, but also in other countries, who would welcome the opportunity to pay tribute to Malta and Gibraltar in a practical way. It is proposed, therefore, to open a fund for the purpose of repairing and extending our Cathedral Centres at Gibraltar and Malta; so that in future years the spiritual and social needs of men in the Services, and of civilians quartered in the Mediterranean area, shall be more adequately provided for.

> *The comprehensive scheme that has been planned includes the repairing of the bomb-damaged Cathedral at Malta; the building at both places of Social Centres, and the furnishing in St. Paul's Cathedral, Malta, of a Shrine of Remembrance to the memory of British men and women who gave their lives in defence of the Island. We express the hope that the sum of £100,000 which is needed will be speedily forthcoming."*

An important and influential addition to the appeal was made by the American General Dwight D. Eisenhower, the Supreme Commander of the Allied Expeditionary Force:

> *"Few of us in the United Nations are unaware of the vital part played in the war by Malta and Gibraltar... Both places have for particular periods served as my Headquarters during this war.*
>
> *I, for one, welcome the opportunity to pay tribute to Malta and Gibraltar in a practical way, and am delighted that you are opening a fund for the purpose of repairing and extending the Cathedral Centres... There can be no better way to say – "Thank You" to Malta and Gibraltar."*

By the end of the year £10,000 had been received, in addition to a special fund of £2,000 raised by the readers of the "Spectator" magazine, for the furnishing of the proposed Memorial Shrine in St. Paul's.

As the Allied armies penetrated deeper into Europe from France after D-Day, and pushed up the leg of Italy in the summer of 1944, Malta ceased to be a war zone. The last air raid alert of the war sounded at 8.43 p.m. on 28th August 1944, and the all-clear fifteen minutes later.[10]

An important milestone in the life of St. Paul's was celebrated on November 1st 1944, the Centenary of the Church's consecration by Bishop Tomlinson. Mrs. Farrie[11] described the day:

> *"Hugh went over the water for Choral at the Cathedral at 10.30., Mary followed a little later armed with her basket of small cakes, 100 – one for every year, for the evening 'at home'. Canon Hicks and Hugh had thought out a beautiful service, Solemn Evensong at 5.30. We all went over – it was a really glorious day not too hot but very bright sunshine, and sparkling water – on the Ferry. Even the Cathedral looked almost full by the time the service began, and the candlelight against the blue and gold cloth panels at the East End was very lovely. There were flowers on the altar and the church's treasure was displayed."*

The service opened with a procession; choir, servers, clergy and the two Canons in copes. Canon Hicks read the bidding prayers from the chancel, and the Governor and Vice-Admiral Malta, read the Lessons. After the reading of the special prayers by Canon Farrie the verger and churchwardens with staves led a procession of cross-bearer, servers in albs carrying lights, visiting clergy, and the two Canons to the Font, where an adaptation of the first prayer from the baptism service was read. After the singing of verses of Hymn 396 (A & M) the procession reformed and returned to the chancel where the collects for Corpus Christi and St. Paul Shipwrecked were read. Finally the Te Deum was sung facing the altar.

After the service an 'At Home' was held in the crypt, which had been attractively prepared. Some refreshments were provided by a number of ladies, and all present had an enjoyable evening. Canon Hicks probably expressed the feelings of many when he wrote:

> *"Everybody was very friendly. An AB named Williams played the piano most divinely and I think the audience would have listened to him all night. His playing of Merbecke at the Eucharist at 10 a.m. (our regular organist being unable to be present) was just perfect, and everyone sang as if they enjoyed it. I've seldom had a more satisfying day."*

Notes

[1] A memorial to Sir David Callender Campbell is in St. Andrew's Scots Church, Valletta.
[2] Of the 11th Battalion, The Lancashire Fusiliers.
[3] She died early in 1943.
[4] Throughout the rest of September, October and early November the medal was taken to a large number of villages throughout Malta to be displayed to the local population.
[5] He had been Verger since 1932.
[6] Memorial plaque in St. Paul's.
[7] He died in Cape Town, South Africa, beginning of March 1963.
[8] Then living at The Croft, Wendover, Bucks.
[9] He was no stranger to St. Paul's having served as a locum tenens in 1933, 1935, 1938 & 1939.
[10] Air Raid alerts over Malta, 1940 – 211; 1941 – 963; 1942 – 2,031; 1943 – 127; 1944 – 8. A total of 3,340 Alerts.
[11] The wife of the Reverend Hugh Farrie. Canon Farrie relinquished his appointment at Holy Trinity Sliema, in the spring of 1945 and was replaced by the Reverend Frederick James Bailey as locum tenens.

Chapter 21

Reconstruction Plans

With the end of the war now in sight, rebuilding plans for St. Paul's could be discussed and decisions taken.

A significant alteration to the interior layout of St. Paul's was proposed and agreed. It was resolved to reconstruct the interior based on the original plan first set out by William Scamp in 1842 placing the altar at the west end, so reversing the change ordered by Bishop Tomlinson, but incorporating modern additions. In the summer of 1945 Mr. A. C. Webb, made a drawing of the proposed Memorial Shrine after viewing the architects plans. It was suggested that all the Royal Navy and Merchant ships actively engaged in the defence of Malta[1], plus the Army units, and Royal Air Force squadrons which served on the island, should have their names engraved on dark oak panelling as a permanent record.

The architect adviser Mr. Hugh Braun F.R.I.B.A. had been stationed on Malta when he was an officer in the Royal Engineers, so he was aware of local conditions and working practices. In his view:

> "this building 'was finished but never furnished'; and it possesses too little of colour, ornament or decoration. Briefly, St. Paul's is an austere building, and we propose to give it the effect of rich furnishing which it needs. There will be gilding on the dark oak; crimson damask cushions in the stalls; flags or standards above them; and heraldry in due place. Two small spur screens, such as are found in some of the London City churches, will form the entrance to the Shrine or West End, but will not obscure the view of it from the nave. Not the least merit of the scheme is the opening up of the Portico upon Queen Adelaide Square, and the repair of the valuable organ. It is hoped also to make improvements to the Clergy House and to the Cathedral Hall."

By the middle of 1946, over £30,000 had been received from the Appeal Funds. Mr. Alban Caröe, of the firm Caröe and Passmore, who would be responsible for carrying out Major Braun's proposals, visited the Island to see for himself the practical aspects of re-orientating the interior of St. Paul's, constructing the Memorial Shrine, and improving the crypt. His company had been involved during the 1938 alterations.

Meanwhile both St. Paul's and Holy Trinity found difficulties in adjusting to the new peacetime conditions. The composition of the congregation at St. Paul's altered as many of its members connected directly or indirectly with H.M. Forces left the island, to be replaced by fresh arrivals of civilians, some for the first time, others resuming their interrupted residence. However, most of the newcomers were taking up residence in villages throughout Malta, or in the Sliema and St. Julians area rather than in Valletta.

There was some alarm amongst the members of St. Paul's in June 1946 when Canon Hicks made it known that the Bishop was thinking of moving him to another position within the Diocese. Canon Hicks himself was unhappy with the idea and told the Church Committee at their meeting on 18th June *'he had informed the Bishop that he had not left his parish in England to be moved every two years and had anticipated staying in Malta as long as he was fit for the job. If it was the Bishop's intention to move him after two years he would look for another Diocese.'*

Major Bruce asked whether a Bishop could appoint anyone without the consent of the churchwardens?, to which Captain Hayles replied that when a previous Bishop had done so a strong protest was lodged and the Bishop in question admitted he was in error in so doing.

Canon Hicks quoted from a book relating to the Diocese which stated that only the Bishop had the right of appointment and dismissal, the churchwardens being solely in an advisory capacity.

However, it was pointed out by a member that the churchwardens are responsible for the stipend of the Chaplain and can refuse to pay it.

At this point Canon Hicks left the meeting and all members of the Church Committee freely gave their views on the matter. Mr. Barrett put it to the meeting *"We unanimously agree to support Canon Hicks in his wish to remain in Malta, and that we will write to the Bishop that he should be confirmed in his appointment, the letter to be signed by every member of the Committee."* All agreed. Canon Hicks returned to the room, and was told of this resolution.

However, there was a change of heart on the part of Bishop Buxton and he let Canon Hicks continue at St. Paul's, so the protest letter was never sent.

On September 9th the Garrison Church of St. Luke, Tigne Barracks, damaged by enemy action during the war, was re-opened which affected Holy Trinity more than St. Paul's since troops from the barracks had been attending services there. However, Holy Trinity was now attracting more new civilian worshippers than St. Paul's due to the popularity and growth of Sliema. Bishop Buxton visited Malta at the end of 1946 to discuss the rebuilding plans for St. Paul's and was invited to dedicate a memorial in St. Luke's to the men of the 68th HAA Regiment, Royal Artillery.

In the autumn of 1946 after fourteen years the Bishop announced that he was resigning from the end of the year on medical advice. Although he had been instrumental in taking decisions regarding the new appearance of St. Paul's it was left to his successor, Cecil Douglas Horsley, to see them implemented.

At the Annual General Meeting in February 1947 the new Bishop commented adversely on the make up of the Church Committee since it was composed entirely of Churchwardens, and he wanted it to be more representative of the whole congregation. A draft constitution for the Council was discussed and the agreed outcome was for One Churchwarden to be appointed by the Chancellor, with One Churchwarden, Secretary, Treasurer, Six Sidesmen, and up to Four other persons all to be elected by members of St. Paul's at the Annual General Meeting.

Accordingly elections were held the following year as per the Bishop's wishes, and the following broad based committee elected:

People's Warden Major A. Cathcart Bruce, Hon. Secretary Mrs. J. Blythe, Hon. Treasurer Captain Trevor Hayles, Sidesmen: Admiral Kelsey, Mr. G. Firman, Major F. H. Rust, Capt. A. Messenger, Capt. Podger, Col. Carter. Other members: Mrs. Godfrey, Mrs. Day, Mrs. Kelsey, and Mrs. Bradley. Mr. Charles Edwards was selected by the Chancellor as his warden.

Apart from shaking up the committee the Bishop Horsley ran into some opposition when he decided that an appeal for funds should be launched in 1948. He wished to seek funds for the Diocese, whereas in Malta they felt that the funds should be for St. Paul's and that any appeal would have more satisfactory outcome if 'St. Paul's Malta' was the focus rather than the 'the Diocese'. A sub-committee was set up and prepared an appeal letter, which was approved by the Church Council. When asked to add his name to it Canon Hicks declined saying that *"he did not wish to as he had been in favour of sending the letter drafted by the Bishop and as the council had decided to prepared their own letter he thought the proper persons to sign were the two wardens."* which is what happened.

Preparations were now made to close the church so that the reconstruction work could begin.

Notes

[1] See Appendix 3

Chapter 22

Re-Hallowing and Memorial Shrine

In September 1948 the team of builders moved into the church and started the dismantling and demolition work. These were the first steps in this mammoth undertaking. The local architects overseeing the project were Mr. Joseph Degaetano of Swieqi and Mr. R. J. D. Cousin, with Joseph Caruana as the main contractor, providing most of the labour. For the skilled tasks local craftsmen were engaged, Giuseppe (Joseph) Marmara and John Sammut, stonemasons, G. Maguire and W. G. Proctor experienced joiners, and sculptor Marco Montebello.

They set to work moving the 'Mason's Screen' from the east end to form a wall of the new chapel of Our Lady and St. George at the west end, building the walls and raising the floor level for the new Chancel. This basic construction work had to be completed before the carpenters and joiners could make a start on the Memorial Shrine.

Another major operation was the transfer of the organ to the west end of the church and re-erecting it on a gallery overlooking the choir. The instrument was rebuilt again, by Hill Norman & Beard Ltd.

Deliveries of timber, stone and marble started to arrive in June 1949. The timber studding and under-framing was prepared in readiness for the panelling, whilst Mr. Montebello was engaged in carving the large and intricate sculpture on the top of the new main altar. The following year when the baldacchino was erected over the font he sculpted a series of Maltese Crosses and winged cherub heads inside the dome.

Meanwhile the woodwork for the Shrine was being prepared in England by Dart & Francis Ltd., of 128 High Street, Crediton, Devon. The English Oak timber was intricately carved by several employees including Frank Dyer, Albert Miller, and Teddy Snell, assisted by joiner Jack Vicary.

The first consignment was sent at the end of October 1949 when eight crates of carved oak panelling, and one crate containing altar embroideries, were shipped on board HMS *Glory*. When submitted to Malta Customs on 12th November, the declaration stated:

> "These items are being carried out to Malta by HMS Glory without charge by the Royal Navy as a help towards the Empire Memorial to the Battle of

Malta. The Memorial is being formed in the Anglican Pro-Cathedral, Malta."

The packages were promptly delivered to St. Paul's where they were opened and under the supervision of Mr. Proctor the panelling for the shrine was erected. Above the panels twelve crests were fixed. They had been carved in oak, coloured and gilded, and each one denoted a branch of the British and Commonwealth Forces and associated Services which had taken part in the defence of Malta.

The work proceeded relatively smoothly over the summer months despite the high temperatures and was sufficiently advanced for a re-opening date to be fixed. It was felt that the 2nd December would be appropriate since it would be the Centenary of Queen Adelaide's death, and this was agreed.

Bishop Horsley invited the Archbishop of Canterbury, the Right Reverend Geoffrey Fisher to attend the re-hallowing of the Cathedral and dedication of the Memorial Shrine, which was much appreciated and gratefully accepted.

Flight-Lieutenant Malcolm Jolly had been appointed the 'Project Officer' in 1946 and spent the next three years monitoring the work, and in particular the re-orientation of the interior. However, in August 1949 he was posted back to England by the RAF so was naturally disappointed not to be in the Cathedral at its re-opening.

Preparations for the big day were put in hand.

"8th November 1949, To Captain H. A. Traill, CBE, R.N., HMS Falcon Malta.

In connection with the Dedication of the War Memorial in St Paul's on 2nd December 1949 at 11.00 a.m., I should be most grateful if you would grant leave from duty on that day as requisite to the following members of the Cathedral Choir:

J. Heale A.A.4.(0) L/FX 669058 HMS Falcon, Kalafrana.
D. J. Woodham, R.E.M.T. L/SFX 856038 HMS Falcon, Lower Camp Hal Far.
P. A. Thorp R.E.T.(AR), L/FX 7832181 HMS Falcon, Hal Far.
D. P. Twiss SA(A), C/MX 859949 HMS Falcon, D Mess Kalafrana.
A. Ette NA/AM(A), HMS Falcon, Lower Camp Hal Far.[1]"

"November 25th 1949, HMS Ricasoli

With reference to your letter dated 21st November 1949, leave from duty will be granted to C.P.O. Photographer W. Hoskin to attend the Dedication Service at St. Paul's Anglican Cathedral, Valletta, on 2nd December 1949."

After WWII a period known as the 'Cold War' began when the Western Nations were in opposition to the Soviet Union's domination of Eastern Europe, behind the Iron Curtain as it was termed. In view of this atmosphere some recommendations regarding relations with the Press were given to the Bishop of Gibraltar.

"Soundings" were taken in Fleet Street. A Press Release was issued on 28th November to the Press Association and Reuters for distribution world wide, but particularly in the United States. It was suggested that it would be appropriate for the Archbishop of Canterbury to lay a cross of flowers at the George Cross itself, since:

> *"among the many reasons for its importance are Russian propaganda in America and elsewhere to the effect that Britain now has lost all interest in her colonies and has forgotten what they did for her in the war;"*

Princess Elizabeth[2] arrived by air to spend Christmas with her husband, the Duke of Edinburgh then serving on the Malta Station in command of the frigate HMS *Magpie,* and had agreed to be present at this ceremony.

The Archbishop arrived at Luqa during Wednesday afternoon of 30th November, and was taken to Admiralty House, South Street, Valletta where he stayed for the first three nights of his tour. A full schedule of events was drawn up for the eight-day visit, comprising a mixture of ecclesiastical duties, social gatherings and official dinners. He was able however to have one day of relaxation sightseeing around Malta, with Chev.Hannibal Scicluna as his guide.

On the day itself, St. Paul's proved too small to accommodate all those wishing to participate in the service, as over 150 official guests had been invited, and the congregation overflowed into the precincts of the church. The motorcade with Princess Elizabeth and Sir Gerald Creasy in the first car arrived just before 11 o'clock where they were met at the church door by Bishop Horsley and Canon Hicks.

Apart from Her Royal Highness and the Governor, those attending also included Earl and Lady Mountbatten of Burma, the Heads of the three Services, Consuls, Matrons from Bighi, Imtarfa and the King George V Hospital, representatives of the Army, Air Force, Navy and Merchant Navy, as well as many civilian and service clergy with their wives from various denominations, and members of local organisations.

The Bishop conducted the service with Canon Hicks, and they were assisted by a large number of clergy including Archdeacon Bailey, the Reverends Stevens, Long, Noakes, Fitzgerald plus Church of England Chaplains and Chaplains from other Churches.

After the re-hallowing service for St. Paul's itself had been performed Canon Hicks escorted Sir Gerald Creasy[3] into the sanctuary where the Governor requested the Archbishop of Canterbury to dedicate the Memorial Shrine.

After performing this act His Grace delivered a stirring sermon, before bringing the service to a close with a blessing of the congregation. With the service over, all the clergy escorted Princess Elizabeth back to the entrance where large crowds of cheering spectators had gathered in the adjacent streets to see her re-enter the car and be driven away[4].

Shortly afterwards the reception in the undercroft commenced, where Dr. Fisher and his wife had the opportunity of meeting many of the Anglican community. Bishop Horsley told the gathering that a letter had been received from General Sir William Dobbie, the Governor during the toughest years of the war, expressing his pleasure that the War Memorial project had been realised.

Due to financial restraints, the work of completing the chancel was delayed, and a year went by before the next delivery of oak panelling was made. It was shipped in October 1950 on HMS *Ocean,* and also included the Bishop's throne, and the oak doors. Three weeks later a smaller consignment comprising the moulded cornices and Queen Adelaide's Coat of Arms arrived on HMS *Tyne*.

Canon Hicks was able to tell the Annual General Meeting in February 1951, that he was satisfied with the work done so far, and hoped the coming year would see the chancel completed except for the back and canopy of the stalls on the pulpit side, for which there were unfortunately no funds available. Other shipments were made in September and November 1951, on HMS *Fort Beauharnais* and HMS *Glasgow* respectively. These contained panelling for the choir stalls, panelling for the Organ Case, the moulded font cover, carved oak canopies for the chancel stalls and the Archbishops Seat, Desk and platform, and a Credence Table.

However, the overall project was still incomplete, and at the AGM in 1952 Canon Hicks repeated his hope *'that the chancel would be finally completed by the end of the year'* but said that approximately £800 would have to be raised for the purpose. The money was slow to come in so it was not until November 1953 that the final shipment arrived from England, but on the 9th December Canon Hicks was able to confirm that all the canopies were now in place and only a few minor jobs remained to be done.

The magnitude of the work carried out can be judged from a letter dated 1st July 1952 sent by Mrs. Blythe, the secretary of the church council to the Diocese of Gibraltar office:

"Dear Sir,

We, the Chancellor, Churchwardens and Council of St. Paul's Anglican Cathedral, Malta, hereby make application for the granting of a Faculty to cover the following works which are in course of completion:

1. Removal of gallery and Chester Organ Case & refitting of Chester Organ Case in 'north' gallery.
2. Erection of stone Reredos & High Altar complete with Dossal and Frame; erection of stone Screen and Pulpit emblazoned with the Arms of St. Paul, and provision of oak desk for pulpit.
3. Removal of Masons' Screen to side Chapel on 'north' of Chancel; insertion in the screen of mosaic of Our Lady presented by the Chaplains of the 8th Army; provision of statuette of Virgin and Child presented by the present Chancellor.
4. Erection of stone Altar in side Chapel complete with Dossal and Frame.
5. Formation of Clergy Vestry on ' south' side of Chancel, with stone wall and double doorway with oak doors.
6. Formation of Chancel floor, finished in marble.
7. Installation of oak panelling round Sanctuary, surmounted by crestings of the Services, gilded and coloured, forming a record of Units engaged in the defence of Malta during the late war.
8. Fitting of oak doors under the Chester Organ Case, surmounted by Coat-of-Arms of Queen Adelaide, gilded and coloured.
9. Installation of Bishop's Seat in the Sanctuary, with carved Coats-of-Arms.
10. Installation of oak Credence Table in Sanctuary (gift of the Architect).
11. Re-erection of Communion Rail in new position.
12. Erection of Bishop's Throne (in oak) and embroidery drapery on ' south' side of Chancel.
13. Erection of Stalls, Canopies and Choir Seating in oak, throughout.
14. Formation of Baptistry at 'east' end, with marble steps and tiled floor; erection of stone Baldacchino with Holy Dove globe, over Font removed from original position; provision of oak Font cover.
15. Provision of four Candlesticks and Altar Cross.
16. Provision of Grilles to Organ Loft.
17. Provision of movable Communion Rail in side Chapel.
18. Appropriate decoration of His Excellency the Governor's pew and pews of Commanding Officers.
19. Installation of ceiling lighting throughout.
20. Gift of two branched Candlesticks."

When the final statement was drawn up the total cost covering all the professional fees, building, electrical and carpentry work, organ, embroideries, taxes, etc. was £26,869.12.1d.

Notes

[1] The RAF formally turned over Hal Far to the Fleet Air Arm in 1946, when it became named as HMS *Falcon*. Ta Qali had been handed over to the Fleet Air Arm a year earlier and named as HMS *Goldfinch*.
[2] Later Queen Elizabeth II.
[3] He had taken up the post of Governor on 13th July 1949 in succession to Sir Francis Douglas.
[4] On the 8th December Princess Elizabeth unveiled the Cenotaph in Floriana.

Chapter 23

1950's Changes in Malta and Britain

Due to postings of Service personnel the Church Committee lost members at short notice and needed to find replacements often before the following Annual General Meeting. This trend continued for more than fifteen years, so it was the civilian members who provided some stability and continuity. Especially Mr. Charles Edwards, Mr. Dyce, Mrs. Hewitt, Mr. K. J. Swann, Mr. F. Taylor, and retired Royal Navy Captain-Paymaster Trevor Hayles[1].

Captain Hayles was first appointed a lay warden in April 1929, and served as honorary treasurer for about 18 years thereafter. However, from 1946 onwards he was unhappy with the opinion of St. Paul's held by the Bishop of Gibraltar so decided to resign as treasurer in October 1948, and from the Church Committee itself in March 1949.

For 1949 the two churchwardens exchanged roles. Canon Hicks asked for Major Cathcart Bruce to be his warden, so Mr. Edwards was elected People's warden. The new secretary was Mrs. R. Harbot, new treasurer Flight-Lieutenant Jolly, and other new members of the committee were Mr. Roberts, Captain Gladstone, Brigadier Gray, and Mr. Anderton. Also during this post-war period there were numerous changes of organist as various Servicemen left Malta, but they included Mr. Littlefield, Flight-Sergeant Connell, Lieutenant Duly, Squadron Leader Livingstone, Midshipman Denby, Leading Writer Botterill and Sergeant Batt.

The question of appointing an assistant to the Verger was discussed. The very faithful Murray Clement was now 82 years old, and was clearly slowing-up, but he had expressed the desire to complete twenty years service to the Cathedral, i.e. next year, so it was agreed let the matter rest. However, fate intervened and Mr. Clement died on 5th August 1950[2].

In December 1952 the current organist Squadron Leader Livingstone informed the church committee that although the organ was rebuilt in 1949 in his opinion specialist advice on repairs should be sought. In view of his comments the organ company of Hill Norman & Beard Ltd, who had carried out the 1949 overhaul was contacted and in a letter dated 16th January 1953[3], they gave estimate of £340. This would cover the cost of sending two of their employees out from England but the men were prepared to work long hours to get the job finished. It was decided to go ahead and although the repairs took slightly longer than anticipated they were completed by 13th May, and the total cost was within the estimate.

The YMCA in Malta which had used the crypt of St. Paul's for many years gave notice that it was closing down on Saturday October 3rd 1953, and that the premises would be handed back to the church Council. The opportunity was taken to buy from the YMCA all the tables, crockery, kitchen utensils, etc., that could cater for about 100 persons, and would be used for future social events by other church groups.

Around this time Canon Hicks made these observations about St. Paul's:

> *"Whatever one may feel about the reorientation of the Cathedral interior it is now an accomplished fact and must be accepted. Those best qualified to judge believe the Choir and Sanctuary are now beautiful; the same can scarcely be said of the Nave where the pews are an eyesore; they are much too large, ugly and uncomfortable and to replace them with smaller, better designed pews of good wood would transform the Nave, but it would be an expensive business.*
>
> *Again the baldacchino over the Font might be seemly in a vast building; in its present setting it seems to me quite out of place and from a practical point of view most perplexing; at baptisms it is almost impossible to see the worshippers half of whom are hidden by pillars."*

On Tuesday 9th February 1954 a special service was held at 5.30 p.m. for the Reverend Thomas Craske to be enthroned as the Bishop of Gibraltar, and installed as Dean of St. Paul's. He had succeeded Bishop Horsley into the post.

The next large gatherings at St. Paul's were somewhat sombre occasions relating to the Royal Air Force. Since October 1953 eight new Shackleton MR.2 aircraft had been delivered to 38 squadron based at Luqa aerodrome. During an exercise with the submarine HMS *Tudor*, aircraft WL794 piloted by Flight-Lieutenant Raymond John Stevenson, crashed into the Mediterranean Sea on 12th February. All the ten RAF men on board[4] perished in this disaster. A memorial service was held for them on Thursday the 18th, at which the Reverend H. L. O. Reece officiated.

Paying her first visit since being crowned Queen Elizabeth II in June 1953, Her Majesty came to Malta to unveil the Commonwealth Air Forces Memorial, which had been erected in Floriana. The 50-foot column of Travertine marble, is topped by a gilded bronze eagle[5]. Fixed at the base are bronze plaques with the names of the 2,301 airmen of the Commonwealth Air Forces who lost their lives in the Mediterranean area during World War II and have no known last resting-place.

On Sunday morning, 2nd May, the eve of this ceremony, she attended St. Paul's for a Memorial Service to all the Officers and Men of the Commonwealth Air Forces who had died during World War II. A large number of top ranking Royal Air Force officers and their wives had flown in from England as well as relatives of the deceased, and many were present in St. Paul's for this service, which was conducted by Canon Alan S. Giles, Chaplain in Chief of the Royal Air Force, assisted by the Reverend T. Madoc-Jones, the Principal Chaplain of the Presbyterian's.

During several meetings held in the summer of 1954 Canon Hicks[6] was asked whether a new Chancellor had been appointed to supersede him, but he had to reply that the Bishop was having difficulty to come up with someone suitable so it was suggested that a locum tenens be found for a few months.

St. Paul's was fortunate that during his period as Governor both Sir Gerald Creasy and his wife were involved with the church and participated in its activities. This favourable state of affairs continued when Sir Robert Laycock took over the Governorship in September 1954.

Bishop Craske's search for a new Chancellor was finally successful and he appointed the Reverend Charles Paton, a former Royal Naval Chaplain, who had served as a locum tenens at St. Paul's during the 1930's. Captain Naish, the People's warden was pleased to inform the members of St. Paul's that the new Chancellor was expected to arrive on 31st May 1955 on board SS. *Arabian Prince*, but regretfully he himself would shortly be leaving and therefore a new People's warden would be needed.

The Reverend Charles Paton duly arrived and was installed as Chancellor and Senior Canon on the Feast of the Nativity of St. John the Baptist, Friday 24th June 1955 by Archdeacon Bailey, the Archdeacon of Malta.

Further installations of new Canons followed on Sunday 29th January 1956 when the Chaplain of Athens, the Reverend Douglas A. Duncan was made a Canon of St. Paul's in the stall of St. Silas and in the same service the Reverend Tom Ryder, of the Royal Air Force, became an associate member of the Chapter and occupied the RAF Chaplains Stall.

At the 1956 AGM the Treasurer informed the meeting that in recent years the figures for income and expenditure were 1954 Income £2,017 – Expenditure £1,250: 1955 Income £2,314 – Expenditure £1,797: but for 1956 the Income forecast £2100, whilst the Expenditure forecast was £2242. At the same meeting, a letter from the Whitechapel Bell Foundry was read stating that the bells could be re-equipped for swinging at a cost of £345, but it was unanimously agreed not to go ahead.

About a year later during a meeting on the 4th June 1957, the subject of a new house for the Chancellor was discussed but it was generally understood that though desirable the cost would be too high and it would be better to spend any money on improving the present residence. As the treasurer stated in his financial report, in 1956 and 1957 the bazaar raised £2,000 or so each year, but due to the reduction in assistance by Servicemen and their families it was not expected to continue at this rate, and he estimated say £850 annually in future as a more realistic figure.

Since it was costing about £2,000 per annum to run St. Paul's, not only was there no surplus money to consider a new house, even finding some to improve the current one would be difficult. There were insufficient funds for repairs to the church roof though it badly needed doing but was estimated to cost several thousand pounds. There was not even enough spare money to engage a full time organist.

Having lain dormant since before the war, the question of finance and the Army churches was reintroduced on 30th September 1957, when Colonel Colquhoun pointed out that the churches used by the Army were not fully maintained by the War Office. In his opinion other Anglican churches on Malta should be able to ask St. Paul's for financial help.

A churchwarden with many years experience on the Church Committee of St. Paul's, Mr. Charles Edwards, said *"throughout his long association with the Cathedral, the Cathedral had always been in financial difficulties"* and went on to point out that the money raised by the Bazaar was virtually the only income and that regretfully the Cathedral was not in a position to give financial aid to other Anglican churches. Lieutenant-Commander Bird, R.N., anticipated that the British Forces would be reduced in the future and that the remaining Anglican community would probably be unable to support the present number of churches. In any event his view was that St. Paul's must remain and its financial position must be safeguarded.

The old adversary prior to WWII the Barracca Church had itself fallen on hard times. A letter from the D.A.C.G., Malta Garrison, sent to the Chaplain General in London dated 31st January 1953[7] explains that it had been closed since early 1950, and should be handed over to the civil authorities.[8] The principle reason for its demise was the re-deployment of British troops to the Pembroke area, so that Casement and Lintorn Barracks at Floriana housed less than 200 men.

Notes

[1] Mr. Edwards lived at 66 Barbara Street, Hamrun, Dr.Dyce c/o 'Twenties Club' Cruxifix Hill Floriana, Mrs. Hewitt Testaferrata Street Msida, Mr. Swann c/o British Council West Street Valletta, Mr. Taylor Villa Lewza, Ta'Misrahlewza Birkirkara.

[2] Murray Clement was born in Brighton 1869. He served as a sergeant in the Royal Artillery. Before becoming Verger he worked in the National Library in Valletta. He started as Verger

in 1933 and during July that year married a Maltese. He is buried in Ta Braxia cemetery Plot A grave No.51.

[3] 3/5 West Street, Lewes, Sussex.

[4] Flt.Lieut.Stevenson, Fly.Off.Albert Smallwood, M/Nav.Charles Hugh Peter Sloan, Flt.Sgt. Wallis Lloyd Rawlinson, Sgt. James Henry Hennel, Sgt. Norman Wyatt Betts, Sgt. Dudley Skinner, Sgt. James Douglas Henderson, Sgt. Peter Francis John Raddon and Sgt. Percy Luke Edland.

[5] The architect of the memorial was Sir Hubert Worthington, and the sculptor of the bronze eagle, Mr. Charles Wheeler.

[6] Canon Hicks died in 1960.

[7] PRO Kew WO.32/15107

[8] It became a Mail Room for the Malta Post Office. The pews and organ were removed sometime in 1950/1951 and taken to St. Luke's Church, Tigne Barracks.

Chapter 24

British Defence Cuts Cause Crisis

Needless to say St. Paul's was not immune from the effects of political changes and decisions made by the British and Maltese Governments and it is necessary to take them into account.

The 1955 General Election in Malta was won by the Labour Party, led by Mr. Dom Mintoff who became Prime Minister. During 1956/1957 discussions took place about the political future of Malta, but these were curtailed when the British Defence Minister, Mr. Duncan Sandys announced drastic cuts in the Defence Budget and *'large reductions in manpower would inevitably curtail the volume of civilian employment in the naval dockyards and the ancillary establishments.'* At this time from a total labour force of around 83,000 some 20,000 Maltese were directly employed by the British Armed Forces[1], so this statement of intent caused considerable alarm.

No satisfactory agreement could be reached between the two Governments so the talks were called off, and in April 1958 Mr. Mintoff handed in his resignation. The Governor met the leader of the Opposition, Dr.Borg Olivier, but he was not prepared to form a Government. Faced with this situation Sir Robert Laycock suspended the Constitution.

With such major issues to deal with, it was surprising that Sir Robert found time to be on the committee of St. Paul's, and give a considered judgement about its future, but he did, and in March[2] sounded out the Bishop of Gibraltar, the Right Reverend Thomas Craske, on the possibility of handing over control of the church to the Royal Navy.

> *"When you visit Malta at the end of April I hope you will be able to discuss the future of St. Paul's Anglican Cathedral.*
>
> *As you know the finances of the Cathedral have been largely dependent upon the Services for contributions. The Heads of Services in Malta have become increasingly concerned at the dimensions of the Annual Bazaar in aid of the Cathedral. This year's bazaar made some £2,000 at considerable cost to the time (and tempers) of Servicemen and their families, who, of course, are also required to support their Garrison or equivalent church. So much so*

that Heads of Services are of the opinion that bazaars on such a scale cannot be held in future, especially in view of the major reductions likely to be made to the three Services in Malta as a result of the latest Defence Policy Review.

As we see it here, the Services ought to attend to their Garrison or equivalent churches and the civilians ought to support the Cathedral. However, the number of civilians is too small to compete, which is why the Services have had to help. In future it seems that, with the best will in the world, the Services will be unable to provide that assistance without which the Cathedral has been unable to manage in the past. The Heads of Services have accordingly been considering ways and means of overcoming these financial hazards. They have reached the conclusion that a satisfactory solution could be achieved if the Royal Navy took over control of the Cathedral.

The Senior Chaplain, aided by an Assistant Chaplain also found by the Services, could be put in charge of the Cathedral under the auspices of the Archdeacon of the Fleet. An important problem is how the Cathedral would retain its valued connection with the Diocese of Gibraltar. It has been suggested that this might be done by adding to the title of the Archdeacon of the Fleet the words "and Archdeacon of Malta."

Nevertheless the suggestion that the Services should take over the Cathedral would appear to be the only worthwhile solution when compared with the alternative. These are either that the Cathedral must be closed (which is unthinkable) or that the Diocese must defray the present financial deficiency and provide a curate.

It would be most convenient if we could reach a firm decision when you visit the Island."

The Governor knew at first hand the amount of time and trouble taken with running the bazaar, since his wife Lady Angela Laycock was the prime organiser in 1957 when it raised £2,242.

Chancellor Paton was taken ill in April 1958. His doctor's verdict was that he needed at least six months rest and had to consider lighter work, therefore there was little hope of him being able to take up his post at St. Paul's again. He left for England by sea on 15th May, to live with his sister at Worthing.

Two weeks later the members of the congregation who attended a meeting on 24th were taken aback to hear the Bishop of Gibraltar's reply to a question regarding a new Chancellor for St. Paul's. He said:

"the current political question marks over Malta affected consideration of and proposals for staffing the Cathedral."

He had presumably met with the Governor, because he said that the civilian church population was only a small minority of the Anglicans and that Service people and their dependants formed a large majority of this population. At the present time he, the Bishop of Gibraltar, has no jurisdiction over 90% of the Anglican population as the Archbishop of Canterbury issues licences to Service Chaplains and it was therefore essential for him to consult with the Archbishop regarding a closer association between the Service Chaplains and St. Paul's. He considered three important questions needed to be answered (a) the likely future of Malta (b) the financial prospects of St. Paul's (c) the possible future deployment of Chaplains on the island, but appears to have left Malta without any firm decision being made.

One manner in which it was decided to raise funds was to establish a 'Friends of St. Paul's' group. Very large numbers of people had lived, served, or passed through Malta, and quite a number of them would have some affection for St. Paul's and would be willing to contribute towards its maintenance. It was felt appropriate that the Duke of Edinburgh should be approached and asked to be the 'First Friend'. He accepted and has continued to give his support to St. Paul's ever since.

In the meantime the Reverend Jack Newton Charles Holland, from the Dockyard Chapel, stood in at St. Paul's, as Canon Paton had still not officially resigned. However by October 1958, the resignation had been received, and the Reverend Henry Rupert Colton was approached to take on St. Paul's for a few months. He later agreed to remain until the end of 1959.

Brigadier Houghton of the Royal Marines who was the Chancellor's warden that year, wrote to the Bishop of Gibraltar:

> *"There is no doubt at all that Colton has done a great work here in Malta. He has brought new life and vigour to the Cathedral and people admire and like his qualities.... I know that they all expect him to be re-appointed to carry on in 1960. I realise that he could do good work elsewhere in the Diocese and you have that side to consider, but from the point of view of Malta and the Cathedral here, my recommendation is that Colton should be fully installed as Canon and given the appointment for several years so as to carry through the work he has started."*

The suggestion was accepted by Bishop Craske and a double installation ceremony was held on Friday 26th June 1959 when the Reverend Colton was made Chancellor and Senior Canon, and the Reverend W. H. S. Chapman, R.N., Honorary Canon to the Senior Royal Naval Stall.

Notes

[1] 'Wings in the Sun' by Air Chief Marshal Sir David Lee., HMSO, 1989. p. 207.
[2] Letter March 1958, St. Paul's archives.

Chapter 25

Royal Marines

During the 1950's the 3rd Commando Brigade Royal Marines was quartered in St. Andrew's Barracks at Pembroke Camp, on the outskirts of St. Julians[1]. It was composed of 40, 42 and 45 Commando, under the command of Brigadier J. L. Moulton.

On Wednesday evening the 26th November 1952 the Duke of Edinburgh arrived at Luqa airport for a week of official engagements on Malta. However for the Marines the most important event was scheduled for Saturday the 29th.

That morning a relatively short though dignified service was held at St. Paul's attended by the Duke, The Governor Sir Gerald Creasy, Admiral Earl Moutbatten of Burma, and Brigadier Moulton. The three Queen's Colours and three Regimental Colours were laid upon the altar, and were consecrated by the Chaplain of the Fleet, the Venerable Archdeacon F. N. Chamberlain. Also present were the Reverend A. R. Thornley, R.N., the Reverend C. E. Dunant, R.N., and the Reverend G. D. Buchanan, R.N., of the Church of Scotland.

The party then left St. Paul's and were driven to Floriana Parade Ground where 67 officers and 1168 men of the 3rd Commando Brigade Royal Marines were drawn up together with their massed bands for a ceremonial parade during which the Duke[2] presented the newly consecrated Colours to each of the three units.

Early the following year on 13th January 1953, Canon Hicks said he had received a letter from Brigadier Moulton proposing that the 3rd Commando Brigade be permitted to put some small memorial in the form of a plaque on the wall of St. Paul's. Canon Hicks explained that the Church as a whole was opposed to the placing of plaques and he thought that a prayer desk for communicants in the side chapel would be far more appropriate. This suggestion was acted upon and a three-place oak prayer desk (prie-dieu) was sent out from England in 1954. It bears the inscription "TO THE GLORY OF GOD AND IN MEMORY OF THE CONSECRATION IN THIS CATHEDRAL OF COLOURS PRESENTED BY H.R.H. THE DUKE OF EDINBURGH TO 40, 42 AND 45 COMMANDOS ROYAL MARINES 29TH NOVEMBER 1952. A small Royal Marines badge is on the left of the inscription, and the dagger emblem on the right.

By 1957, Brigadier Moulton[3] had been succeeded by Brigadier R. W. Madoc, and Canon Hicks by Canon Paton, when the following letter dated 4th February, was sent:

"My dear Canon

Malta has been virtually the permanent home of 3rd Commando Brigade, Royal Marines since 1947 and during all our operations in the Mediterranean away from Malta our families and rear parties have remained here. During recent operations in Cyprus and Port Said a number of Officers and Other Ranks from this Formation were killed.

It is the wish of all ranks of 3rd Commando Brigade, Royal Marines that a memorial to these Officers and Other Ranks be erected in St. Paul's Anglican Cathedral. On behalf of all ranks of 3rd Commando Brigade, Royal Marines I would like to offer to the Cathedral a screen for this Chapel, which could be dedicated as a permanent memorial to our dead."

The proposal contained in this letter was accepted, and Canon Paton got in touch with Covell & Matthews, of 34 Sackville Street, London W.1., who were the Architects and Planning Consultants, for the Diocese of Gibraltar. Mr. Ralph G. Covell supervised this project.

The first meeting of the Memorial Committee was held on Friday 9th August 1957, attended by Brigadier Madoc, Canon Paton, Lieut-Colonel Tweed, Major Willasey-Wilsey, and Captain Wall. The contents of a Book of Remembrance were discussed, and it was decided that the names would be recorded in date of death sequence. Personal details would also be given, number, rank, initials, name, decorations if any, and unit. All denominations would be recorded together in the same book.

A week later at the 15th August meeting, it was agreed that the country in which death took place would be shown, and that the names of the Iban Trackers who died whilst serving with the Brigade in Malaya would also be recorded.

The work of producing this book was given to Mr. W. M. Gardner, A.R.C.A., F.R.S.A., and upon completion contained the following inscription:

"IN PROUD THANKSGIVING AND IN GRATEFUL MEMORY OF ALL WHO HAVE GIVEN THEIR LIVES IN OUR COUNTRY'S CAUSE WHILE SERVING IN THE 3RD COMMANDO BRIGADE ROYAL MARINES SINCE THE SECOND WORLD WAR.
THEIR NAMES ARE INSCRIBED WITHIN THIS BOOK.[4]"

By the middle of February 1958, work in St. Paul's had begun. The dwarf wall, which was to support the screen, was under construction, and the wrought iron screen itself was in the process of being manufactured locally.

The stone wall had a dagger design carved on it and the iron screen was mounted on top. In the centre above the gates were metal figures of the crucifixion, sculpted in England by Mr. Charles W. Lewis, of Fetcham, Surrey. Later the Royal Marines badge was added. At waist height the gates were inscribed:

FROM CHRIST THEY INHERIT A HOME OF
UNFADING SPLENDOUR

At a special service on Friday 4th July 1958 the Chapel of Our Lady and St. George was dedicated by the Chaplain of the Fleet as the Royal Marines Memorial Chapel, and a small brass plate on the adjacent pilaster records this occasion. General Sir Campbell Hardy, the Commandant General, Royal Marines was present at the ceremony.

The gates and screen were painted light blue and gold for the 150th Anniversary of the Cathedral in 1994. This restoration work was funded by the Bassingthwaighte family in memory of departed family members: Edith Louise 1960, Reginald Harry 1965, Edward King 1965, and Frank Albert 1985.

The Royal Marines also held their Remembrance Day Service at St. Paul's. This service was held on the Sunday which fell on or nearest the 23rd April, St. George's Day. The date commemorates St. George's Day, 1918, when the 4th Battalion, under Lieut-Colonel B. N. Elliot D.S.O., took a leading part in the attack on the German naval base at Zeebrugge. The Marines landed on the Mole and successfully blocked the entrance to the canal then destroyed the Mole. In this operation eleven officers, including Lieut-Colonel Elliot, and one hundred and nine NCO's and men lost their lives, two hundred and thirty-three were wounded, and thirteen taken prisoner. Two Victoria Crosses[5] were awarded to the Royal Marines for this gallant action.

This service always included The Royal Marine's Prayer:

"O Eternal Lord God, who through many generations hast united and inspired the members of our Corps, grant Thy blessing we beseech Thee on Royal Marines serving all round the globe.

Bestow thy Crown of Righteousness upon all our efforts and endeavours and may our Laurels be those of gallantry and honour, loyalty and courage.

We ask these things in the name of Him whose courage never failed, our Redeemer,

Jesus Christ, Amen."

Notes

[1] Opposite the barracks was Jessie's bar, the favourite rendezvous of Royal Marines, which now hosts the monthly meetings of the Royal Marines Association (Malta Branch).

[2] In 1953 the Duke of Edinburgh became Captain General of the Royal Marines, in succession to the late King George VI.
[3] Author of 'The Royal Marines' published in 1972.
[4] This Book is no longer in St. Paul's, probably stolen.
[5] Sgt. Norman Augustus Finch, R.M.A., later Lieut. Born Handsworth Birmingham 26th December 1890, died Portsmouth, Hants, 15th March 1966. Captain Edward Bamford, R.M.L.I., later Major. Born London 28th May 1877, died Shanghai 29th September 1928. Both medals are now in the Royal Marines Museum at Eastney.

Chapter 26

Independence for Malta

As had been anticipated the Dockyard Church had been forced to close down at the end of 1958, so the congregation and Sunday School run by the Reverend Holland and his wife were welcomed at St. Paul's.

Sir Robert Laycock left Malta on 28th May 1959, to be replaced by Sir Guy Grantham who had served in the Mediterranean with the Royal Navy and was well acquainted with the island and St. Paul's. The following year saw a change of Bishop when at the 6 p.m. service on Thursday 14th July 1960 the Right Reverend Stanley Eley, was enthroned as the twelfth Bishop of Gibraltar and installed as Dean of St. Paul's, in place of Bishop Craske.

The Anglican Church Commission held one of its sporadic meetings on Wednesday 29th August 1962, attended by the then current members Bishop Eley, Admiral Sir Deric Holland-Martin Captain H. W. Barratt, Norman Hill Esq., Brigadier C. E. de Wolff and Canon Colton.

On the Agenda was the future of the two Anglican churches. The minutes show that:

> *"The Commander in Chief (Admiral Holland-Martin) said that the general opinion was that we should keep the Cathedral and suggested that there would not be sufficient numbers of Anglicans in the future to maintain two churches and that it was therefore a question of either the Cathedral or Holy Trinity."*

In the discussion that followed Captain Barratt considered the Cathedral provided a better centre than Holy Trinity, but Bishop Eley was in favour of Holy Trinity as against the Cathedral. He went on to say that the Cathedral might have to close *"and that it was not really a Cathedral at all"*. The closure of the cathedral was imminent but for a very different reason.

In 1958 the church Council commissioned the London Fumigation Co.Ltd. to carry out a full inspection of the roof. When the report was delivered the members were disturbed at its findings, which showed that the roof timbers had been attacked by long horn beetle, death watch beetle, etc., and that the alternative recommendations were either to carry out a full fumigation or renew the roof entirely. Both would involve the outlay of a considerable amount of money that was just not available.

The Cathedral roof continued causing concern over the next few years but by the summer of 1962 it was discovered that the beetle damage to the timbers was so serious that the roof was in a dangerous condition, and now there was no alternative but to strip off the old roof entirely and replace it. Faced with this crisis it was decided to close the Cathedral at the end of September.

The contract for the new roof was given to Taylor Woodrow Ltd., under the control of the local Maltese architects Mortimer and De Giorgio. Mr. Arthur Mortimer personally supervised the work and most generously dispensed with his fee. A timetable of work was drawn up showing the approximate date for the completion of each phase, with a finishing date of mid-December 1963. So well did the work proceed that it was actually completed by September.

The estimated cost of the repairs was between ten and eleven thousand pounds, but whilst the Cathedral was closed, the opportunity was taken to carry out a few other small alterations so the total cost was a little over £12,000. An appeal for funds was launched in the United Kingdom under the signature of the Bishop of Gibraltar, the Governor and others, but the response was below expectations. On the other hand the money received from Malta far exceeded the forecast so by the beginning of 1964 the total amount had been raised.

Whilst the repairs were being carried out the usual church services, and even weddings, were held in the Crypt.

Since the work was completed by September, a Service of Re-Hallowing and Thanksgiving was held on Sunday 27th October 1963, led by Bishop Stanley Eley. Once the congregation had taken their seats the Bishop together with the clergy and choir went in procession to the entrance door of the church for the ceremony to begin. It opened with a Fanfare of Trumpets, and whilst the assembled worshippers sang the hymn *'All People that on Earth do Dwell'* the procession moved down the church to the Chancel.

The Bishop then said *"Brethren we are come together in the presence of Almighty God, and the whole company of heaven to re-hallow this Cathedral Church of St. Paul to God's glory and to give thanks for all His mercies."* The procession went in turn to the Pulpit, the Font, the Lectern, and the Altar, in front of each the Bishop recited a re-hallowing prayer. Meanwhile the congregation sang the Hymn *'We love the place, O God, Wherein thine honour dwells'*.

The Morning Service then began, during which the first lesson was read by the Commander-in-Chief Mediterranean, the second by H.E. the Governor, with the Address given by Bishop Eley.

Just prior to the final Blessing, the Reverend Robert William Pope, R.N. was licensed as acting Chancellor of the Cathedral.

Although the 1911 statutes instituted by Bishop Collins made provision for the appointment of Lay Canons at the 'Collegiate' Church of St. Paul, none were appointed until 1963 when on Christmas Day Mr. Charles Edwards was installed by the Bishop of Gibraltar. He had been an active worker and member of St. Paul's congregation for over 50 years, so the honour was richly deserved.

As already described the Royal Marines connection with St. Paul's was strengthened in 1958, and at the beginning of 1961 the Royal Air Force expressed a wish to increase its association with the church. The small Chapel of the Ascension, which had been linked with the RAF since before WWII, was dedicated as the Royal Air Force Chapel at Evensong on Saturday the 1st April 1961. This date was chosen since the Royal Air Force came into being on the 1st April 1918.

The Order of Service was:

Processional Hymn: "Praise my Soul, the King of Heaven"
Psalm 122: "I was glad when they said unto me 'We will go into the House of the Lord.'"
First Lesson: Job 19, verses 21 27, read by Padre Harries.
Office Hymn: "Ye Choirs of New Jerusalem."
Second Lesson: John 2, verses 13 22, read by Wing Commander Slade.
Hymn: "Praise to the Holiest"
Sermon: By the Chaplain-in-Chief
Hymn: "Christ the Lord is Risen Again"
Whilst this hymn was being sung the Venerable Francis William Cocks, the RAF Chaplain-in-Chief, the Chancellor and Padre Henry Rayner Mackintosh Harries went up the flight of stairs leading to the Chapel of the Ascension. The Dedication Prayers were recited.
Hymn: "Thy Hand O God Hath Guided".

During the singing of this last hymn the Clergy returned to the Altar, whilst a collection took place amongst the assembled worshippers. The service was brought to an end with a Blessing, and the congregation left the church to the music of the RAF March, played by the band of the Royal Air Force.

For the first time in Malta since 1955 a General Election was held during February 1962 but under a new Constitution. It was won by the Nationalist Party, headed by Dr.George Borg Olivier, who made it clear from the first moment that he wanted discussions with the British Government which would lead to independence for Malta. The Governor, Sir Guy Grantham left office four months later, so it was left to his successor Sir Maurice Dorman to continue the political dialogue with the Maltese Prime Minister, and eventually in 1964 the British Government took the decision to grant independence to Malta.

The time and date set was midnight on Sunday 20th September 1964. The Duke of Edinburgh arrived on the island for this momentous occasion. A 'Malta Independence Service' was held at St. Paul's at 10 o'clock that Sunday morning. Besides Prince Philip and the current Governor with Lady Dorman, the assembled worshippers also included three former Governors, Lord Douglas, Sir Robert Laycock, and Sir Guy Grantham. Of the other 220 specially invited guests, more than the seventy-five percent were Army, Navy and Air Force Officers and their families, including a number of WRNS. The Acting Chancellor the Reverend Robert Pope and the Bishop of Gibraltar conducted the service. The First Lesson was read by the Sir Maurice Dorman, the Second by the Duke of Edinburgh, and the Bishop of Gibraltar, the Right Reverend Stanley Eley, gave the Sermon.

It was to be a long day for the Duke, that evening there was a State Banquet at the Phoenicia Hotel prior to the actual ceremony itself that took place at the Independence Arena in Floriana. Here a dazzling number of displays were given before an excited and packed audience, but as the clock ticked away close to midnight His Grace the Archbishop of Malta left the Royal Box and walked to the foot of the flagstaff where he read a prayer of dedication then blessed the Maltese flag held by Lieutenant A. J. Cassar Reynaud of the Royal Malta Artillery. The Governor and Maltese Prime Minister then took up their position by the flagstaff. The arena was in darkness only a spotlight illuminated the Union Jack, the bands played 'Auld Lang Syne', followed by 'God Save the Queen'. The Union Jack was lowered by Lieutenant S. C. Thorpe of the Royal Sussex Regiment[1], and seconds later the Maltese flag was flying at the top of the flagpole whilst the bands played the Maltese National Anthem. The crowds were then treated to an extravagant fireworks display.

So from 21st September 1964 Sir Maurice Dorman ceased to be the Governor, but remained on Malta with the new title of Governor-General until 22nd June 1971[2].

Notes

[1] Chosen because the Kings Colour of the 35th Regiment flew from the ramparts of Valletta on 5th September 1800, when the French surrendered.

[2] He was succeeded by Sir Anthony Mamo as Governor-General.

Chapter 27

Memorial Services

Though Malta was now an independent country its ties with Britain were still strong as 164 years of shared experiences and history do not vanish overnight.

There was therefore a sense of loss when on the 24th January 1965 Sir Winston Churchill who had led Britain to victory during the Second World War died two months after celebrating his ninetieth birthday. No one in Malta of the wartime generation would ever forget listening to his distinctive voice on the radio during the grim days of 1940/1942.

Whilst his impressive State funeral was taking place in London on Saturday morning, the 30th, a memorial service was held in St. Paul's. It was unique since it brought together men and women of several religious denominations to worship in the same building. Archbishop Gonzi of Malta had given his permission for Roman Catholics to attend and he was represented by the Reverend Professor Gerald J. Seaston, Chaplain to the Forces.

Leading Maltese politicians present were the Deputy Prime Minister Dr. G. Felice[1], the Minister of Education Dr. A. Parnis, Minister of Justice Dr. T. Caruana Demajo, Minister of Health Dr. P. Borg Olivier, together with the Speaker of the House of Representatives Mr. Paolo Pace. Members representing the Opposition Party were the Hon. Mabel Strickland, and Dr. H. Ganado.

Canon Pope, Chancellor of St. Paul's opened the service with prayers, followed by the singing of the 23rd Psalm. The First Lesson was read by Vice Admiral Cole, and the Second by Sir Maurice Dorman. Canon Pope then gave a short sermon praising Sir Winston's qualities of leadership and his efforts to maintain a stable peace once the war was over.

Later that year on 24th August the Commanding Officer of the Royal Malta Artillery, Colonel G. Z. Tabona, presented a crucifix to St. Paul's in memory of Sir Winston on behalf of the Officers and Men of the regiment. It was attached to the pillar alongside the pulpit.

In 1968 it was agreed that a new lectern would be commissioned and dedicated in memory of Sir Winston Churchill. The design by Mr. Godson, a member of St. Paul's, called for a combination of English Oak and Maltese stone. The wood was worked by Mr. Saviour Tonna of Rabat, and the stonework was cut and laid by another Maltese craftsman Mr. Fortune Vassallo.

A special service was held at 11 o'clock on Wednesday morning 29th May 1968, to unveil and dedicate the lectern. It was a truly ecumenical gathering of clergy that took part in the service, the Venerable Douglas James Noel Wanstall, the Archdeacon of Malta, the Reverend Henry George Warren Macdonald, Acting Chancellor, the Reverend David Gordon Davies Chaplain of Holy Trinity, the Reverend W. J. Walter Royal Naval Chaplain, the Reverend Robert David Ebbitt, DACG, the Reverend Peter Owen Wingfield Levingston RAF Chaplain, the Reverend P. O. Price Methodist Chaplain, the Right Reverend Andrew, Bishop of Troy Orthodox Church, His Lordship Mgr. E. Gerada representing His Grace the Archbishop of Malta.

Another man held in high esteem by the Maltese was Admiral Andrew Cunningham and after his death, a special service was held on Friday 28th April 1967 for the unveiling and dedication of a plaque in his memory. Appointed Commander in Chief Mediterranean Fleet in June 1939, it was through his determination and against heavy odds that convoys were sent to Malta, even though they did so under hazardous circumstances.

St. Paul's was full to capacity; the congregation was composed of leading dignitaries from Diplomatic, Government and Military circles. Attending from the foreign corps, were the Ambassadors of Italy and West Germany, with the Charge d'Affaires' of France, Israel, and Libya. From Malta Sir Maurice Dorman, Dr. Borg Olivier, the Most Rev. Mgr. Coleiro representing His Grace the Archbishop, and the Chief Justice Sir Anthony Mamo.

Apart from the VIP's, men who had served the late Admiral in a personal capacity were also invited to attend, Royal Naval cooks and stewards, these were Francis Abela, Carmel Aquilina, Alfred Gauci, Paul Montebello and Philip Sammut.

The 50-minute service was conducted by Bishop Eley assisted by Archdeacon Wanstall, the Reverend Donald Young, Fleet Chaplain and Acting Chancellor of St. Paul's, plus the Reverend D. G. Davies, Chaplain of Holy Trinity Sliema.

The Lesson was read by Rear Admiral R. M. Dick, Chief of Staff to Admiral Cunningham during the war, and the Address was given by Admiral Sir John Hamilton, the current Commander-in- Chief, Mediterranean.

Whilst the congregation was singing the hymn 'O Come Ye Servants of the Lord' a small group formed up in procession behind the Bishop, then walked down the nave and turned left to the pilaster on which could be seen a White Ensign surrounded by laurel leaves. As Lady Cunningham drew the flag to one side, the white marble plaque in memory of her husband was revealed. The Bishop read the Dedication after which the assembled worshippers said the Lord's Prayer.

Outside the church in Independence Square, buglers of the Royal Marines sounded the 'Last Post', which was followed by the Highland lament 'The Flowers of the Forest' played by Petty Officer Gordon Williams on the bagpipes. The buglers then sounded 'Reveille'. The Bishop led the small group back to their places and he brought this simple service to an end with a blessing.

The last British Commander-in-Chief Mediterranean left Admiralty House in South Street, Valletta, during 1967 and re-located to Villa Portelli at Kalkara. The building was later re-opened and now houses the Museum of Fine Arts. On the walls either side of the grand staircase visitors can see large panels listing the British C-in-C's from 1792 and although many may be forgotten, several names will be familiar from their involvement with St. Paul's.

For the next five years St. Paul's was without a civilian Chancellor. Though the church was not handed over to the Royal Navy, as had been proposed by Sir Guy Grantham back in 1958, Royal Naval Chaplains became Acting Chancellors, Robert Pope 1964–1965, Lancelot MacManaway 1965–1966, Donald Young 1966–1967, and Henry MacDonald 1967–1969.

It was apparent that a permanent civilian Chancellor was required but would mean finding the necessary money for his stipend since the Naval Chaplains had been funded by the Royal Navy. In March 1969 Sir Maurice Dorman, the Governor-General, wrote to several prominent members of St. Paul's congregation asking them to consider becoming guarantors for a Chancellor's stipend by donating £10 per year. He mentioned that about 150 people were being approached and continued:

> *"The need for some such scheme is clear. For the first time for a number of years, the Cathedral has to finance its own Chancellor. Hitherto, we have had the generous assistance of a Senior Fleet Chaplain whose emoluments have not been the Cathedral's responsibility. With the rundown of the Services this help can no longer be given to us.*
>
> *The Bishop has appointed a man of wide experience, whom, I am confident, you will come to admire and respect – the Reverend Gordon Hyslop, a Cambridge man, for twenty years in the Royal Air Force and for eleven years Assistant Chaplain in Chief. On retirement he went to East Africa as Chaplain to one of the constituent parts of Uganda University and then as Director of Religious Education in Kenya. He is married and will take up duties after Easter."*

The political situation on Malta changed in June 1971 when the Labour party headed by Mr. Dom Mintoff won the General Election. He wished to follow a policy of neutrality and non-alignment, and therefore wanted the total withdrawal of all foreign troops and navies from Malta. He issued an ultimatum

ST PAUL'S ANGLICAN CATHEDRAL
VALLETTA

Morning Service
& Dedication & Unveiling
of the Submarine
Memorial Plaque

Sunday 17 November 1974
1030

on 29th December 1971 that all British Forces were to be out of the island by the 31st, but this deadline was extended to the 14th January 1972[2]. Under such conditions large numbers of British Service wives and children were flown out of Malta mostly on VC10 aircraft from Luqa to Brize Norton, before the 14th. After difficult negotiations a new agreement was signed allowing Britain, as part of NATO, to continue using bases on Malta until 31st March 1979.

The 'Friends of St. Paul's Anglican Cathedral' was originally founded in 1958, shortly before illness forced Canon Paton to leave Malta, but due to interregnums, the constant changes of Church Council membership, and in 1962 the pressing problem of funding the new roof, this group was not very active. However, it gradually increased in membership and in 1971 was combined with the Chancellor's stipend fund scheme organised by the outgoing Governor-General, Sir Maurice Dorman. The honorary secretary, Victor Lewis, wrote to members of the stipend fund that year soliciting support from them to be entered on the 'Roll of the Friends of the Cathedral', which is on permanent display in the Cathedral.

The last memorials to be placed at St. Paul's relating to WWII were to the submariners of the Royal Navy. The first on Sunday 17th November 1974, saw the dedication and unveiling of a plaque fixed to the base of the tower overlooking Marsamxett Harbour. It commemorates the close ties between the Maltese people and the men of the 10th Submarine Flotilla who were based on Manoel Island for three years during WWII, with the Lazaretto Buildings as their Headquarters.[3]

The unveiling was performed by Vice Admiral Sir Arthur Hezlet, a former Flag Officer Submarines. Fifty British and Allied submarines were lost in the Mediterranean theatre of war, but during that campaign some 300 awards for gallantry were won including, 5 Victoria Crosses.[4] The memorial was sponsored by the Flag Officer Submarines with the support of the Submarine Old Comrades Association under their President Rear Admiral Sir Anthony Miers, VC.

The second, almost a year later when a window was dedicated by the Bishop of Gibraltar, John Satterthwaite[5], on 2nd November 1975 in the Chapel of Our Lady and St. George. The window consists of small plain glass panels, similar to the other windows in the cathedral, was presented by relatives, shipmates and friends in memory of the Officers and Men of the 10th Submarine Flotilla and other submarines operating from Malta, who lost their lives during WWII.

Notes

[1] The Prime Minister Dr. Borg Olivier was in London for the State funeral.

[2] Not only the British Forces were affected. On 3rd March 1972 the Malta Government informed the King's Own Malta Regiment that they were to be disbanded from 1st April.
[3] Known by the name HMS *Talbot*.
[4] Cdr.John Wallace Linton, HMS *Turbulent*. Cdr.Anthony Cecil Capel Meirs, later Rear Admiral, HMS *Torbay*.
[5] Lt-Cdr.Malcolm David Wanklyn, HMS *Upholder*. P. O. Thomas William Gould and Lieut. Peter Scawen Watkinson Roberts, HMS *Thrasher*.
[6] He was appointed to the Bishopric in 1970.

Chapter 28

British Forces Farewell to Malta

At the Annual General Meeting in 1972 Dr. Rex Cheverton was elected a Churchwarden for the first time, and joined Mr. Kenneth Biddis who had already served as a Churchwarden since 1969. These two worked together during the transition back to a completely civilian congregation, and the partnership lasted until 1982.

The same year it was felt more appropriate to call the area beneath the church the 'Undercroft' instead of 'Crypt' as heretofore, since in Maltese churches and especially Cathedrals, the 'Crypt' was traditionally used for used for burials, and a distinction needed to be made. However, it should be mentioned in passing that on at least a couple of occasions a friendly 'ghost' has allegedly been seen in the Undercroft. Since it is the site of the old Auberge D'Allemagne, and with the typical English sense of humour he was nicknamed 'Fritz'.

The following year Chancellor Hyslop resigned, and the vacancy was filled by the Reverend Howard Stacey Cole[1] who took up the post on 28th December 1973.

On the 30th March 1974 the following obituary notice appeared:

> Sidney Larkins.
> A distinguished steeplejack of Nelson's Column fame will be widely mourned. During 1969[2] at a critical period in the history of St. Paul's Anglican Cathedral, Valletta, when the famous spire was in need of attention he gamely came to the rescue. It was typical of Mr. Larkins generosity and kindly nature that he personally sought Bank of England permission to bring out with him the material needed to re-gild the cross. He asked that this undertaking should be regarded as a gift to the Cathedral, and he even occupied himself with the project while lying sick in bed at a Malta hotel. Now he has reached beyond the spire, but his memory will long remain.

On the political scene the Malta Government declared that Malta and its dependencies would become a Republic from 13th December 1974, but would remain a member of the Commonwealth, and a new National flag was created. During the time that Malta was a British colony the currency in circulation was British Sterling pounds, shillings and pence, but from 1972 the Malta Government introduced their own decimal currency the Maltese Liri (pound), identified with the symbol £M. From Independence Day, 21st September 1964, the postage stamps of Malta ceased to bear the Queen's head.

During 1975, the Church Council formed the opinion that Queen Adelaide should be remembered by having a banner showing her coat of arms on display in the Chancel. Firstly the College of Arms was contacted, and subsequently they approached Jane Urwick to make it. Apart from deciding that it should be four feet square and hang from a horizontal pole, she was given a free hand. After carrying out considerable research into German heraldry, she managed to complete the banner itself in about fifteen weeks. It was erected on the left-hand side of the Chancel, and dedicated by the Bishop Satterthwaite on the 2nd November.

Chancellor Cole left St. Paul's in June 1977 and was followed as Chancellor by the Reverend David Inderwick Strangeways.[3] Shortly after his taking charge a modification was made in the sanctuary. In July 1978, the altar was moved forward from the back wall so that the Celebrant at the Sung Eucharist service could stand behind it facing the congregation, instead of with his back to them as previously.

The date for the total withdrawal of British Forces was drawing near. The Commander of British Forces on Malta was Rear Admiral Oswald Cecil, and it was under his cool and clear headed leadership that the British withdrawal was achieved with goodwill on all sides. In 1800 General Thomas Graham, the Commander of British and Maltese Forces had used the Palazzo D'Aurel[4] in Gudja as his headquarters, so it was with a sense of history that Admiral Cecil held his final Staff Meeting in this same building in February 1979. For over two hundred years it has been the home of the same family, and Gino Trapani-Galea-Ferol, the 10th Baron of San Marciano[5], is in residence at the present time.

The guided missile destroyer HMS *London* dropped anchor in Grand Harbour and on March 12th the Admiral transferred his flag from Fort St. Angelo to HMS *London*. A series of farewell events took place culminating with a ceremony at the Freedom Monument[6] just prior to midnight on 31st March 1979, when a young sailor from HMS *London* lowered the Union Jack, and a Maltese dockyard worker raised the Maltese flag.

In spite of bad weather the bastions and quays were thronged next morning when HMS *London* sailed out of Grand Harbour, so ending the Royal Navy's link with Malta after 180 years.

Notes

[1] He died at Sherborne 18th December 1988.
[2] September 1969.

[3] An ex-Army Officer, he had served in Malta in 1933, with the 1st Battalion Duke of Wellington's Regiment. During WWII he was involved with strategic and tactical deception of the Germans in the Near and Middle East. After the war he served in Khartoum, Greece and Malta. In 1957 he retired from the Army and took holy orders. He died in August 1998, aged 86 years.

[4] Bettina D'Aurel was a lady-in-waiting to Queen Maria Carolina, the wife of King Ferdinand IV of the Two Sicilies, on whose behalf the British were fighting to remove Napoleon's French troops from Malta. General Graham entertained Admiral Nelson there in May 1800.

[5] The First Baron of San Marciano was created on 14th June 1726 by Grandmaster Manoel de Vilhena.

[6] In front of St. Lawrence's Church, Vittoriosa.

Chapter 29

St. Paul's and Holy Trinity United

All over the world Anglican Christians had used the 1662 Book of Common Prayer, which was based on two earlier books written by Thomas Cranmer[1] in 1549 and 1552. After 1900 some countries without an Anglo-Saxon heritage introduced variations, but still the 1662 Prayer Book remained the norm. However, it was being questioned whether the language of Cranmer was appropriate in the twentieth century. In everyday speech the words 'thee', 'thou', 'lo', 'beget', etc. were no longer used and it was thought that the language of worship should be plain, direct and clear.

After much discussion within the Church of England the result was the Alternative Service Book 1980[2]. When introduced by the Chancellor Strangeways at St. Paul's a few of the worshippers found this change unacceptable and regretfully ceased attending the Cathedral. He had completed four years in office and left at the end of May 1981. The new man to take control was Archdeacon John Walter Evans.

Since their origins in 1844 and 1867 respectively, the Anglican congregations at St. Paul's and Holy Trinity in Sliema kept their separate identities, but co-operated where and when possible. Each church had its strengths and weaknesses, its ups and downs, but those attending regular worship generally felt more comfortable with this arrangement.

However, faced with a decline in church attendances and financial problems, it was decided in 1983 that for administrative purposes the two churches should be combined, and the term Chaplaincy Laity was introduced. In February 1985, a few months before his retirement after 43 years in the Ministry, Archdeacon John Evans proposed to the Church Council that there should be just one electoral roll to cover St. Paul's and Holy Trinity, which was accepted by the Council though not welcomed by all the churchgoers themselves.

Archdeacon Evans departed in August 1985, and a series of locum tenens again were needed. Archdeacon Gordon Davies, Canon David Dixon and the Reverend James Packer took the services at St. Paul's over the course of the next twelve months.

At the AGM held on the 17th April 1986 when a single electoral role was used Mr. George Robins was elected Chaplain's Warden and Colonel W.A.R.Hutton as People's warden for the Cathedral, with Mrs. Jean Bartolo, Mrs. Peggy Kirkpatrick, Mr. John Lloyd, and Lady Doreen Thorp from St. Paul's as Council members.

Churchwarden Hutton informed the meeting that the Reverend Kenneth William Alfred Roberts had accepted a three-year contract and would be coming in June. He duly arrived and was installed as Chancellor on Sunday 14th September 1986.

Bishop John Satterthwaite visited Malta from the 12th to the 16th March 1987, and at the next Chaplaincy Council meeting, Canon Roberts read a letter from him concerning a matter, which the Bishop had raised with the churchwardens during his visit.

"Hearing reports of growing activity of Freemasonry in Malta I explained that there must be no official connection between Freemasonry and either of our two churches in Malta. If any private individuals have personal links with Freemasonry that is to be regarded as an entirely private matter and one which is in no way connected with the Pro-Cathedral of St. Paul or to Holy Trinity Sliema.[3]"

In view of the Bishop's instruction a proposed donation from a Freemason's charity in England was declined, even though it was known that the same charity was making grants to Cathedrals of the Church of England with the Archbishop of Canterbury's approval. In view of the difficult financial circumstances of the Anglican chaplaincy the Council members were unhappy at the Bishop's directive and sought amplification from him but without result.

For many years it had been the customary to hold a Summer Garden Fete at the residence of the British High Commissioner in aid of St. Paul's, but with the advent of increased terrorist activity throughout the world, the imposition of security controls prevented this event continuing.

However the income from the 1987 Fete, which had been held on 6th June whilst Stanley Duncan was the British High Commissioner, amounted to £M1360 which was most welcome.

When giving his report to the gathering for the AGM on 26th April 1988, Canon Roberts stressed the theme of one united Anglican community in Malta, with a joint monthly magazine, joint fund raising and a joint Chaplaincy Council.

At the same meeting Mr. George Robins handed in his resignation as a Churchwarden due to his long absences from Malta, and Captain Norman Cockshoot was elected in his stead. Mr. Robins expressed a wish to donate some gift to St. Paul's in remembrance of his wife Lucy, who had passed away in 1986. A faculty was requested to erect lamp standards on the choir stalls, and Joinwell Ltd. was given the order to manufacture them. The twenty-four lights were installed and dedicated in July 1988.

In the course of carrying out research about the Msida Bastion Cemetery in Floriana on behalf of Din L'Art Helwa, Mr. Reginald Kirkpatrick became interested in the Births, Deaths and Marriage records of St. Paul's. Knowing that the registers and many papers relating to the history of the church were not correctly preserved Canon Roberts asked him to become honorary archivist. He accepted, and in 1988 wrote and published a small booklet describing the history, architecture and memorials in the Cathedral.

Canon Roberts only stayed for three years, departing on 9th January 1989. Five acting Chancellors then ran St. Paul's. Canon William Roan for ten weeks, the Reverend Russell Harrison for eight weeks, Canon John Whitelaw for four weeks, Archdeacon George Davies for seven weeks, then the Reverend Harrison again for six weeks.

During his time as the acting Chancellor William Roan issued a one-page newssheet and members of St. Paul's were saddened to read in the January 1989 edition that Mr. Kenneth Biddis had died at Portsmouth. He had come to Malta in 1968, and was a churchwarden at St. Paul's from 1969 to1982.[4]

A permanent Chancellor was sought and the Reverend Philip John Cousins accepted the position. He was installed as Chancellor and Senior Canon on Sunday morning 29th October 1989, by the Right Reverend John Satterthwaite, Bishop of Gibraltar.

Notes

[1] He was Archbishop of Canterbury from 1533, but during the reign of Mary was burnt at the stake as a heretic on 21st March 1556.
[2] For a full description of events leading up to the ASB 1980, and explanation of the ASB, see 'Anglican Worship Today', Collins, 1980.
[3] Minutes of Chaplaincy Council Meeting 13th April 1987.
[4] Also was honorary veterinary surgeon to the S.P.C.A.

Chapter 30

Royal Visit

Chaplaincy funds were at a low ebb so once again it was necessary to issue a Restoration Appeal to help meet the maintenance costs of the church buildings. It was launched in the summer of 1990, with Air Commodore Malcolm Jolly as Chairman. He was pleased to report at the 1991 AGM held on 17th April that:

> "We have already reached £20,416 which is 80 percent of our original target of £25,000 sterling in barely nine months."

The rate of donations slowed slightly thereafter but within eighteen months around £26,000 was raised. The task was made harder by Bishop John Satterthwaite's directive dated 19th March 1987, which was still in force.

At the same meeting it was agreed to open a subscription list to purchase a new silver chalice in memory of Mrs. Jean Bartolo who had worked hard for the Cathedral and the Diocese. The money was soon raised so the chalice was ready to be dedicated the following year during the St. Paul Shipwreck service on 10th February 1992.

At the end of May 1992, Queen Elizabeth flew to Italy to join the Royal Yacht *Britannia* for a State Visit to Malta. On the 29th she unveiled the large Siege Bell Memorial close to Lower Barracca Gardens in Valletta. During the afternoon just before 3 o'clock she paid a short private visit to St. Paul's, accompanied by the Duke of Edinburgh, and their aides. The Bishop of Gibraltar escorted the Royal party through the Cathedral into the lounge of the Chancellor's Lodge, where members of the Church Council with their spouses were gathered. Together with Canon Cousins and his wife Janet, they were able to have an informal conversation with Her Majesty over tea.

In 1979 around 150,000 tourists visited Malta. The majority were British, often ex-Servicemen and their families, either reviving old memories or coming to see where Dad served when he was in the Forces. Throughout the next ten years tourism grew considerably and became the largest single contributor to the Maltese Exchequer. It continued to grow and was close to 800,000 by the early

Nineties. Most visitors came from European countries but others from further afield.

Canon Cousins introduced a system of Cathedral Stewards to be on duty during the afternoons to welcome tourists and if necessary answer their questions. Small information boards, similar to table-tennis bats were produced which could be handed out to visitors and gave them some brief notes about the Cathedral's history and memorials. These were produced in several European languages.

The increase in the number visitors to the island also benefited St. Paul's. At the 10.30 Sunday morning service quite a number of holidaymakers help to swell the congregation especially in the winter months.

Canon Cousins was an advocate of women taking a greater role in the religious rites of the church, and urged that *"We need women Servers, women Lay Assistants and a proper welcome to visiting women Deacons to preach or assist in the sanctuary. These matters were all decided long ago by the parent Church of England "*[1]

In the Oxford English Dictionary the word 'ecumenical' is defined thus: 'of or representing the whole Christian world; seeking world-wide Christian unity; hence ecumenism.'

The Sunday Times of Malta[2], reporting the Memorial Service for Sir Winston Churchill in 1965 opened its article with the words *"For the first time ever"*, and continued: *"...a congregation of Catholics, Anglicans and men and women of other religious denominations prayed together under one roof in St. Paul's Anglican Cathedral, Valletta."*

Attitudes and suspicions continued to change, rather slowly at first, but certainly over the last ten years considerable progress towards co-operation amongst all Christian people has been made.

In 1991 Canon Cousins was delighted to report:

> *"Ecumenically it has been a good year above all because of the visit to Malta of Pope John Paul II in May when we took part in an ecumenical meeting with him in Mdina Cathedral. But we were also privileged to host at St. Paul's both the Week of Prayer for Christian Unity Service in January, and the Women's World Day of Prayer Service in March. We also took part in a 'Songs of Praise' programme televised by the BBC in conjunction with our Roman Catholic friends"*

Henry Mallia had served as the Verger of St. Paul's for twenty years and as a sign of appreciation he was presented with a Video Recorder on behalf of the grateful congregation. He was a popular figure, but sadly a few months later in 1993 he died from a heart attack.

Notes

[1] Due to the pressure for female equality in all walks of life, many felt that the decision by the Church of England to allow the Ordination of Women had been made purely for 'politically correct' reasons. It was highly controversial and many clergymen and laity could not accept this outcome and left the Church of England. This decision also caused difficulties in the relationship to the Roman Catholic Church.

[2] 31st January 1965.

Chapter 31

150th Anniversary of Consecration

With the 150th Anniversary of the Consecration of St. Paul's on the far horizon, a committee was set up in 1992 to decide upon and to arrange all aspects of the celebrations. The first meeting was held on the 4th November, with Lady Doreen Thorp as Chairman, but she later decided to step down, and Air Commodore Malcolm Jolly took over.

Under his leadership a meeting took place on 14th January 1994, when the items which had been considered throughout the previous year were reviewed; Location, Menu and Guest list for a Dinner on the 31st October; Procedure and Form of the Service in St. Paul's on the 1st November; Reception following the Service; Commemorative Souvenirs.

Over the next months with much hard work, sometimes very frustrating, all the arrangements were put into place and everything was ready for the big day. Many people had been busy doing tapestry work on new kneelers in a variety of colourful designs, either as their own contribution or doing the needle-work on behalf of other sponsors. Over 100 were completed.[1]

The Archbishop of Canterbury, the Right Reverend George Carey[2] arrived in Malta on 31st October 1994 by air from London accompanied by his wife Eileen. They had come to take part in the celebrations, and stayed as guests of the British High Commissioner, Sir Peter Wallis at the official residence, Villa de Giorgio, San Pawl tat Targa.

The same evening they attended the Sesquicentenary dinner at the Phoenicia Hotel, Floriana. Some 288 diners, which was the maximum that could be accommodated, were present. Among the large number of distinguished guests, were the President of Malta, Dr. Ugo Mifsud Bonnici with his wife, His Grace the Archbishop of Malta, the Right Reverend Monsignor Annetto Despasquale – Vicar General, H.E.Archbishop Pierre Luigi Celela – Apostolic Nuncio, Sir Peter and Lady Wallis – British High Commissioner. The Right Reverend John Hind, Bishop of Gibraltar in Europe presided, and the top table was completed by Mrs. Hind together with Canon Cousins and Mrs. Cousins.

The next afternoon Archbishop Carey went to visit Mdina where he had the pleasure of meeting again Archbishop Mgr. Mercieca of Malta, and together they entered The Metropolitan Cathedral of St. Paul, for ecumenical prayers. He then returned to Valletta to prepare for the Consecration Anniversary service at St. Paul's, due to commence at 6.30p.m. The Auberge d'Aragon across the Square from St. Paul's was put at his disposal for robing. Arrangements had been made for the service to be recorded and shown later on Malta Television.

Just before six o'clock, Barbara Engerer, Lileth Andersen, and Jean Attard climbed the rickety wooden stairs to the first floor of the belfry and by deftly manipulating the six bell handles they rang a selection of chimes for half an hour.

By the time the service was due to start the church was full to capacity, and the congregation included the President of Malta together his wife. The service was taken by the Bishop of Gibraltar, assisted by the Archdeacon of Italy and Malta, the Right Reverend Eric Devenport, and Canon Philip Cousins.

The Old Testament Lesson from Jeremiah was read by Churchwarden Mr. Tony Savage and the Epistle by Air Commodore Malcolm Jolly. In Dr. Carey's sermon he expressed pleasure at the growth of co-operation between the Anglican and Roman Catholic faiths. The Intercessions were led by Canon Cousins, and included a prayer for the church's founder and benefactor the Dowager Queen Adelaide.

After the Intercessions, Lady Doreen Thorp offered the new kneelers for the Archbishop's blessing. During the distribution of Holy Communion the augmented choir sang a setting of psalm *'O how amiable are thy dwellings'* conducted by Hugo Agius Muscat the organist at St. Paul's. Following *'All people that on earth do dwell'* the choir sang the Te Deum composed by Mrs. William Frere for the 1844 consecration.

At the end of the service all the clergy, including the Archbishop, followed by the distinguished guests left the church in procession into Independence Square and St. Paul's church bells, played by Josephine Earp, rang out 'Canterbury Surprise' in joyous celebration.

As souvenirs of this historic event a range of engraved glasses, printed tea towels, and bookmarks bearing a portrait of Queen Adelaide were produced and offered for sale. A Commemorative Postage Stamp on first day cover was issued by the Maltese Post Office.

The Archbishop left for England the next day and was presented with a painting of the Cathedral, commissioned from local artist Mrs. Joy Micallef, as a memento of his visit.

Notes

[1] The kneelers became very popular and have continued to be produced, so that the figure is now over 200.

[2] Archbishop Carey was born in Bow, East London on 13th November 1935. He married in 1960, and has two sons and two daughters. He spent two years, 1954–1956, doing National Service in the Royal Air Force, as a wireless operator. He was ordained in 1962, and prior to becoming Archbishop of Canterbury in 1991, he had been the Bishop of Bath and Wells from 1987–1991. He lets it be known that he is an Arsenal supporter.

Chapter 32

St. Paul's Interior Appearance 1999

As we approach the Millenium how does St. Paul's appear to the visitor today. Externally very little has changed since the church was originally built.

On the north side facing Marsamxett Harbour is the tower and graceful spire housing the belfry, joined to the main building by a short passage. Before WWII the spire was only illuminated for special occasions such as the Jubilee of King George V and the Coronation of King George VI, but nowadays it can be clearly seen every night on the Valletta skyline as it is continuously floodlit. Affixed to the base of the tower is the plaque commemorating the close ties between the Maltese and the men of the Royal Naval submarines, who were based on Manoel Island during WWII.

At the rear of the church after a narrow terrace confined by black iron railings, is 12 feet wide flight of stone steps down to Marsamxett Street, with the door to the Undercroft about halfway down on the right. On the other side of the steps are 'St. Paul's Modern Buildings', which were erected in 1908 on the site of Beverley's Hotel, where Sir Walter Scott stayed in 1831.

The Portico of St. Paul's is supported by six Ionic columns above which is the inscription:

D.O.M. ECCLESIAM HANC COLLEGIAM ADELAIDA REGINA GRATO ANIMO DICAVIT MDCCCXLIV. (Queen Adelaide with a grateful heart dedicated this Collegiate Church to Almighty God 1844)

Due to Bishop Tomlinson's alterations, the two main doors of St. Paul's under the portico now only serve as decorative panels, since they are almost never opened, and visitors have to use the door at the northwest end from Strada Ponente (West Street). The building on the other side of the Square the Auberge d'Aragon, which was known for a time as 'Gibraltar Palace' when the Bishop had it as his residence, is now used as offices by the Ministry of Economic Services.

The Square itself has had a few name changes. At the time of the church's construction it was called, Piazza Celsi, a corruption of Piazza Gelsi (Mulberry Square). Later it was re-named very appropriately, Queen Adelaide Square, but this was subsequently changed to Independence Square. In the centre is the Freedom Monument to Dun Mikiel Xerri and other Maltese patriots who rose against the French occupation in 1799 but were captured and shot. This memorial was unveiled by the President of Malta, Agatha Barbara, on 31st July 1986.

Coming up the steps from Strada Ponente, one enters the building and there is a small lobby with notice boards on the walls including a light oak board listing the Chaplains and Chancellors since 1844. Above the inner door is a large painting received in 1995 on permanent loan from the Fine Arts Museum[1] of "Christ among the Children", thought to be the work of Giuseppe Cali's son.

Once inside St. Paul's it still appears plain in comparison with the Maltese churches. However, the history and events commemorated within cover a very wide spectrum. Above the door is a marble tablet in memory of Major Leonard Barrett, Royal Artillery. For several years he had been a Churchwarden, and died in Valletta on 17th July 1898, aged 40 years. Hanging from a staff above the tablet is the flag of St. George donated in 1989 by the British Residents Association.

On the left hand side of the door is a brass plate in memory of Attilio Sceberras, the late Lieutenant-Colonel of the 98th Prince of Wales' Regiment. Born in Malta on 26th July 1826, he joined the 80th (Staffordshire Volunteers) Regiment as an Ensign on 21st April 1846 transferring to the 70th (Surrey) Regiment in 1849. He was Adjutant of the 70th in India during 1857/1858, and was present at Peshawar when the native garrison mutinied, and the 70th helped to disarm them. Later he was involved when the 51st Bengal Native Infantry mutinied in August 1857 and were annihilated. During this conflict his charger was shot beneath him. He was awarded the Indian Mutiny medal. He joined the 98th Regiment in 1860 and remained with them until retirement in 1880, having being appointed to the rank of Lieut-Colonel on 14th September 1878.

On the right hand side is a brass tablet in memory of Maye Fremantle, the wife of Sir Arthur Fremantle, Governor of Malta. An officer in the Coldstream Guards, he was sworn in as Governor during January 1894 and served until December 1898. He married Maye Hall, the daughter of Richard Hall in 1864. She was engaged in philanthropic work whilst in Malta, in particular the introduction of Military midwives. She died on 16th August 1898. In addition to this tablet the marble altar steps, now in the Chapel of Our Lady and St. George, were given in her memory.

Left Hand Aisle
In the first bay is a memorial to William Hardman. A white marble tablet with incised lettering coloured gold, and an elaborate ornamental border. He was

born in Liverpool on 21st August 1838, and for 53 years was a resident in Malta. For many years he was a Churchwarden, and together with his wife[2], a benefactor of the church. He died in London on 22nd November 1907.

From the pilaster hangs the flag of the Gibraltar Diocese, the Cross of St. George with the Arms of the Diocese in the top of the hoist.

Below are three tablets. The first one in white marble is to Lieutenant Bertram Holman, Royal Artillery, the Aide-de-Camp to Sir Arthur Fremantle, the Governor of Malta. He died in London on 4th November 1896, aged 24 years.

The next in brass in memory of Evelyn Emily Grenfell. She was born in London, the daughter of General Robert Blucher Wood, and married General Sir Francis Grenfell in 1887. Her husband was Governor of Malta from 6th January 1899 until 18th March 1903. She suffered from ill health, and died at the Governor's Palace in Valletta on the 21st June 1899, aged 43 years. She was buried in Ta Braxia cemetery.

The Bishop of Gibraltar, Bishop Sandford wrote to the Churchwarden Mr. Gale on 26th April 1901:

"My Dear Mr. Gale, Though I hardly consider that memorial tablets improve the appearance of a church and much prefer memorial windows, as the other members of the Commission have acceded to the request of the Governor that he should be allowed to erect a tablet in St. Paul's Church to the memory of Lady Grenfell, I at once give my consent."

The third tablet is also brass by Comper. Elizabeth Ann Coldwell[3], M.B.E., R.R.C., sometime Q.A.I.M.N.S., the first wife of Captain Godfrey J. Coldwell, a Churchwarden of St. Paul's. She was Honorary Secretary of the Malta Girl's Friendly Society, and from 1928 to 1931, when the Coldwell G.F.S. Hostel was opened, her house was used for its meetings. She was born on 17th January 1874 and died on June 12th 1936. Her white marble grave can be seen in Ta Braxia cemetery.

In the next bay is a large white marble memorial tablet to Sir Edward and Lady Houlton. Incised letters coloured gold, surrounded by an elaborate ornamental border. Dame Hyacinth Henriette Houlton, born 10th February 1825 and died 3rd February 1897, was the only daughter of Richard Wellesley Esq. She married in 1860 Sir Edward Victor Lewis Houlton, G.C.M.G. He was the youngest son of John Torriano Houlton, of Farley Castle, Somerset, where he was born on 4th March 1823. He served as Chief Secretary to the Government of Malta from 20th September 1855 to 1883, and died 24th August 1899 in London. Bishop Sandford wrote of him:

"He will be sorely missed by many friends at Malta and elsewhere, and by none more than by myself, whom he uniformly treated with courtesy, kindness

and affection, and often aided by his counsels, during the twenty-five years of our friendship."

On the adjacent pilaster is a white marble heart-shaped shield, with a crown above the inscription and an anchor beneath, with black lettering to a young Midshipman, John L. Gordon Paterson, (Jack), of HMS *Bacchante,* who died of typhoid fever, on 20th January 1905, aged 18 years 6 months. His tomb in Ta Braxia cemetery is very distinctive. The whole of the white marble top is carved and features a large draped Union Jack, on which is a Midshipman's cap, belt and sword also carved in white marble.

Above this tablet hangs a tattered almost threadbare RAF ensign, which flew at the Royal Air Force Aerodrome at Luqa from 1940 to 1942, during the height of the blitz on Malta by the Italian Regia Aeronautica and the German Luftwaffe.

In the next bay is a large white marble memorial to George Tomlinson D.D., with incised letters coloured gold, and an ornate surround. He was the first Bishop of Gibraltar. Born 12th March 1794, and died 6th February 1863. Many details about his relationship with St. Paul's have been mentioned in earlier chapters.

High on the next pilaster is the flag of the Republic of Malta and below a marble tablet to the memory of Sir Edward Peter Stubbs Bell, Q.C., Knight of Grace of the Order of St. John. He had been Legal Secretary in Malta 1941–1945, and Chief Justice of Northern Rhodesia. Born 10th May 1902, he died 18th June 1957.

In the next bay is the memorial to the Venerable John Cleugh, who devoted his life to serving the Anglican community on Malta. He was Chaplain to the Government from 1824 to 1877, and Archdeacon of Malta from 1864 until his death on 25th March 1881, aged 89 years. At first he was in charge of the Government Chapel and later of St. Paul's. This memorial was erected in 1885. When the Archdeacon Cleugh retired in 1877 Bishop Sandford wrote:

> *"His great experience, good sense, manly honesty, and calm judgement, rendered him a valuable adviser to the Bishops of this See; the kind, prompt, and efficient assistance which he has often given to myself will be always gratefully remembered; while the firm, upright and consistent manner in which he has maintained the dignity of his office have made him respected by all residents of the island, Englishmen and Maltese, members of our own Church, and Roman Catholics. He carries with him upon his retirement the esteem and affection of all for whose good he has laboured for half a century."*

and upon his death four years later:

> "A well-known and honoured name has been lost this year to the roll of British Chaplains abroad. On the evening of Friday March 25, the gentle spirit of the Ven.John Cleugh D.D., Archdeacon of Malta passed away.... Mr. Cleugh was the first Chaplain of this church, and here single-handed he fulfilled the duties of his office till 1877, when declining health and old age compelled him to resign the charge. Rarely, even in the summer was he absent from Malta, his adopted country, except now and then for a month or so during the extreme heat, when he would retire to the neighbouring island of Gozo, returning each week for the duties of Sunday..... His great experience, his intimate acquaintance with the annals of the colony, his moderation, good sense, and calm judgement, rendered him an invaluable friend and counsellor. A spirit of peace marked his every act and word.
>
> Though he was firm and conscientious in maintaining the principles and doctrines of the church to which he belonged, yet during a continuous residence of fifty-seven years in a Roman Catholic community, he was never known to give offence. He had no enemies, but was held in highest esteem by the whole Maltese population. Golden opinions he won from all classes, by his uprightness of life, by his kindliness of nature, by the fidelity with which he discharged the duties and upheld the dignity of his high office. His fund of anecdote, geniality of temper, and courtesy of manner made him a general favourite in society. The readiness with which he relieved the needy, and gave counsel to those who sought his aid endeared him to countless hearts".

Archdeacon Cleugh and his wife were buried in the Ta Braxia cemetery, but the top of their granite tomb was badly split and damaged when a bomb landed nearby during WWII.

Beneath this tablet is a small glass case containing a book listing the 'Friends of St. Paul's Cathedral'. Alongside, in a metal holder is the Standard of the Malta Branch of the Royal British Legion. Above is the national flag of Australia presented by the Australian High Commissioner in 1992.

The Chapel of Our Lady and St. George

The ornate screen and gates given by the Royal Marines have already been described. Set in the left-hand wall is the cast of an inscribed stone from the Auberge d'Allemagne discovered when the foundations of Chancellor's House were being dug. In translation it reads:

> "Brother James Spar, of Germany, Grand Bailiff of the Order of St. John of Jerusalem. 1571"

Above it is a framed photograph of 'The Memorial Chalice to Jean Bartolo 1926–1990'.

From the centre of the ceiling hangs a brass sanctuary lamp which was a gift from the officers and men of HMS *Phoenicia*.

The white marble altar steps carry the inscription:

'IN MEMORY OF LADY LYON FREMANTLE 1898'

Before WWII they were located in the sanctuary. Behind the altar is a panel of blue and silver brocade similar to that in the baptistry, but the design has smaller crowns.

On the altar sits the Tiarks Crucifix. Geoffrey Lewis Tiarks (1909–1987), was a Royal Naval Chaplain from 1934 to 1947[4]. On 14th November 1934 whilst serving on HMS *London*, he married Betty Lyne Stock in St. Paul's, and the couple held their wedding reception on board his ship. Three weeks earlier, on 27th October, he had officiated at a wedding in St. Paul's between ERA Arthur Goulden R.N., of HMS *Coventry* to Elsie Picton of Parkstone, Dorset.

The crucifix is believed to be of Flemish origin, and is carved from Rosewood and Blackwood. It was donated to St. Paul's by his widow, Betty Tiarks, and was brought from England to Malta on board the Royal Yacht *Britannia* during a goodwill visit in January 1997.

On the right hand side of the Chapel is a stone screen erected by the Freemasons of Malta in memory of Alfred Bumstead[5], whose marble memorial tablet is high up beneath the stone cross. He died 18th December 1906, aged 36 years.

In the centre of the screen is a panel of coloured mosaic depicting the Virgin and Child, which was used in the temporary churches for the British Forces in Italy between 1943 and 1945, and was presented to the Cathedral by the Chaplains of the Eighth Army. In the right hand niche is a figure of the Virgin and Child, donated by Mrs. Hicks, the wife of the Chancellor from 1944 to 1954.

The Chancel

Adjoining the Chapel of Our Lady and St. George is the left-hand spur screen, comprising two individual pillars and a pair at the centre. Within it is the pulpit, with the carved and coloured arms of St. Paul on the front.

On the pillar adjoining the pulpit is the crucifix given by the Royal Malta Artillery in memory of Sir Winston Churchill, with a small brass plate below suitably inscribed.

Running along the wall are six Canon's Stalls, and in front of them two rows of Choir Stalls. Above each of the Canon's Stalls is a Saint's name or decorative emblem, with the name of the designated occupant carved on the back of the seat. In August 1997 the Bishop of Gibraltar conferred saint's names on five Stall's so that all twelve now bear the name of a saint. These are shown in brackets. From the pulpit towards the altar, the sequence of stalls is: Dean – the Bishop of Gibraltar St. Paul: Archdeacon of Malta St. Silas: Canon St. Polycarp: Naval Chaplain (St. Helena): Army Chaplain (St. Catherine of Siena): RAF Chaplain (St. Agnes).

Mounted on the choir stalls are lamps presented and dedicated in July 1988 in memory of Lucy Robins, the wife of Mr. George H. Robins, who had been a Churchwarden of St. Paul's.

Beyond and above the stalls is the organ. The organ case is older than the Cathedral, having been built originally by Father Smith (c.1630-1708) for Chester Cathedral. Below the organ pipes, are the Royal Coat of Arms of Queen Adelaide, and the large Banner of Queen Adelaide.

A double doorway leads into a storeroom, which has an exit into Strada Ponente. Pre-1949 this was the entrance into St. Paul's. To the left of the doors is an alcove containing a framed sketch of Queen Adelaide, by Sir Martin Archer Shee, and below a description of Queen Adelaide's banner and to the right another alcove containing a framed white embroidered cloth. The embroidery is in gold and silver thread, and is a collection of religious symbols. Above each alcove is mounted a wooden panel, the left hand one records that the new roof was constructed during 1962/1963, and the right hand one that the re-hallowing of the Cathedral took place in 1949.

The adjoining wall of the Sanctuary is the start of the Memorial Shrine. It has four panels, which combined are about sixteen feet long, and ten feet high, listing Army Units; similar panelling on left hand side of the altar has three panels listing Naval Units, and to the right side three more panels of Naval Units, then to complete the Shrine on the right hand side of the Sanctuary, one panel of Royal Air Force Squadrons, and three panels listing Merchant Navy ships. Above all these panels are the carved and coloured badges of the Army, Queen Alexandra's Imperial Military Nursing Service, the Royal Navy, Queen Alexandra's Royal Naval Nursing Service, the Royal Australian Navy, the Royal Marines, the Royal Air Force, the Royal Australian Air Force, the Royal Canadian Air Force, the South African Air Force, and the Merchant Navy.

On the left side of the altar is the Archbishop's Desk. The altar itself was built as part of the new design for the church in 1949. The Malta Times reported the death on 12th July 1988 of Maltese sculptor, Marco Montebello[6], aged 73 years, and confirmed *"his works include the altar at St. Paul's Anglican Pro-Cathedral"*. Though not visible, the foundation stone laid by Queen Adelaide in 1839 is located in the wall behind the altar.

Queen Adelaide's Banner

The left-hand half refers to her husband King William IV. It is divided into four sections, 1 England, 2 Scotland, 3 Ireland, 4 England. On top of these is an escutchen of Hanover: Gules, 2 lions passant guardant in pale or – Brunswick. Or, seme of hearts gules, a lion rampant azure – Luneburg. Gules, a horse running argent – Westphalia, and overall an inescutcheon charge with the Golden Crown of Charlemagne, the badge of the Archtreasurership of the Holy Roman Empire. The whole ensigned with the Royal Crown of Hanover. The right-hand half refers to Queen Adelaide.

1. Azure, a lion rampant barry argent and gules – Landgraviate of Thuringia.
2. An escarboucle Or and a scutcheon argent – Cleves.
3. Or, a lion rampant sable – Meissen.
4. Or, a lion rampant sable, crowned gules – Julich.
5. Escutcheon, barry Or and sable, a rautenkranz vert – Saxony.
6. Argent, a lion rampant gules, crowned azure – Berg.
7. Azure, an eagle displayed, crowned Or – Palatinate of Saxony.
8. Or, two pales azure – Landsberg.
9. Sable, an eagle displayed Or – Palatinate of Thuringia.
10. Or, seme of hearts gules, a lion rampant sable crowned gules – Orlamûnde.
11. Argent, three bars azure – Eisenberg.
12. Azure, a lion passant per pale Or and argent – Pleissen.
13. Argent, a rose gules – Altenburg.
14. Gules plain – The enjoyment of Sovereign Rights.
15. Argent, three leaves of nenuphar gules – Brena.
16. Or, a fess chequy argent and gules – Mark.
17. Gules, a column argent crowned Or, impaling; Or, on a mount vert a cock sable, wattled gules – Römhild/Henneberg.
18. Argent, three chevrons gules – Ravensberg.

In front of the altar, on the riser of the second step appear the words:

> TOWARDS THE COST OF THE ALTAR AND REREDOS THE EDITOR OF THE SPECTATOR RAISED THE SUM OF TWO THOUSAND POUNDS AS A MEMORIAL TO THOSE WHO FOUGHT IN THE BATTLE OF MALTA 1940–1943

The Communion Rail Gates were a gift in 1989 from Mr. Trevor Rodger, Hon. secretary of the Church Council, and later a Churchwarden.

On the right of the altar is kept a small oak credence table inscribed LAUS DEO on the front, which was a gift from the architect, Alban Caroe. Next to it is a three-place oak prayer desk (prie-dieu) presented by the Royal Marines in 1954.

The door on the right gives access to a lobby. Alongside is the Bishops Throne; its alcove is attractively lined with heraldic embroidery. A large motif of the Arms of the Diocese is in the centre, with the initials of the earlier Bishops of Gibraltar around the perimeter.

The six Canon's stalls on this side of the Chancel are: Bishop's Chaplain (St. Ignatius of Antioch): Chaplain of Holy Trinity Sliema (St. Titus): Canon St. Mark: Canon St. Barnabas: Canon St. Timothy: Chancellor St. Luke.

The right hand spur screen contains the 'Winston Churchill Lectern', described previously.

Right Hand Aisle

On this side of the building from the double doors of the Vestry, high on the first pilaster hangs the Red Ensign. There is no memorial in the first bay.

On the neighbouring pilaster is the Union Jack, below it is the only pictorial memorial in the Cathedral, a fine mosaic of St. Michael by Powell. It is in memory of Admiral of the Fleet, John Michael de Robeck. Born 10th June 1862, died 20th January 1928. He commanded the Naval forces in the Dardanelles during 1915 and was C-in-C Mediterranean Fleet 1919–1922. The memorial was improved shortly before WWII by the addition of the blue border.

In the next bay is the large memorial to the Venerable and Reverend John T. Howe Le Mesurier, who for thirty-three years was Chaplain to the Forces, and Archdeacon of Malta 1843 to 1864. His services to the Anglican community, especially in the early days have already been mentioned. Born 18th August 1785, he died 29th September 1864. His wife, Martha Le Mesurier, died in 1839, aged 52 years, and was buried in Msida Bastion cemetery, Floriana. He spent his later years living on the Isle of Wight where he died. A large panel in his memory was placed on the side of his wife's tomb, and can be seen there.

Affixed to the next pilaster is the flag of the United States of America, the Stars and Stripes, and below it a marble tablet in memory of Henry Roger Hancox, who was killed whilst serving as a pilot in the Fleet Air Arm at Malta on 11th February 1926, aged 27 years. He had been active in WWI, in many theatres of that war including Jutland, Dover Patrol, Zeebrugge, Gallipoli and the Caspian Sea.

In the next bay is a large memorial. Henry Lumsden Gale was born in Plymouth, Devon, on the 24th July 1833, and died at Eastbourne, Sussex, on the 16th September 1904. He lived in Malta for 43 years, and had been a Churchwarden at St. Paul's for twenty-five years.

On the following pilaster are memorials to two distinguished Admirals, but from different eras, Fisher and Cunningham.

The bronze tablet is to Admiral Sir William Wordsworth Fisher. During his service career Admiral Fisher, a distinguished sailor and loyal churchman, served in the Mediterranean on many occasions; on HMS *Hawke* 1896–98, HMS *Canopus* 1901–3, he was Chief of Staff to Admiral De Robeck (the C-in-C Mediterranean 1919–22), Rear-Admiral First Battle Squadron 1924–25, Second in Command Mediterranean Fleet 1930–32 and Commander-in-Chief 1932–36. He died in 1937. Above these memorials hangs the flag flown by him in HMS *Barham,* when Rear Admiral, First Battle Squadron, Mediterranean Fleet 1924–1925, laid up without ceremony at Easter 1939.

The white marble tablet to Admiral of the Fleet Viscount Cunningham of Hyndhope, was dedicated and unveiled in 1967, at a ceremony which has already been described.

At the end of the aisle is the second vestry. To the left of the door is a brass memorial plate recording the names of NCO's and men of the 3rd Battalion Royal Garrison Regiment, who died whilst stationed on the island between September 1901 and April 1904. Above the door flies the White Ensign.

Baptistry
As explained in an earlier chapter pre-1949 this area was the Sanctuary, when the six pilasters were carved and gilded, in an attempt to make the Sanctuary more decorative. The curved wall contains the five panels covered with blue and gold fabric, and below each panel is an oak bench. These were presented by the Corps of Royal Engineers to mark their special connection with Malta, having served on the island continuously from 1798 to 1979.

The white Carrara marble font is inscribed: DEO. OPT. MAX. IOANNES. GUL. BOWDEN. ANGLUS. SUB. COELLO. METITENSI. REVALESCENS. AD.MDCCCXL. and stands in the centre, with a moulded oak cover. It is under a domed white stone canopy supported by six columns.

There is a framed portrait of Queen Adelaide on each side of the baptistry.

Chapel of the Ascension
Up a flight of stairs from the lobby behind the altar, and overlooking the choir is the little Chapel of the Ascension and the Holy Angels. The memorial window was erected by relatives and friends of men who lost their lives in a flying accident in 1926. It is the only stained glass window in the Cathedral, and the figure of Christ ascending appears in the upper centre.

When the Italian Air Force commenced bombing in 1940, the iron window frames were bent by blast. Canon Nicholls had the window removed and laid flat in the West Gallery. Fortunately, only slight damage was done to the actual glass, so it was possible to replace the window after the war.

It was hoped that the Chapel would be especially linked with the Royal Air Force, and before WWII occasional RAF services were held, though the intention was not fully realised until 1961. Two RAF weddings took place here in 1936, on 18th November the marriage of Flying Officer Shepherd-Smith, followed on 23rd December by Leading Aircraftsman Young, both officiated by Canon Nicholls. The Chapel was at one time the 'Upper Room' of Toc H Malta.

At the rear of the altar is a light blue wrought iron reredos with the RAF badge in the centre, and a panel of frosted glass behind, which was installed in 1961.

When the Royal Air Force Chapel at Luqa airport was closed down during March 1979 their altar frontal was transferred to this Chapel in St. Paul's. It was presented by Air Commodore H. D. Hall[7], who supervised the withdrawal of the RAF from Malta. The altar front is light blue with the gold coloured RAF badge in the centre flanked with the dates 1918 and 1978, and was produced to celebrate the Diamond Jubilee of the Royal Air Force.

During services the organist is seated here. Not only can he see what is happening in the Chancel but also has a good view of the congregation.

Notes

[1] This painting had been commissioned by Mrs. J. R. Hemsley in 1916, and had hung above the Altar in the Pembroke Garrison Chapel, which was closed with the withdrawal of British troops. It is thought that this work was mainly by painted by the son of Giuseppe Cali.

[2] Mrs. Hardman, who died in 1913 at the age of 76, was born in Malta, the daughter of a merchant named Corlett. She was baptised in the Palace Chapel, confirmed, and in 1863 married in St. Paul's. Her first husband, Mr. J. Whitaker, died in 1883, and in 1885 she was married to Mr. Hardman.

[3] Her distinctive white marble tomb is in Ta Braxia cemetery.

[4] He was appointed Bishop of Maidstone in 1969, and served in that post until 1976.
[5] On his gravestone in Ta Braxia cemetery it says, 'of Hastings, Sussex. P.M.P.Z. SEC. OF D.G. MARK LODGE AND S.E. OF D.G. CHAPTER OF MALTA'.
[6] Born in Qormi.
[7] On the morning of 1st April 1979 when HMS *London* made the final departure from Malta for the Royal Navy after 180 years, Air Commodore Hall took off from Luqa and flew a lone Nimrod aircraft over Grand Harbour in salute before heading for Gibraltar.

Chapter 33

Latest Events

In the December 1994 issue of the Parish magazine Canon Cousins humorously asked:

'Is there life after the Sesquicentenary?'

Well, yes, most decidedly.

- Canon Cousins himself left Malta in October the following year to carry on his work as a Clergyman at Llandudno in North Wales.
- The Reverend Canon Alan Geoffrey Woods arrived and was installed as Chancellor and Senior Canon on Saturday 10th February 1996, the Feast of St. Paul Shipwrecked.
- In 1997 Dr. Alexander (Andy) Welsh took over as Churchwarden from Mr. Trevor Rodger, and joined Mr. Tony Savage.
- Ecumenism has continued and improved.
- Along with millions of people throughout the World, when the Maltese woke up on Sunday morning 31st August, they were stunned to hear the news that Lady Di, as she was more familiarly known, had been killed in a car crash in the early hours of the morning in Paris. Over 400 men, women and children filled St. Paul's for an 'Ecumenical Service of Thanksgiving for the life of Diana, Princess of Wales 1961–1997' on 6th September 1997. Canon Woods was assisted at this service by the Reverend Colin Westmarland of St. Andrew's Scots Church and the Reverend Father Charles Carabott, Chaplain to the English Speaking Catholics. The collection which was made for the Princess Diana Memorial Fund and forwarded to England was a remarkable £M 700 plus (around £1,200 sterling).
- 2nd October 1998, saw an 'Ecumenical Service of Thanksgiving in celebration for 200 years of close relations between Malta and the United Kingdom and the 180th Anniversary of the Institution of The Order of St. Michael and St. George' attended by H.R.H. Prince Andrew, the Duke of York.
- When Bishop Annetto was consecrated as Auxiliary Bishop of Malta on 2nd January 1999 in St. John's Co-Cathedral, Canon Woods was invited to represent the Anglican Church.

- One of the local band clubs 'Is-Società Filharmonica Nationale 'La Valette'' who traditionally play funeral marches during the Good Friday procession, needed a venue at short notice to hold a concert during Easter Week 1999, and were offered the use of St. Paul's. It was very well attended by the families and friends of the musicians as well as the general public.
- The popularity of Malta as a holiday destination continues to grow. In 1999 including day visitors from cruise ships the number of tourists topped one million one hundred thousand.

Queen Adelaide died 150 years ago on 2nd December 1849, and as we reflect upon this fact, we can declare without any doubt that many thousands of men and women have had their lives enriched due to her generosity and piety in providing this church for Anglican worship. The building nowadays bears the official title 'St. Paul's Anglican Pro-Cathedral', but it will forever remain Queen Adelaide's Church.

POSTSCRIPT

As already mentioned over 1,100,000 tourists now set foot on Malta. Though the majority are Europeans, others arrive from Australia and New Zealand, North and South America and the Far East.

Visitors to St. Paul's either to join the congregation for Sunday morning service, or during the week as sightseers are always most welcome.

The Cathedral does not benefit from any endowment and receives no financial support from the Church Commissioners in England. The Anglican community on Malta has to meet all expenses, including the stipend of the Chancellor, and is entirely dependent on donations, subscriptions, collections and fund raising activities. Being outside the UK it does not qualify for support from the British National Lottery Fund.

If you would like to help in maintaining Queen Adelaide's Church, please write to:

> The Secretary
> Friends of St. Paul's Cathedral
> Independence Square
> Valletta VLT 12
> Malta

Appendix 1

Diocese of Gibraltar

In 1787 the first colonial Bishop, The Bishop of Nova Scotia was consecrated, and in the years following further bishoprics were established, though not in sufficient numbers to meet the growing demand. A letter of April 24th 1840 sent to the Archbishop of Canterbury, by the Bishop of London mentioned:

> *"Malta as the station of a Bishop, who might exercise a salutary superintendence over those of our clergy who officiate as chaplains in the seaports and towns upon the coast, or near the coast of the Mediterranean; and perhaps Gibraltar"*

The S.P.C.K. sent one of its secretaries, the Reverend George Tomlinson, on a mission of goodwill to the Patriarch and Prelates of the Greek Church, and his friendly reception encouraged the establishment of a Mediterranean Bishopric which should, among its other functions, further improve relations with the Eastern Churches.

However, the next overseas bishopric to be established was in New Zealand, but a report of a meeting held in Whitsun week at Lambeth Palace states:

> *"Our next object will be to make a similar provision for the congregations of our own communion, established in the islands of the Mediterranean, and in the countries bordering upon that sea; and it is evident that the position of Malta is such as will render it the most convenient point of communication with them, as well as with the Bishops of the ancient Churches of the East, to whom our Church has been for many centuries known only by name.*
>
> *We propose, therefore, that a See be fixed at Valletta, the residence of the English Government and that its jurisdiction extend to all the Clergy of our Church residing within the limits above specified. In this city, through the munificence of Her Majesty the Queen Dowager, a Church is in course of erection which when completed, will form a suitable Cathedral"*

Nevertheless there were civil as well as ecclesiastical reasons why it was later recommended that the Mediterranean Diocese be founded at Gibraltar instead of Malta. There already existed a Roman Catholic Bishop of Malta, who was not only acknowledged but also nominated by the British Government. Upon taking advice, Queen Victoria declared her intention of founding an Episcopal See at Gibraltar, and nominated the Reverend George Tomlinson to be the first Bishop.

Provision was made however for the Collegiate Church of St. Paul in Valletta to become a Pro-Cathedral for the Diocese; the Episcopal Coat of Arms includes the Maltese Cross in addition to the Rock of Gibraltar.

The Letters Patent which established the See of Gibraltar were dated August 21st 1842, and provided for the See City to be Gibraltar; the Church of the Holy Trinity there was to become a Cathedral. Dr. George Tomlinson, the first Bishop, was to be subject to the Archbishop of Canterbury. His powers at Gibraltar were set out, and it was stated that he and his successors

> *"may perform all the functions peculiar and appropriate to the office of bishop within all churches, chapels, and other places of worship within our island of Malta and it's dependencies, which now are, or may hereafter be founded, set apart, or used for the service of Almighty God, according to the ritual of the said united Church of England and Ireland, and more especially within the church now or late founded by the pious munificence of our dearly beloved Queen Adelaide, The Queen Dowager, in the city of Valletta and also by himself or themselves, or by the Archdeacon or Archdeacons, or the Vicar-General, or other officer or officers hereinafter mentioned, exercise jurisdiction spiritual and ecclesiastical within the said cathedral church of the Holy Trinity, and throughout the said Diocese of Gibraltar, and also within the churches, chapels, and other places aforesaid, in the island of Malta and its dependencies, according to the ecclesiastical laws now in force in England."*

> It also declared: *"That the Bishop of Gibraltar and his successors may exercise and enjoy full power and authority to grant licences to officiate to all Rectors, Curates, Ministers, and Chaplains of all the churches, or chapels, or other places, within our said possessions of Gibraltar and Malta, wherein Divine Service should be celebrated according to the rites and liturgy of the Church of England."*

In addition to Malta and Gibraltar, the Bishop was to supervise the clergy and other members of the Church of England in Spain, Southern France, Italy, part of Austria, Greece, part of the Turkish Empire, North Africa west of Tripoli, and the Islands of the Mediterranean as the Bishop of London had previously exercised.

Though the limits of the Diocese have changed over the years, the Bishop of Gibraltar still has a vast and scattered area to supervise with peculiar difficulties to surmount.

As Bishop Knight commented. The Government chapels, of both Garrisons and Dockyards, are independent of the Bishop of Gibraltar. If he ministers to them it is by invitation. The Bishops of Gibraltar have throughout the years always welcomed opportunities of serving the Forces of the Crown, and the assistance of Navy and Army chaplains was often generously given to the Civil chaplains.

In 1980 the Diocese was enlarged to include the former jurisdiction of North and Central Europe, and was re-named the 'Diocese in Europe', though the Bishop is called 'Bishop of Gibraltar in Europe'. It now extends from the Azores in the West and including the Canary Islands and Madeira, the whole of mainland Europe (excluding the U.K. and Ireland), the islands of the Mediterranean (except Cyprus which is under the Anglican Province of the Middle East), Morocco, Turkey and the former Soviet Union countries. In 1981 a second Pro-Cathedral was established when the church of Holy Trinity Brussels was given the status Pro-Cathedral.

Appendix 2

1895 Declaration

"At a meeting of representatives of those interested in the maintenance of all the rights and privileges of the Protestant inhabitants of Malta and 'Her Majesty's Land and Sea Forces' in the Collegiate Church of St. Paul, Valletta, held in the Library of the above Church on Tuesday May 21st 1895 and at which were present the Archdeacon, Captain Ewart A.M.S. (representing H.E. the Governor), Captain Aldrich R.N., (representing the Admiral Commander in Chief), H. L. Gale Esq. (delegate appointed by the Church Commission) and William Hardman Esq. (delegate appointed by the Churchwardens) it was resolved and unanimously agreed to, in view of the vacancy about to take place in the Chaplaincy to Government:

1. That efforts should be made to provide a Stipend of £300 a year (exclusive of the usual fees for Marriages, Burials, etc) for a Civilian Chaplain for St. Paul's Church and Congregation.
2. That this Stipend of £300 shall be paid by the Churchwardens from the offertory.
3. That there shall be Guarantors for any deficiency in the offertory fund for this purpose to the extent of £250 per annum.
4. That after the payment of £150 for the year's expenses of Divine Worship the full amount of the above Stipend of £300 shall be the next charge upon the offertory fund.
5. That at the close of each year the Guarantors shall be liable for any deficiency (if any) that may so exist and shall pay in equal proportions and according to the amount of their Guarantee what is required of them to the Churchwardens or their account.
6. That while it is desirable that the period during which the Guarantors shall be responsible should be fixed at three years, the period may be either for one, two or three years, and as they shall signify in writing to the Churchwardens or the Committee to be appointed for that purpose.
7. That the appointment of the Chaplain be for three years, and shall be made by the Bishop.

8. That a fund for the endowment of the Chaplaincy be at once initiated and that H.E. the Governor, and Admiral Commander in Chief and the Bishop be invited to be Patrons of a Committee to be nominated by this conference to open such Fund to secure contributors and to receive the Donations that may be made to it, and that the Patron of the Chaplaincy shall always be the Bishop.
9. That the Services at 11.0 a.m., and 6.0 p.m. on Sundays shall be conducted as at present with the aid of an Organist and Surpliced Choir.
10. That there shall be an Annual Meeting of the Congregation on the 3rd Monday in January of each year for the purpose of electing six Churchwardens and so that two such Churchwardens shall be Civilians, and represent the Civil Community, two Military Officers to represent the Military, and two Naval Officers to represent the Naval communities respectively.
11. That the Chaplain-in-charge of St. Paul's and Congregation, being present shall be the Chairman at all meetings of the Churchwardens and at the Annual Meeting for the election of Churchwardens and shall have a casting Vote in cases where such casting Vote would be decisive. In his absence the chair shall be taken by the Churchwarden selected by those present.
12. That all sittings in the Church shall be free, but there shall be a general Offertory at all services on Sundays and Holy Days and which offertory shall be entirely at the disposal of the Churchwardens for the expenses of Divine Worship, for the Stipend of the chaplain, the aid of the Sick and Poor and other purposes to which such a fund is usually devoted.
13. That the Pews of the Governor and Admirals in St. Paul's be maintained and that there shall be 100 sittings always reserved for allotment to the Civil Community, 100 to Military Officers and their families, and 100 to Naval Officers and their families, and that these sittings shall be in the Benches immediately at the back of the Governor's and Admirals' Pews and in as proportionately an equal position an is practicable and with the usual appeal to the Bishop where there is dissatisfaction, and that the remainder of the sittings shall be allotted by the Churchwardens at their discretion.
14. That 'Her Majesty's Land and Sea Forces' as such shall attend St. Paul's Church only at such times and in such numbers as there shall be accommodation for them and after application to the Churchwardens, who shall state the number that can be accommodated and the period during which such accommodation can be provided.
15. That the Ordinance No. VI, 1876 appointing a Church Commission shall be amended by the Council of Government and receive the sanction necessary to make it legal so that (1) all members of the Commission shall be members of the Church of England (2) that two of the members shall always be

Civilians (3) that the Admiral Commander-in-Chief shall be an ex-officio member of it, or, should he not be a Member of the Church of England, then the next Senior Naval Officer on the Station who is such a member of the Church of England (4) that the Plate, Registers, Furniture (Organ, Benches, etc.) and Library shall be included in the Property vested by the Ordinance in the Commission.

16. That these proposals having been agreed to by the H.E. the Governor, the Admiral C-in-C, the Archdeacon, the delegate elected by the Church Commission for that purpose, and the delegate elected by the Churchwardens for that purpose, be submitted to the Bishop of Gibraltar for his sanction and approval.

17. That the date at which the Chaplaincy shall be vacated by the present holder of it shall be fixed only when such progress has been made in carrying out the foregoing proposals as is approved by the Bishop.

18. That the following Committee be forthwith appointed to give effect to Paragraphs 1 and 3. The Archdeacon, Mr. Hardman, Mr. Gale, a Naval officer to be appointed by the Admiral Commander in Chief, and a Military officer to be appointed by H.E. the Governor; and

19. That this committee, with power to add to their number, be the Committee referred to in Paragraph 8." Sir Victor Houlton and the Reverend W. K. R. Bedford later joined this Committee.

Appendix 3

Memorial Shrine Units

Captain C. K. S. Aylwin, R.N., visited Malta for the Siege Bell Memorial dedication by Queen Elizabeth II, and whilst there photographed the Memorial Panels in St. Paul's relating to Maritime Forces.

After checking with Naval Historical Branch of M.O.D., the Public Record Office, and Guildhall Library, he found differences between the names shown in St. Paul's, and his lists for the period 11th June 1940 to 13th May 1943, the Siege Period. He wrote to Canon Cousins and sent details of the differences.

(A) *Maritime Forces named in the Cathedral, which did not opoerate in support of Malta during the siege 10th June 1940 to 13th May 1943.*

1. *Naval Ships*

ALBERNI (R.C.N.)	FOXTROT	OAKLEY
AL GOMA (R.C.N.)	GENTIAN	PARRAMATTA (R.A.N.)
ARGONAUT	GRIMSBY	PENSTEMON
ATHERSTONE	GROVE	PORCUPINE
AUCKLAND	HOBART (R.A.N.)	PORT ARTHUR (R.A.N.)
AZALEA	HOLCOMBE	PRESCOTT (R.C.N.)
BADDECK (R.C.N.)	IERAX (GK)	PRIMULA
BERMUDA	JUPITER	PUCKERIDGE
BOREAS	KENT	QUALITY
BRILLIANT	KING SOL)	QUANTOCK
BROCKLESBY	KITCHENER (R.C.N.)	QUIBERON
CALPE	LAMERTON	REGINA (R.C.N.)
CALYPSO	LATONA	REIGHTON WYKE
CAMROSE (R.C.N.)	LAUDERDALE	ROCHESTER
CONVOLVULUS	LEANDER	SANDWICH
COREOPSIS	LEITH (R.N.Z.N.)	SCARBOROUGH
DELHI	LIDDERSDALE	SCYLLA
DEPTFORD	LOYAL	SNAPDRAGON
EGGESFORD	MAN O'WAR	SUMMERSIDE (R.C.N.)
ERNE	METEOR	SPORTSMAN (S/M)
EXETER	MILNE	TANGO
FLAMINGO	NASTURTIUM	TYNDEDALE
FLEETWOOD	NEWFOUNDLAND	VETCH

VILLE DE QUEBEC (R.C.N.)	WISENDA	WYVERN
WAYBURN	WOODSTOCK	YARRA (R.A.N.)
WHEATLAND		

2. *Fleet Air Arm*
822 and 881 Squadrons

3. *Merchant Vessels*
BANTRIA	ERIDGE (see below)	IRENEE DU PONT
MEROE	RUNO	

4. *Ships correctly shown in support of Malta but with incorrect details*
LANG	Should be LONG (under US Navy)
UNDA	Should be UNA
TORBAY	Incorrectly stated to be Greek
RFA PLUMLEAF	Incorrectly listed under Merchant Vessels
OHIO	Stated to be Panamanian, but flew British Flag with British Crew

5. *Summary of ships named which did not operate in support of Malta*
Never in Mediterranean	7
In Levant and Eastern Mediterranean only	17
In Operation Torch and North Africa	56
M.V. named (S.S. Eridge) which never existed	1
	81

(B) *Maritime Forces which operated in support of Malta during the siege, 10th June 1940 to 13th May 1943, but are not named in the Cathedral.*

1. *Naval Surface Ships*
ACHATES	CHAKLA	ICARUS
AMAZON	CHERRYLEAF (R.F.A.)	IMHOFF (SA)
ANCIENT	DESPATCH	INCONSTANT
APHIS	DINGLEDALE (R.F.A.)	INDOMITABLE
BEDOUIN	EASTON	INGLEFIELD
BERWICK	ECHO	INTREPID
BEVERLEY (ex-US)	EDINBURGH	JAUNTY
BEVERLEY (Hunt)	EMPIRE PATROL	KENYA
BIRMINGHAM	GEORGETOWN	KEPPEL
BOKSBURG (SA)	GLENGYLE	KUJAWIAK (POL)
BRAMHAM	HARVESTER	LEDBURY
BROWN RANGER (R.F.A.)	HAVELOCK	LONDON
CAIRO	HECTOR VII	MALCOLM
CENTURION	HELLESPONT	MARINE

MATCHLESS	ORIBI	SOMALI
MIDDLETON	PIORUN (POL)	SOUTHAMPTON
MOOR	PRINCE OF WALES	ULSTER PRINCE
NEWCASTLE	SALISBURY (ex-US)	VANSITTART
NIGERIA	SALVONIA	VICTORIOUS
NORMAN	SEAHAM	WESTCOTT
ONSLOW	SKUDD V	WOLVERINE

2. Submarines

0.21 (DU)	PROTEUS	THRASHER
0.23 (DU)	RAINBOW	TRAVELLER
0.24 (DU)	REGULUS	TRIAD
ISIRIS	TACTICIAN (P.314)	TRITON (GK)
OSWALD	TALISMAN	TRIUMPH
P.222	TEMPEST	TRUANT
PANDORA	TERRARCH	TRUSTY
PERSEUS	THORN	UNDAUNTED
PHOENIX		

3. Fleet Air Arm Squadrons

800	809	831
800X	815	832
800Y	817	880
800Z	819	884
804	827	885
806		

4. Merchant Vessels

ALAVI	FORT TADOUSSAC	PONTFIELD
AMERIKA	KING EDWIN	PRIMULA (FIN)
ARDEOLA	KIRKLAND	ROBERT MAERSK
BALTARA	KNIGHT OF MALT	SETTLER
BRITISH TRUST	MARIT MAERSK	SVENDOR (NOR)
CITY OF LONDON	MASIRAH	TADORNA
EL NIL (EG)	NOVASLI (NOR)	TROCAS
EMPIRE DEFENDER	OCEAN VOYAGER	TROILUS
EMPIRE GARRICK	ORNA	TUREBY (DAN)
EMPIRE PELICAN	OZARDA	TWEED
ERINPURA	PARRACOMBE	ZEELAND (DU)
FORT ST.JAMES	PIERRE S. DU PONT	

Appendix 4

Anglican Civil Clergy of Malta

Chaplains to the Government
1807	Francis Laing
1814–1824	John Castleton Miller
1824–1877	John Cleugh, D.D.
1877–1878	Henry White M.A.
1878–1895	Edward Ambrose Hardy M.A.

Church and Pro-Cathedral of St. Paul
1844–1877	John Cleugh D.D.
1877–1878	Henry White M.A.
1878–1895	Ambrose Hardy M.A.
1896–1901	Arthur Babington Cartwright M.A.
1901	Frank Bullock Webster – Locum tenens
1901–1903	Franklyn de Winton Lushington M.A.
1903–1905	Daniel Collyer M.A.
1905	Charles Samuel Gustavus Lutz – Locum tenens
1906–1907	Charles George Gull M.A.
1907–1908	Walter Naish M.A. – Locum tenens
1908–1910	William Evered
1908–1909	Somers Percy Smith-Heriz M.A. – Locum tenens
1910	James Houssemayne Du Boulay M.A. – Locum tenens
1910	Edward Hay Crane Cawood M.A. – Locum tenens
1910	Richard Courtier-Forster – Locum tenens
1910–1912	Arthur Fowler Newton M.A., Chancellor
1912–1913	William Emery Barnes D.D., M.A. – Locum tenens
1913	Francis Peel Mears – Locum tenens
1913–1919	Frederick Davies Brock, Chancellor
1919	Erasmus Austin Ommanney M.A. – Locum tenens.
1919–1922	Archibald Hugh Conway Fargus M.A., Chancellor
1922–1926	Arthur Cyprian Moreton M.A., Chancellor
1925–1926	George Charles May M.A. – Locum tenens

1926–1931	Noel Ambrose Marshall, Chancellor
1931–1944	Reginald Morton Nicholls M.A., Chancellor
1942–1944	Harold Edward Stevens M.A. – Locum tenens
1944–1954	Francis William Hicks B.A., Chancellor
1955–1958	Charles Paton OBE., Chancellor
1959–1963	Henry Rupert Colton M.A., Chancellor
1964–1965	Robert William Pope L.Th., R.N., Acting Chancellor
1965–1966	Launcelot MacManaway Q.H.C., M.A., R.N., Acting Chancellor
1966–1967	Donald Young OBE, R.N., Acting Chancellor
1967–1969	Henry George Warren MacDonald M.A., B.D., R.N., Acting Chancellor
1969–1973	Gordon Hyslop CBE, O.St. J., M.A., Chancellor
1973–1977	Howard Cole Q.H.C., B.Sc., Chancellor
1977–1981	David Inderwick Strangeways DSO, OBE, M.A., Chancellor
1981–1985	John Walter Evans M.A., Chancellor
1986–1989	Kenneth William Alfred Roberts, Chancellor
1989–1995	Philip John Cousins M.A., Chancellor
1996	Alan Geoffrey Woods TD, FCCA., Chancellor

Bishops of Gibraltar

1842–1863	George Tomlinson
1863–1868	Walter John Trower
1868–1874	Charles Amyand Harris
1874–1903	Charles Waldegrave Sandford
1904–1911	William Edward Collins
1911–1920	Henry Joseph Corbett Knight
1921–1927	John Harold Greig
1927–1933	Frederick Nugent Hicks
1933–1946	Harold Jocelyn Buxton
1947–1954	Cecil Douglas Horsley
1954–1960	Thomas Craske
1960–1970	Stanley Eley

Bishops of the Diocese of Gibraltar in Europe

1970–1993	John Richard Satterthwaite
1993	John William Hind

Index

Abela, Francis 155
Abercrombie, Sir Ralph 2
Adams, Captain 30
Adelaide, Queen 2, 9, 11–14, 16, 17, 19, 25, 27–29, 36, 58, 59, 77, 102, 103, 133, 161, 170
Alderman, Edward 1
Alexander, General 125
Allan, J. V. 32
Andersen, Lileth 170
Anderson, Mr. 69
Anderton, Mr. 138
Anglican Church Commission 54, 58, 70, 122, 150
Aquilina, Carmel 155
Archer Shee, Sir Martin 178
Army
  Border Regiment 65
  Coldstream Guards 173
  Lincolnshire Regiment 92
  Rifle Brigade 92
  Royal Artillery 4, 65, 74, 93, 122, 123, 130, 173, 174
  Royal Engineers 65, 93, 129, 181
  Royal Garrison Regiment 66, 100, 181
  Royal Malta Artillery 153, 154, 177
  Royal Malta Fencibles 49
  Royal Sussex Regiment 153
  Sherwood Foresters 65
  West Kent Regiment 116
  1st Loyal North Lancashire Regiment 81
  18th Regiment 34
  42nd Royal Highlanders 30
  70th (Surrey) Regiment 173
  80th (Staffordshire Volunteers) Regiment 173
  88th Regiment 30, 40
  98th Prince of Wales's Regiment 173
  100th Regiment 38
Army Scripture Readers 74
Arnaud, Lieutenant, R.N. 71
Aspinall, Hon. J. 29
Attard, Jean 170
Auberge d'Allemagne 14, 85, 86, 101, 160, 176
Auberge d'Aragon 26, 170, 172
Auberge d'Italie 9
Backhouse, Admiral 92

Badger, Rev. G. P. 29
Bailey, Archdeacon 134, 140
Baillie, Rev. John 33
Baker, Mr. 69
Ball, Sir Alexander 1, 2
Balneavis, Colonel 29, 35
Barbara, Agatha, President of Malta 173
Barnes, Mrs. 97
Barnes, Rev. 77
Barracca Chapel 53, 71, 79, 82, 83, 87, 90, 94, 109, 141
Barratt, Captain H. W. 150
Barrett, Allan Lufton 94, 122, 123, 130
Barrett, Major Leonard, R. A. 173
Barron, Major-General H. 71
Bartolo, Mrs. Jean 164, 166, 177
Bassingthwaighte, Albert King 148
Bassingthwaighte, Edith Louise 148
Bassingthwaighte, Frank Albert 148
Bassingthwaighte, Reginald Harry 148
Batt, Sergeant 138
Bayley, Colonel 29
Beck, Robert Nicholas 40

Beckett, Major-General C. T. 122, 123
Bedford, Lieutenant R.N. 30
Bell, Sir Edward Peter Stubbs 175
Bernhard, Prince of Saxe-Weimar 11
Best, Sir Thomas Vans 86
Bible Society 7
Biddis, Kenneth 160, 165
Bighi Naval Cemetery 64
Bighi Naval Hospital 4, 107
Bird, Lieut-Cdr., R.N. 141
Bishop of Troy 155
Blackborne, Rev. J. 74
Bland, Dorothea 11
Blythe, Mrs. J. 131, 135
Bonham-Carter, Sir Charles 93
Bonham-Carter, Lady 102
Bonnici, Dr. Ugo Mifsud, President of Malta 169, 170
Borg, Sir George 123
Borg Olivier, Dr. George 143, 152, 155
Borg Olivier, Dr. P. 154
Botterill, Ldg-Writer, R.N. 138
Bouverie, Sir Henry 9, 13, 14, 27, 30
Bowden, J. W. 30, 100
Boyd, Major 65, 66
Bradley, Mrs. 131
Brandreth, Captain 19
Braun, Hugh 129
Brock, Rev. Frederick Davies 77, 79, 80
Brooke, Major William Halliday 81
Brown, Rev. Algernon Leslie 75
Browne, Rev. Wiliam Bevill 53
Bruce, Major A. Cathcart 130, 131, 138
Buchanan, Rev. G. D., R.N. 146
Bumstead, Alfred 177
Burial Ground, Floriana 26, 33
Burns & McIver 39, 41
Burrell, Mr. 114
Burrell, Mrs. 114
Bushe, Colonel 69
Butler, Charles James 34
Butler, Jane 34
Butler, Nathaniel Charles 34
Buxton, Rt. Rev. Harold Jocelyn, Bishop of Gibraltar, 89, 94, 101, 122, 123, 125, 130
Byron, Lord 2

Cali, Giuseppe 173
Calleja, G. 42
Cameron, Colonel 65, 66
Camilleri, Rev. Michael Angelo 32
Campbell, General Sir David Graham 93
Campbell, David Callender 122
Campbell, Lady 97
Carabott, Rev. Charles 184
Carey, Rt. Rev. George, Archbishop of Canterbury 169, 170
Caroe, Alban 129, 180
Caroe, W. D. 101, 102
Caroe & Passmore 101, 129
Carter, Colonel 131
Cartwright, Rev. Arthur Babington 60, 65, 66
Caruana, Archbishop 32, 81
Caruana, Joseph 132
Caruana Demajo, Dr. T. 154
Cassar Reynaud, Lieut. A. J. 153
Caward, Rev. Edward 74
Ceci, Dr. 37
Cecil, Rear Admiral Oswald 161
Celela, Archbishop Pierre Luigi 169
Central Civil Hospital 46, 55, 120
Chadwick, Rev. C. Egerton 89, 94
Chamberlain, Archdeacon F. N., R.N. 146
Chamberlain, Joseph 59
Chapman, Rev. W. H. S. 145
Chapple, H. G., R.N. 65
Cheverton, Dr. Rex 160
Church Missionary Society 7, 9
Churchill, Winston 125, 154, 167, 177
Clarence, Duke of 11, 12
Clayton, Miss 90
Clayton, Rev. John 89, 90
Clement, Murray 93, 111, 124, 138
Cleugh, Rev. John 3, 8, 17, 26, 34, 37–40, 43, 45, 47–49, 54, 55, 100, 175, 176
Cocks, Rev. Francis William, R. A. F. 152
Cockshoot, Captain Norman 164
Coldwell, Mrs. Elizabeth Ann 97, 101, 174
Coldwell, Captain Godfrey J. 94, 96, 119, 122, 174
Cole, Rev. Howard Stacey 160, 161
Cole, Vice-Admiral 154
Coleiro, Mgr. 155

Collins, Rt. Rev. William Edward, Bishop of Gibraltar 68, 69, 71–73, 75, 77, 86, 101, 152
Collis & Williams 115
Collyer, Rev. Daniel 68–70
Collyer, Sapper J., R. E. 93
Colquhoun, Colonel 141
Colton, Rev. Henry Rupert 145, 150
Colville, Captain, Hon. S., R.N. 69, 70
Congreve, General 83, 85
Connell, Flt-Sgt, R. A. F. 138
Conventual Church of St John 5
Cosserat, Rev. David Peloquin 2
Cousin, R. J. D. 132
Cousins, Mrs. Janet 166, 169
Cousins, Rev. Philip John 102, 165–167, 169, 170, 184
Covell & Matthews 147
Covell, Ralph G. 147
Cranmer, Thomas 163
Craske, Rt. Rev. Thomas, Bishop of Gibraltar, 139, 140, 143, 145, 150
Creasy, Sir Gerald 134, 135, 140, 146
Crutchley, Captain V. A. C., R.N. 94
Cumberland, Captain 30
Cunningham, Lady 155
Cunningham, Sir Andrew 125, 155, 181
Curzon-Howe, Admiral 71

Dart & Francis Ltd. 132
Davies, Rev. D. G. 155
Davies, Archdeacon Gordon 163, 165
Day, Mrs. 131
de Robeck, Admiral John Michael 180
de Wolff, Brigadier C. E. 150
Degaetano, Joseph 132
Denbigh, Countess of, 30
Denby, Midshipman 138
Despasquale, Mgr. Annetto 169
Devenport, Archdeacon Eric 170
Diana, Princess of Wales 184
Dick, Rear-Admiral R. M. 155
Dill, Sir John 113
Dimech, Ferdinand 36
Disraeli, Benjamin 2
Dixon, Canon David 163

Dobbie, General 109, 124, 135
Dockyard Chapel 4, 64, 80, 87, 90, 109, 145, 150
Dorman, Lady 153
Dorman, Sir Maurice 152, 153–156, 158
Douglas, Lord 153
Drummond, Henry 7
Du Cane, Sir John 88
Du Cane, Lady 97
Duly, Lieutenant 138
Dunant, Rev. C. E., R.N. 146
Duncan, Rev. Douglas A. 140
Duncan, Stanley 164
Dyce, Mr. 138
Dyer, Frank 132
Dyke, Captain, R.N. 65
Dyson, Lieutenant 69
Dyson, Mrs. 69

Ebbitt, Rev. R. D. 155
Eden, Anthony 113
Edinburgh, Duke of 134, 145, 146, 153, 166
Edmonds-Smith, Rev. Ernest 80, 83, 87
Edward VII, King of England 74
Edwards, Captain, R.N. 69, 70
Edwards, Charles 119, 122, 123, 131, 138, 141, 152
Eisenhower, General Dwight D. 127
Eley, Rt. Rev. Stanley, Bishop of Gibraltar 150, 151, 153, 155
Elgin, Lord 70
Elizabeth, Princess 134, 135
Elizabeth II, Queen 139, 166
Elliot, Lieut-Colonel B. N. 148
Emmerson & Murgatroyd 37, 39, 41
Engerer, Barbara 170
Ette, A., R.N. 133
Evans, Archdeacon John Walter 163
Evered, Rev. William 71

Fargus, Rev. Archibald Hugh Conway 80–82
Farrie, Rev. Hugh 122, 123, 126–128
Farrie, Mrs. 127
Felice, Dr. G. 154
Fergusson, General 36
Firman, Gordon 122, 123, 131

Fisher, Admiral Sir John 65, 66, 92
Fisher, Admiral Sir William Wordsworth 181
Fisher, Rt. Rev. Geoffrey, Archbishop of
    Canterbury 133–135
Fisher, Master 81
Fitzclarence, children 12
Fitzgerald, Rev. 134
Fleri, Mrs. 32
Fletcher, Mr. 29
Fletcher, Sir Henry 59
Forbes-Bentley, Sqdn. Ldr., R.A.F. 86
Foss, Rose 106
Fowles, Mr. 47
Foyles 103
Free Church of Scotland 32
Fremantle, General Sir Arthur 56, 58, 59, 65,
    173, 174
Fremantle, Lady Maye, 100, 173
Frere, John Hookham 2
Frere, Mrs. William 30, 170
Friars, Mr. 100
Gale, Henry Lumsden 54, 55, 60, 65, 66, 68,
    100, 174, 181

Gale, Mrs. 112
Galitzia, Caruana 119
Galiwey, Rev. Thomas Gifford 29
Ganado, Dr. H. 154
Gardner, W. M. 147
Gauci, Alfred 155
Gedge, Rev. Arthur Augustus Lynn 71
Geoghegan, Ernest 69, 72, 73
Geoghegan, Mrs. 118
George I, Duke of Saxony-Meiningen 11
George III, King of England 11
George IV, King of England 12
George V, King of England 92, 93, 172
George VI, King of England 125, 172
Gerada, Mgr. E. 155
Germanos, Bishop of Thyateira 89
Gethin-Jones, Rev. J. G. 123
Giaponne, Margaret 49
Gibraltar 12, 28, 52, 75, 89
Gibson, Alfred 42, 47
Gieves & Co. 109
Giles, Canon Alan S. 140

Girl Guides 97
Girls Friendly Society 97, 174
Gladstone, Captain 138
Glenelg, Lord 14
Gobat, Rev. Samuel 34
Godfrey, Mrs. 131
Godson, Mr. 154
Goll & Co. 69, 101
Gonzi, Archbishop 153, 154
Gordon, Captain Frederic 65
Gordon Paterson, Midshipman John L. 70,
    175
Gordon Paterson, Mrs. 69
Gort, Lord 123, 124
Goulden, Arthur, R.N. 177
Government Chapel 4, 6–8, 27, 28, 77, 175
Gozo, 36, 64
Graham, General Sir Thomas 161
Grant, Sir Patrick 52
Grantham, Sir Guy 150, 152, 153, 156
Gray, Brigadier 138
Gray & Davison 55
Green, Rev. 43
Greig, Rt. Rev. John Harold, Bishop of
    Gibraltar, 82, 83, 86
Greig, Sir Hector 16, 29
Grenfell, Lady Evelyn Emily 174
Grenfell, Lieut-General Sir Francis 65, 174
Griffiths, W. A. 94
Gull, Rev. Charles George 70–72

Haines, Rev. Walter Charles 71
Hall, Air Commodore H. D. 182
Hall, Richard 173
Hamilton, Lieut-Colonel 118
Hamilton, Admiral Sir John 155
Hancox, Henry Roger 181
Hankey, Sir Frederick 8
Harbot, Mrs. R. 138
Hardman, Aloisa Annetta, 62, 74
Hardman, J. & Co. 47, 48
Hardman, William 60, 62, 65, 66, 68, 69, 74,
    100, 173
Hardy, General Sir Campbell 148
Hardy, Rev. Edward Ambrose 54–57, 59, 64
Hare, Rev. 2

Harper, Charles 41, 45
Harries, Rev. H. R. M., R.A.F. 152
Harris, Rt. Rev. Charles Amyand, Bishop of
    Gibraltar 50, 52, 54
Harrison, Mr. 101
Harrison, Rev. Russell 165
Hastings, Marquess of 8
Havelock, George 56
Hayles, Paymaster-Captain Trevor, R.N. 94,
    102, 122, 130, 131, 138
Hayles, Mrs. 97
Heale, J., R.N. 133
Hewitt, Mrs. 138
Hezlet, Vice-Admiral Sir Arthur 158
Hicks, Rev. Francis William 126–128, 130,
    131, 134, 135, 138–140, 146, 147
Hicks, Rt. Rev. Frederick Cyril Nugent,
    Bishop of Gibraltar 86, 87
Hicks, Mrs. 177
Higginson, Sir George 36
Higgs, Captain 115
Hill, G. M. 50
Hill, Norman 150
Hill, Norman & Beard Ltd. 132, 138
Hillman, Rev. 39
Hind, Rt. Rev. John, Bishop of Gibraltar 169
HMS Ajax 116
HMS Alexander 2
HMS Ark Royal 110, 115
HMS Bacchante 175
HMS Barham 181
HMS Camperdown 64
HMS Canopus 181
HMS Chrysanthemum 85
HMS Coventry 177
HMS Eagle 88
HMS Edinburgh 115
HMS Egmont 70
HMS Fearless 115
HMS Formidable 29
HMS Fort Beauharnais 135
HMS Gallant 109
HMS Glasgow 135
HMS Glory 132
HMS Hastings 12, 103
HMS Hawke 181

HMS Hood 93
HMS Illustrious 109, 110, 111, 118
HMS Keppel 92
HMS Leander 69
HMS London 161, 177
HMS Magpie 134
HMS Manchester 115
HMS Nelson 115
HMS Ocean 135
HMS Phoenicia 177
HMS Prince of Wales 115
HMS Renown 115
HMS Southampton 110
HMS Sphinx 104
HMS Talbot 119
HMS Tudor 139
HMS Tyne 135
HMS Verity 92
HMS Victoria 64
HMS Warspite 94
HMS Wishart 93
HMS Wren 93
Holland, Rev. J. N. C. 145, 150
Holland-Martin, Admiral Sir Deric 150
Holman, Lieutenant Bertram, R. A. 174
Holy Trinity Church, Gibraltar 12
Holy Trinity Church, Sliema 53–55, 71, 72,
    74, 76, 82, 84, 89, 90, 104, 109, 122, 125,
    130, 150, 155, 163, 164
Horsley, Rt. Rev. Cecil Douglas, Bishop of
    Gibraltar, 131, 133–135, 139
Hoskin, W., PO, R.N. 133
Houghton, Brigadier, R. M. 145
Houlton, Lady Hyacinth Henriette 100, 174
Houlton, Sir Edward Victor Lewis 54, 60, 61,
    62, 174
Houlton, John Torriano 174
Howe, Earl 16, 28
Howe, Rev. 43
Hughes-Hallet, Admiral 66
Hunter-Blair, Major-General 80
Hurst, O. J. 72, 78
Hutton, Colonel W. A. R. 164
Hyslop, Rev. Gordon 156, 160

Icely, Rev. J., R.N. 74

Imperial Hotel, Sliema 109
Imtarfa Military Cemetery 64
Inglefield, Admiral 64
Inglott, Mr. 45

Jackson's Steam Bakery 37
Jesuits Church 5, 6, 8
Jolly, Air Commodore Malcolm, 133, 138, 166, 169, 170
Jordan, Mrs. 11, 12
Jowett, Rev. William 7

Kalkara Naval Cemetery 64
Keeling, John 7
Kelsey, Admiral 131
Kelsey, Mrs. 131
Kennedy, Mr. 38
Kimm, Mr. 65
King George V Hospital 111, 118, 134
Kirkpatrick, Mrs. Peggy 164
Kirkpatrick, Reginald 165
Knight, Rt. Rev. Henry Joseph Corbett, Bishop of Gibraltar 76, 79, 80, 81, 86

La Vallette Band Club 184
Laing, Rev. Francis 2
Lamb, Captain 38, 39
Lamb, Mrs. 38, 39
Lankesheer, Richard 16, 18
Larkins, Sidney 160
Lay, Hugh 103
Lay, Mrs. 103
Laycock, Lady Angela 144
Laycock, Sir Robert 140, 143, 150, 153
Leatham, Admiral Sir Ralph 123
Legh, R. C. 42
Le Marchant, Sir John Gaspard 37
Le Mesurier, Rev. John Thomas Howe 2, 4, 8, 16, 29, 39, 48, 49, 100, 180
Le Mesurier, Martha 180
Leonard, Mr. 30, 46, 47
Levingston, Rev. P. O. W., R.A.F. 155
Lewis, Charles W. 148
Lewis, Victor 158
Littlefield, Mr. 138
Liverpool, Lord 6

Livingstone, Sqdn-Ldr, R.A.F. 138
Lloyd, John 164
Lockwood, Mr. 66
Lodwick, Gnr. J. G., R. A. 123
Lomas, Fleet Surgeon, R.N. 70
London Fumigation Co. Ltd. 150
London Missionary Society 7
Long, Rev. 134
Lowndes, Isaac 7
Luftwaffe 175
Luke, Sir Harry 92, 94
Lushington, Rev. Franklyn de Winton 66, 68

MacDonald, Rev. Henry, R.N. 155, 156
Mackenzie, John 9
MacManaway, Rev. Lancelot, R.N. 156
Madoc, Brigadier R. W. 147
Madoc-Jones, Rev. T. 140
Maguire, G. 132
Maitland, Sir Thomas 2, 3, 5, 7, 8
Mallia, Henry 167
Malta & Mediterranean Gas Co. 47, 76
Malta Bible Society 7
Malta Protestant College 34, 50
Mamo, Sir Anthony 155
Marmara, Giuseppe (Joseph) 132
Marshall, Rev. Noel Ambrose 83–85, 87, 88, 96, 101
Marson, Padre 110
Martin, Mr. 40
Mattock, R. W. 39, 40
May, Fleet Surgeon, R.N. 65
McIver, Charles 39
Mears, C. &. G. 31
Merchant ships
    Essex 110
    Port Chalmers 115
    Sydney Star 115
Mercieca, Archbishop 169
Mercieca, Silvio 126
Messenger, Captain A. 131
Methodist Church 7, 32
Methuen, Lord 79, 80
Micallef, Mrs. 112
Micallef, Mrs. Joy 170

Miers, Rear-Admiral Sir Anthony 158
Mifsud, Mgr. 56
Miller, Albert 132
Miller, Rev. John Castleton 2, 3
Mintoff, Dom 143, 156
Missions to Seamen Society 64
Mitford, Colonel 48
Monk, Mr. 55
Montague, Colonel 47
Montebello, Marco 132, 178
Montebello, Paul 155
Monteith, Master 81
Montgomery, General 125
Moore, Mr. R. G. A. 69
Moreton, Rev. Arthur Cyprian 81–86
Morris, Rev. Samuel Sheppard Oakley 64
Morrison, Rev. 74
Mortimer, Arthur 151
Mortimer & De Giorgio 151
Mosse, J. K., Fleet-Paymaster R.N. 65
Moulton, Brigadier J. L. 146, 147
Mountbatten, Earl 134, 146
Mountbatten, Lady 134
Msida Bastion cemetery 180
Mules, Rev. Philip 29, 30
Munster, Earl of 123
Muscat, Hugo Agius 170
Muscat, Saverio 66
Mussolini 105, 107

Naish, Captain 140
Napoleon 1
Naudi, Dr. Cleardo 7
Newton, Rev. Arthur Fowler 73, 75–77
Nicholls, Lieutenant Anthony H., R.N. 104, 110
Nicholls, Mrs. Phyllis 97, 104, 109, 111–114
Nicholls, Rev. Reginald Morton 88, 89, 92–95, 101, 102, 104, 105, 109, 113, 122, 124, 125, 182
Nicolle, Hedley 94, 108, 109
Noakes, Rev. 134

O'Callaghan, Major-General D. 65, 66, 100
O'Dell, Rev. M. C. 53
O'Reilly, Bernard 34

O'Reilly, Charlotte 34
O'Reilly, Mrs. Mary 34
Ohlson, Captain B. J. 94, 119, 122, 123
Ohlson, Mrs. 123
Ommaney, Rev. E. A. 80, 81
Organ 41, 45, 47, 55, 69, 88, 101, 132, 138, 178
Orpen, Mrs. Anthony 81
Owen, Admiral Sir Edward 29

Pace, Paolo 154
Packer, Rev. James 163
Pargeter, Rev. William 2
Paris, Mr. E. 102
Parnis, Dr. 119
Parnis, Dr. A. 154
Paton, Rev. Charles 140, 144, 145, 147, 158
Patten, Colonel 72
Paulson, Webster 50
Pearce, Mignon Blanche Jane 89
Phillips, Captain 120
Picton, Elsie 177
Pierce, Cdr. F., R.N. 70
Pieta Military cemetery 69
Pisani, Dr. 38
Plasket, Sir Richard 7, 8
Plumer, Lord 80–83
Plumer, Marjorie Constance 81
Podger, Captain 131
Ponsonby, Sir Frederick 8, 9
Poole, Lance-Bdr. J., R. A. 123
Pope, John Paul II 167
Pope, Leo XIII 56
Pope, Rev. Robert, R.N. 151, 153, 154, 156
Pound, Admiral Sir Dudley 92, 93
Powell & Sons 103
Price, Rev. P. O. 155
Proctor, W. G. 132, 133

Raves, Bertram 65, 66
Rawlings, Rear-Admiral 116
Reece, Rev. H. L. O. 139
Refalo, Professor M. A. 82
Regia Aeronautica 105, 175
Reid, Mr. 69
Ricketts, Cdr., R.N. 65
Ridley, Major-General Sir William 50

Riechelmann, Carl Franz 39, 55
Rimmer, Lieutenant F. W. 122, 123, 124
Ripon, Lord 56
Roan, Rev. William 165
Roberts, Mr. 138
Roberts, Rev. Kenneth W. A. 164, 165
Robins, George H. 164, 178
Robins, Lucy 165, 178
Robinson, Walter Stanley 56, 65, 69, 72, 73, 78, 85, 101, 102
Robson, Thomas J. & Co. 45–47, 55, 101
Rodger, Trevor 180, 184
Roosevelt, President 125
Royal Air Force 86, 89, 90, 92, 94, 95, 124, 133, 139, 140, 152, 153, 155, 175, 178, 182
Royal Marines 93, 145 148, 152, 156, 176, 178
Royal Yacht Britannia 166, 177
Rule, William Harris 7
Rundle, Sir Leslie 73, 76, 79
Russell, Staff-Captain Guy, R.N. 123
Rust, Major F. H. 131
Rutter, Lieutenant John 49
Rutter, Thomas Joshua 35
Ryder, Rev. Tom 140

Salvation Army 74
Sammut, John 102, 132
Sammut, Joseph 126
Sammut, Philip 155
Sandford, Rt. Rev. Charles Waldegrave, Bishop of Gibraltar 54, 56, 59, 61, 64, 65, 68, 97, 174, 175
Sandie, Lieutenant J. G. 81
Sandys, Duncan 143
Satterthwaite, Rt. Rev. John, Bishop of Gibraltar 158, 161, 164–166
Savage, Anthony 170, 184
Scamp, Adelaide Frances Melita, 31
Scamp, Harriet 31
Scamp, William 19, 21, 24, 25, 31, 85, 129
Sceberras, Lieut-Colonel Attilio 173
Schlienz, Rev. Christopher Frederick 9
Scicluna, Chev. Hannibal 134
Scobie, General Mack 123
Scence, Robert Clement 19, 26, 27, 100

Scott, Sir Walter 2, 172
Seaston, Rev. Gerald J. 154
Seddall, Rev. Henry 34
Seymour, Sir Michael Culme 58
Shand, Barrack Sergeant 39
Shaw, Rev. Henry Jenkins 76, 82
Sheffield, Lady 16, 30
Shell, Rev. A 87
Shepperd-Smith, Flying Officer 182
Sheridan, Captain, R.N. 94
Sill, Colonel 69
Simmons, General Sir Lintorn 56
Slade, Wing-Cdr, R. A. F. 152
Smith, Reginald 119
Smith, Thomas Corlett 66, 69
Smith, William Jemison 37, 48
Smith, Rev. 43
Snell, Teddy 132
S. P. C. K. 13, 19, 26, 46, 62
Sparkes, Mr. 29, 30
St. George, Marchioness of 38
St. Giacomo Church 8, 9
St. Luke's Church, Tigne 74, 130
St. Paul's Church 27–30, 34, 37–43, 45, 47–50, 52–62, 64–66, 68–90, 92–97, 100–109, 111–116, 118–120, 122–136, 138–141, 143–148, 150–152, 154–156, 158, 160, 161, 163–167, 169 170, 172, 182, 184, 185
Stanley, Lord 28
Stanmore, Lord 65
Staper, Richard 1
Starkey, John W. 65, 66, 69, 72, 76, 101
Stevens, Rev. H. E. 124, 125, 134
Stevenson, Flight-Lieut. R. J. 139
Stewart, Admiral Houston 37
Stewart, Hon. R. Strother 90
Stock, Betty Lyne 177
Stoddart, Sir John 13, 14
Stones, Dr. 118, 119
Storks, Sir Henry 49
Strangeways, Rev. David Inderwick 161, 163
Strickland, Hon. Mabel 154
Stringer, Colonel 66, 100
Stuart, Sir Patrick 27–30, 33
Submarines 119, 158, 172

Swann, K. J. 138

Ta Braxia Cemetery 43, 55, 64, 119, 174, 175, 176
Tabona, Colonel G. Z. 154
Tatcher, Leading Seaman John 89
Taylor, F. 138
Taylor Woodrow Ltd. 151
Thompson, Mr. 48
Thompson, Rev. 43
Thornley, Rev. A. R., R.N. 146
Thorp, Lady Doreen 164, 169, 170
Thorp, P. A., R.N. 133
Thorpe, Lieutenant S. C. 153
Tiarks, Rev. Geoffrey Lewis 177
Toc H 86, 87, 94, 97, 125, 182
Tomlinson, Rt. Rev. George, Bishop of Gibraltar 26, 27, 29, 32, 33, 36, 37, 43, 45, 46, 52, 100, 127, 129, 172, 175
Tonna, Rev. Francis 34
Tonna, Saviour 155
Traill, Captain H. A., R.N. 133
Trapani-Galea-Ferol, Baron Gino 161
Treaty of Paris 1814 1
Trower, Dr. Walter John 46, 49, 50, 52
Trudgeon, T. D. 122, 125
Tweed, Lieut-Colonel 147
Twelves, Alfred 65, 66, 69, 72
Twelves, Henry 65, 66, 68–70, 80, 85
Twiss, D. P., R.N. 133
Tryon, Admiral Sir George 64
Tylden, Colonel 29
Tyler, Lieut-Colonel L. N. 123

Urwick, Jane 161

Vassallo, Fortune 155
Venn, Rev. R. T. 94
Verdala, Grand Master 1
Vicary, Jack 132
Victoria, Queen 12, 13

Waldron, Leonard, Stf.-Sgt., R.A. 93
Walker, Rev. Francis Joseph 81
Wall, Captain 147
Wallis, Sir Peter 169
Walter, Rev. W. J. 155
Wanstall, Rev. D. J. N. 155
Watson, Admiral 66
Watson, Rev. A., R.A.F. 89
Webb, A. C. 129
Webster, Rev. F. Bullock 66
Welsh, Alexander (Andy) 184
Wesleyan Church 74
Westhrop, Mrs. 38
Westmarland, Rev. Colin 184
White, Rev. Henry 55
Whitechapel Bell Foundry 140
Whitehouse, Rev. Francis Cowley 76
Whitelaw, Canon John 165
Whitmore, Colonel George 8
Willasey-Wilsey, Major 147
William IV, King of England 2, 9, 12, 17, 102
Williams, P. O. Gordon, R.N. 156
Williams, AB, R.N. 128
Wisely, Rev. 43
Wood, Rev. J. Ryle 30
Wood, General Robert Blucher 174
Wood, Colonel Elliott 58, 59, 65
Woodham, D. J., R.N. 133
Woods, Canon Alan Geoffrey 184
Worcester, Captain, R.N.R. 69, 72
Wrench, Rev. H. O. 38
Wright, Mr. 69
Wyatt, Midshipman P. 90

Xerri, Dun Mikiel 173

Young, Leading Aircraftsman 182
Young, Rev. Donald, R.N. 156
YWCA 97, 139

Zammit, Professor 86